# "EVERYTHING IS FINE NOW THAT LEONARD ISN'T HERE . . ."

A Book of Readings on the Management of Disturbing Behavior in the Classroom

Edited by

L. J. Stoppleworth

Central Connecticut State College

**MSS Information Corporation**
655 Madison Avenue, New York, N.Y. 10021

**Library of Congress Cataloging in Publication Data**

Stoppleworth, L    J    comp.
    Everything is fine, now that Leonard isn't here.

    CONTENTS: Szasz, T.  The myth of mental illness.—
Gelbur, A. S. and Anker, J. M.  Humans as reinforcing
stimuli in schizophrenic performance.—Farina, A. and
others.  Mental illness and the impact of believing
others know about it.  ₍etc.₎
    1.  Handicapped children—Education—Addresses,
essays, lectures.  I.  Title.  ₍DNLM: 1.  Child
behavior disorders—Collected works.  2.  Education,
Special—Collected works.  3.  Psychology, Educational
—Collected works.  LC4661 S883e  1973₎
LC4015.S76        371.9        73-7931
ISBn 0-8422-0316-8

# CONTENTS

# PREFACE

Many classroom teachers can empathize fully with the feeling of relief expressed by the teacher in the phrase used as the title of our book of readings. Nonetheless, even though Leonard was gone from his room, his disturbing behavior still posed problems for his parents, his present teacher, in fact most everyone in his immediate environment. Hopefully, the judicious use of this book of readings will provide some basic tools for those who must deal daily with Leonard and others like him, tools which can be utilized to successfully manage disturbing behavior.

This book takes the point of view that most disturbing behavior in the classroom is learned behavior; that it is maintained in existence by the consequences that it receives from its immediate environment. This view diverges considerably from the traditional psychological and psycho-analytical belief that disturbed behavior is a result of intra-psychic conflicts and/or internalized repressed dynamic forces. The articles selected for inclusion here say little or nothing about initial etiological factors in the behavior disturbances of children. The editor feels that not enough is known about the relative truth of the various theories of genetic, bio-chemical, neurological or psycho-dynamic etiologies of behavior (and particularly, of the interactions between them) for any one of them to have complete claim to our allegiance. What is known, however, is that, whatever the precipitating factor was for the disturbed behavior in the past, the frequency, intensity and duration of such behavior in the present is definitely influenced by the kinds of consequences the behavior calls forth from its immediate surroundings.

In the first part of this book, representative articles have been included to illustrate divergent ways of looking at disturbed behavior in general, including the effects of labels and stigma, and the sociological influences on the identification of deviant behavior. The second part of the book is devoted exclusively to a consideration of various environmental consequences for disturbing behavior in educational settings.

The first essay by Szasz is the kicking off point for divergency in viewing disturbed behavior. Traditionally, mental illness has been seen as the cause of disturbed and disturbing behavior. If, however, as Szasz maintains, there is no such thing as an internal disease mechanism with its locus solely within the disturbed individual then we must look elsewhere for a rational explanation of disturbed behavior. Gelburd and Anker represent a trend in institutional research which indicates quite clearly that behavior previously thought to be under the complete control of internal dynamics proves to be quite susceptible to simple manipulation of the environment. And, further, that people labeled as schizophrenic, which by many definitions meant out of contact with reality, are in fact quite cognizant of the effect that their behavior has on their environment. (For a further delineation of this topic see, Braginsky, B., Braginsky, D., and Ring, K., eds. *Method of Madness*, New York: Holt, Rinehart and Winston, Inc., 1969)

Farina and his associates demonstrate that labelling a person as mentally ill stigmatizes that individual and that this stigmatization affects his social interaction in a negative manner. Thus, not only does Szasz doubt the validity of the concept of mental illness as a rationale for disturbed behavior, but Farina demonstrates that the label alone is cause enough for disturbed social interactions.

Reger follows with a consideration of the implications for educational procedures in special education when the 'medical' model of viewing behavior is used. A study by Mercer shows that the way in which a child is identified, labeled, grouped and routed into a career as a deviant has not so much to do with any measurable 'internal' characteristics of the individual as it has to do with 'external' socio-cultural biases which impinge upon the judgment of those professionals doing the identifying and the labelling.

Thus, it is seen, in a brief fashion, to be sure, that there is a trend of thought which attempts to explain disturbed behavior on an ecological and environmental basis rather than on the basis of internal psychological dynamics. In the remaining articles in this book attention will be turned specifically to the implications that this trend of thought has for professionals in educational settings.

Rhodes begins this second section with the point of view that the behavior of children in school is regarded more as disturbing than as disturbed. The implications of the semantic connotations of those two suffixes, '—ing' and '—ed', the one, present, active and outer-directed, and the other, past, passive, and inward-directed are readily seen in the actions taken, as a result of two quite different ways of looking at behavior, to remediate the behavior involved.

The traditional method of attempting to 'cure' or 'heal' emotional disturbance has been to diagnose the past cause, and then to treat the patient to help him get his inner dynamic tensions into adjustment. Levitt casts serious doubt on the efficacy of these various types of psychotherapy with children. When behavior is believed to be the result of some inherent condition, diagnostic categorization and labelling occurs. Combs and Harper found that labelling exceptional children does affect the educators' perception of them and Jones' study reveals that the child, once labeled, comes to accept the label with consequently more negative attitudes toward school, particularly if the label was acquired by means of placement in a special education class. Jones also points out that labels have the effect of lowering the teachers' expectations of a child so stigmatized.

One educational 'treatment' of exceptional child behavior has been special class placement. Dunn reviews much of the available literature (up to 1968) on special education for the mildly retarded and he concludes that many special class placements are unnecessary and possibly or even probably harmful. He forcefully points up a dilemma facing special education. If the traditional view of exceptionality as something inherently different, a condition or even a disease state, is accepted then it follows that the needs of the exceptional child are beyond the educational management of the regular classroom teacher. If however the view is accepted that the exceptional child's behavior, be it social or academic, is only quantitatively different from that of the normal child rather than qualitatively so, then it stands to reason that with some extra help, many regular classroom teachers could adequately manage the instruction of many of these children. However, most teachers, having been sold the idea that exceptionality implies radical differences which only other more fully trained professionals can handle, continue to refer a fair share of their day-to-day management problems to these professionals.

Vacc shows that the special educator's hope (and the hope and prayer of the regular classroom teacher who initiates the referral) that special class placement for disturbing children would be beneficial has not been borne out by research results. Buehler, Patterson and Furniss indicate quite clearly that residential institutions which are set up to correct severely disturbed delinquent behavior do just the opposite in that 'the social living system of [the] correctional institution tends to reinforce delinquent responses and to punish socially conforming responses.'

Thus there are at present strong indications that the whole gamut of the conceptualization of exceptional behavior, from viewing it as caused by internal dynamics and/or deficits, to the identification, diagnosing and labelling of it for remedial purposes, to the special treatment methods ranging from psychotherapy to special class placement to institutionalization is shot through with intense and persistent problems. Identification and diagnosis are shaky, special class placement has dubious benefits and institutionalization has the most dubious benefits of all. The net result of this (and certain trends in educational fiscal policies) will put the education of the exceptional child, and, more particularly, for the purposes of this book, the disturbing child, for the most part right back in the hands of the regular classroom teacher.

Can the regular classroom teacher be given the tools to deal adequately with the problems of social and educational behavior management which will inevitably be presented to her. The theorists and practitioners who hold the view that behavior is maintained in existence by the consequences it receives from its environment have strong reason to believe that the tools are already available. Madsen, Becker and Thomas set the tone here in a study which demonstrates that the teacher's own behavior in the classroom is perhaps the most dominant factor in accounting for the kinds and quantities of behavior produced in that room.

A study by Hall *et al.* points up the fact that in the regular classroom milieu the teacher holds in her hand potent social reinforcers which can be used to increase the rate of study behavior simply by the giving and withholding of teacher attention. Broden and her associates also show that one powerful environmental reinforcer for disruptive behavior is teacher attention. The attention of the teacher to appropriate behavior and withdrawal of attention from inappropriate behavior serve as measurable determinants of the increase and decrease of such behavior.

O'Leary and his group demonstrate that even the varying of the intensity of a single facet of the teacher's behavior such as the loudness or softness of reprimands can have an effect on the production of positive or negative behavior.

Teacher attention is shown by Thomas and his associates to be capable of *producing* disruptive behavior by virtue of the fact that in school it seems inevitable that some teachers will pay considerably more attention to negative behavior than to positive behavior. That their intense efforts to eradicate disruptive behavior have the paradoxical effect of maintaining it in existence and even increasing it is doubly frustrating to these teachers.

Hasazi and Hasazi have also studied the effects of attention on error behavior. They showed that a particular digit-reversal behavior of a child who had been diagnosed as a learning disability case was not in fact the result of some perceptual deficit, but was being maintained in existence by the amount of remedial attention which was being paid to the error by all concerned. When the attention to the error behavior was removed, the error behavior disappeared. McKenzie *et al.* also demonstrate that academically disabled behavior can be brought under the control of social and environmental reinforcers.

A study by O'Connor is representative of research showing more subtle influences of the environment on behavior. O'Connor illustrated the effects of symbolic modeling on the subsequent behavior of individuals who observed the modeled behavior. He increased the rate of positive social interaction of children who previously exhibited withdrawing behavior simply by showing the children a film in which appropriate social behaviors were modeled.

Graubard's work indicates that the reaction of the peer group of an individual to his behavior is a strong determinant of the character and frequency of that behavior. The residential institutional environment need not be reinforcing for delinquent behavior as is shown by the research conducted by Phillips and his colleagues in *Achievement Place*, their halfway house for adolescent juvenile delinquents. Their work is a good example of the use of a token economy to achieve modification of inappropriate and anti-social behaviors.

In summary, then, it is apparent that we, in education, possess the technology with which to manage much of the disturbing behavior we are presented with each day. It is hard to know why we do not utilize this technology more fully. Perhaps, even in the face of considerable research evidence showing that behavior can be changed, we are still 'psyched-out,' conditioned by a Freudian pessimistic belief that behavior, and disturbed behavior in particular, is in fact, a 'condition' which will remain relatively immune to our efforts to change it. However, education is behavior change, the text books tell us. It remains for us who teach every day to put that statement of philosophy into practice. The behavior of the disturbing child makes a persistent demand on our daily supply of energy. Our problem then becomes how to use this energy to manage the disturbing behavior in an efficient and satisfying and educationally productive way.

PART I

# THE MYTH OF MENTAL ILLNESS

### THOMAS S. SZASZ

MY aim in this essay is to raise the question "Is there such a thing as mental illness?" and to argue that there is not. Since the notion of mental illness is extremely widely used nowadays, inquiry into the ways in which this term is employed would seem to be especially indicated. Mental illness, of course, is not literally a "thing"—or physical object—and hence it can "exist" only in the same sort of way in which other theoretical concepts exist. Yet, familiar theories are in the habit of posing, sooner or later —at least to those who come to believe in them —as "objective truths" (or "facts"). During certain historical periods, explanatory conceptions such as deities, witches, and microorganisms appeared not only as theories but as self-evident *causes* of a vast number of events. I submit that today mental illness is widely regarded in a somewhat similar fashion, that is, as the cause of innumerable diverse happenings. As an antidote to the complacent use of the notion of mental illness— whether as a self-evident phenomenon, theory, or cause—let us ask this question: What is meant when it is asserted that someone is mentally ill?

In what follows I shall describe briefly the main uses to which the concept of mental illness has been put. I shall argue that this notion has outlived whatever usefulness it might have had and that it now functions merely as a convenient myth.

## MENTAL ILLNESS AS A SIGN OF BRAIN DISEASE

The notion of mental illness derives it main support from such phenomena as syphilis of the brain

AMERICAN PSYCHOLOGIST, 1960, Vol. 15, pp. 113-118.

12

or delirious conditions—intoxications, for instance —in which persons are known to manifest various peculiarities or disorders of thinking and behavior. Correctly speaking, however, these are diseases of the brain, not of the mind. According to one school of thought, *all* so-called mental illness is of this type. The assumption is made that some neurological defect, perhaps a very subtle one, will ultimately be found for all the disorders of thinking and behavior. Many contemporary psychiatrists, physicians, and other scientists hold this view. This position implies that people *cannot* have troubles—expressed in what are *now called* "mental illnesses"—because of differences in personal needs, opinions, social aspirations, values, and so on. *All problems in living* are attributed to physicochemical processes which in due time will be discovered by medical research.

"Mental illnesses" are thus regarded as basically no different than all other diseases (that is, of the body). The only difference, in this view, between mental and bodily diseases is that the former, affecting the brain, manifest themselves by means of mental symptoms; whereas the latter, affecting other organ systems (for example, the skin, liver, etc.), manifest themselves by means of symptoms referable to those parts of the body. This view rests on and expresses what are, in my opinion, two fundamental errors.

In the first place, what central nervous system symptoms would correspond to a skin eruption or a fracture? It would *not* be some emotion or complex bit of behavior. Rather, it would be blindness or a paralysis of some part of the body. The crux of the matter is that a disease of the brain, analogous to a disease of the skin or bone, is a neurological defect, and not a problem in living. For example, a *defect* in a person's visual field may be satisfactorily explained by correlating it with certain definite lesions in the nervous system. On the other hand, a person's *belief*—whether this be a belief in Christianity, in Communism, or in the idea that his internal organs are "rotting" and that his body is, in fact, already "dead"—cannot be explained by a defect or disease of the nervous system. Explanations of this sort of occurrence—

assuming that one is interested in the belief itself and does not regard it simply as a "symptom" or expression of something else that is *more interesting* —must be sought along different lines.

The second error in regarding complex psychosocial behavior, consisting of communications about ourselves and the world about us, as mere symptoms of neurological functioning is *epistemological*. In other words, it is an error pertaining not to any mistakes in observation or reasoning, as such, but rather to the way in which we organize and express our knowledge. In the present case, the error lies in making a symmetrical dualism between mental and physical (or bodily) symptoms, a dualism which is merely a habit of speech and to which no known observations can be found to correspond. Let us see if this is so. In medical practice, when we speak of physical disturbances, we mean either signs (for example, a fever) or symptoms (for example, pain). We speak of mental symptoms, on the other hand, when we refer to a patient's *communications about himself, others, and the world about him*. He might state that he is Napoleon or that he is being persecuted by the Communists. These would be considered mental symptoms *only* if the observer believed that the patient was *not* Napoleon or that he was *not* being perseucted by the Communists. This makes it apparent that the statement that "*X* is a mental symptom" involves rendering a judgment. The judgment entails, moreover, a covert comparison or matching of the patient's ideas, concepts, or beliefs with those of the observer and the society in which they live. The notion of mental symptom is therefore inextricably tied to the *social* (including *ethical*) *context* in which it is made in much the same way as the notion of bodily symptom is tied to an *anatomical* and *genetic context* (Szasz, 1957a, 1957b).

To sum up what has been said thus far: I have tried to show that for those who regard mental symptoms as signs of brain disease, the concept of mental illness is unnecessary and misleading. For what they mean is that people so labeled suffer from diseases of the brain; and, if that is what they mean, it would seem better for the sake of clarity to say that and not something else.

## Mental Illness as a Name for Problems in Living

The term "mental illness" is widely used to describe something which is very different than a disease of the brain. Many people today take it for granted that living is an arduous process. Its hardship for modern man, moreover, derives not so much from a struggle for biological survival as from the stresses and strains inherent in the social intercourse of complex human personalities. In this context, the notion of mental illness is used to identify or describe some feature of an individual's so-called personality. Mental illness—as a deformity of the personality, so to speak—is then regarded as the *cause* of the human disharmony. It is implicit in this view that social intercourse between people is regarded as something *inherently harmonious,* its disturbance being due solely to the presence of "mental illness" in many people. This is obviously fallacious reasoning, for it makes the abstraction "mental illness" into a *cause,* even though this abstraction was created in the first place to serve only as a shorthand expression for certain types of human behavior. It now becomes necessary to ask: "What kinds of behavior are regarded as indicative of mental illness, and by whom?"

The concept of illness, whether bodily or mental, implies *deviation from some clearly defined norm.* In the case of physical illness, the norm is the structural and functional integrity of the human body. Thus, although the desirability of physical health, as such, is an ethical value, what health *is* can be stated in anatomical and physiological terms. What is the norm deviation from which is regarded as mental illness? This question cannot be easily answered. But whatever this norm might be, we can be certain of only one thing: namely, that it is a norm that must be stated in terms of *psycho-social, ethical,* and *legal* concepts. For example, notions such as "excessive repression" or "acting out an unconscious impulse" illustrate the use of psychological concepts for judging (so-called) mental health and illness. The idea that chronic hostility, vengefulness, or divorce are indicative of mental illness would be illustrations of the use of ethical norms (that is, the desirability of love,

15

kindness, and a stable marriage relationship). Finally, the widespread psychiatric opinion that only a mentally ill person would commit homicide illustrates the use of a legal concept as a norm of mental health. The norm from which deviation is measured whenever one speaks of a mental illness is a *psychosocial and ethical one.* Yet, the remedy is sought in terms of *medical* measures which—it is hoped and assumed—are free from wide differences of ethical value. The definition of the disorder and the terms in which its remedy are sought are therefore at serious odds with one another. The practical significance of this covert conflict between the alleged nature of the defect and the remedy can hardly be exaggerated.

Having identified the norms used to measure deviations in cases of mental illness, we will now turn to the question: "Who defines the norms and hence the deviation?" Two basic answers may be offered: (*a*) It may be the person himself (that is, the patient) who decides that he deviates from a norm. For example, an artist may believe that he suffers from a work inhibition; and he may implement this conclusion by seeking help *for* himself from a psychotherapist. (*b*) It may be someone other than the patient who decides that the latter is deviant (for example, relatives, physicians, legal authorities, society generally, etc.). In such a case a psychiatrist may be hired by others to do something *to* the patient in order to correct the deviation.

These considerations underscore the importance of asking the question "Whose agent is the psychiatrist?" and of giving a candid answer to it (Szasz, 1956, 1958). The psychiatrist (psychologist or nonmedical psychotherapist), it now develops, may be the agent of the patient, of the relatives, of the school, of the military services, of a business organization, of a court of law, and so forth. In speaking of the psychiatrist as the agent of these persons or organizations, it is not implied that his values concerning norms, or his ideas and aims concerning the proper nature of remedial action, need to coincide exactly with those of his employer. For example, a patient in individual psychotherapy may believe that his salvation lies

16

in a new marriage; his psychotherapist need not share this hypothesis. As the patient's agent, however, he must abstain from bringing social or legal force to bear on the patient which would prevent him from putting his beliefs into action. If his *contract* is with the patient, the psychiatrist (psychotherapist) may disagree with him or stop his treatment; but he cannot engage others to obstruct the patient's aspirations. Similarly, if a psychiatrist is engaged by a court to determine the sanity of a criminal, he need not fully share the legal authorities' values and intentions in regard to the criminal and the means available for dealing with him. But the psychiatrist is expressly barred from stating, for example, that it is not the criminal who is "insane" but the men who wrote the law on the basis of which the very actions that are being judged are regarded as "criminal." Such an opinion could be voiced, of course, but not in a courtroom, and not by a psychiatrist who makes it his practice to assist the court in performing its daily work.

To recapitulate: In actual contemporary social usage, the finding of a mental illness is made by establishing a deviance in behavior from certain psychosocial, ethical, or legal norms. The judgment may be made, as in medicine, by the patient, the physician (psychiatrist), or others. Remedial action, finally, tends to be sought in a therapeutic —or covertly medical—framework, thus creating a situation in which *psychosocial, ethical,* and/or *legal deviations* are claimed to be correctible by (so-called) *medical action.* Since medical action is designed to correct only medical deviations, it seems logically absurd to expect that it will help solve problems whose very existence had been defined and established on nonmedical grounds. I think that these considerations may be fruitfully applied to the present use of tranquilizers and, more generally, to what might be expected of drugs of whatever type in regard to the amelioration or solution of problems in human living.

### THE ROLE OF ETHICS IN PSYCHIATRY

Anything that people *do*—in contrast to things that *happen* to them (Peters, 1958)—takes place in a context of value. In this broad sense, no

17

human activity is devoid of ethical implications. When the values underlying certain activities are widely shared, those who participate in their pursuit may lose sight of them altogether. The discipline of medicine, both as a pure science (for example, research) and as a technology (for example, therapy), contains many ethical considerations and judgments. Unfortunately, these are often denied, minimized, or merely kept out of focus; for the ideal of the medical profession as well as of the people whom it serves seems to be having a system of medicine (allegedly) free of ethical value. This sentimental notion is expressed by such things as the doctor's willingness to treat and help patients irrespective of their religious or political beliefs, whether they are rich or poor, etc. While there may be some grounds for this belief—albeit it is a view that is not impressively true even in these regards—the fact remains that ethical considerations encompass a vast range of human affairs. By making the practice of medicine neutral in regard to some specific issues of value need not, and cannot, mean that it can be kept free from all such values. The practice of medicine is intimately tied to ethics; and the first thing that we must do, it seems to me, is to try to make this clear and explicit. I shall let this matter rest here, for it does not concern us specifically in this essay. Lest there be any vagueness, however, about how or where ethics and medicine meet, let me remind the reader of such issues as birth control, abortion, suicide, and euthanasia as only a few of the major areas of current ethicomedical controversy.

Psychiatry, I submit, is very much more intimately tied to problems of ethics than is medicine. I use the word "psychiatry" here to refer to that contemporary discipline which is concerned with *problems in living* (and not with diseases of the brain, which are problems for neurology). Problems in human relations can be analyzed, interpreted, and given meaning only within given social and ethical contexts. Accordingly, it *does* make a difference—arguments to the contrary notwithstanding—what the psychiatrist's socioethical orientations happen to be; for these will influence his ideas on what is wrong with the patient, what deserves comment or interpretation, in what possible directions change might be desirable, and so forth. Even in medicine proper, these factors play a role, as for instance, in the divergent orientations which physicians, depending on their religious affiliations, have toward such things as birth control and therapeutic abortion. Can anyone really believe that a psychotherapist's ideas concerning religious belief, slavery, or other similar issues play no role in his practical work? If they do make a difference, what are we to infer from it? Does it not seem reasonable that we ought to have different psychiatric therapies—each expressly recognized for the ethical positions which they embody—for, say, Catholics and Jews, religious persons and agnostics, democrats and communists, white supremacists and Negroes, and so on? Indeed, if we look at how psychiatry is actually practiced today (especially in the United States), we find that people do seek psychiatric help in accordance with their social status and ethical beliefs (Hollingshead & Redlich, 1958). This should really not surprise us more than being told that practicing Catholics rarely frequent birth control clinics.

The foregoing position which holds that contemporary psychotherapists deal with problems in living, rather than with mental illnesses and their cures, stands in opposition to a currently prevalent claim, according to which mental illness is just as "real" and "objective" as bodily illness. This is a confusing claim since it is never known exactly what is meant by such words as "real" and "objective." I suspect, however, that what is intended by the proponents of this view is to create the idea in the popular mind that mental illness is some sort of disease entity, like an infection or a malignancy. If this were true, one could *catch* or *get* a "mental illness," one might *have* or *harbor* it, one might *transmit* it to others, and finally one could get *rid* of it. In my opinion, there is not a shred of evidence to support this idea. To the contrary, all the evidence is the other way and supports the view that what people now call mental illnesses are for the most part *communications* expressing unacceptable ideas, often framed, moreover, in an unusual idiom. The scope of this essay allows me to do no more than mention this alternative theoretical approach to this problem (Szasz, 1957c).

This is not the place to consider in detail the similarities and differences between bodily and mental illnesses. It shall suffice for us here to emphasize only one important difference between them: namely, that whereas bodily disease refers to public, physicochemical occurrences, the notion of mental illness is used to codify relatively more private, sociopsychological happenings of which the observer (diagnostician) forms a part. In other words, the psychiatrist does not stand *apart* from what he observes, but is, in Harry Stack Sullivan's apt words, a "participant observer." This means that he is *committed* to some picture of what he considers reality—and to what he thinks society considers reality—and he observes and judges the patient's behavior in the light of these considerations. This touches on our earlier observation that the notion of mental symptom itself implies a comparison between observer and observed, psychiatrist and patient. This is so obvious that I may be charged with belaboring trivialities. Let me therefore say once more that my aim in presenting this argument was expressly to criticize and counter a prevailing contemporary tendency to deny the moral aspects of psychiatry (and psychotherapy) and to substitute for them allegedly value-free medical considerations. Psychotherapy, for example, is being widely practiced as though it entailed nothing other than restoring the patient from a state of mental sickness to one of mental health. While it is generally accepted that mental illness has something to do with man's social (or interpersonal) relations, it is paradoxically maintained that problems of values (that is, of ethics) do not arise in this process.[1] Yet, in one sense, much of

---

[1] Freud went so far as to say that: "I consider ethics to be taken for granted. Actually I have never done a mean thing" (Jones, 1957, p. 247). This surely is a strange thing to say for someone who has studied man as a social being as closely as did Freud. I mention it here to show how the notion of "illness" (in the case of psychoanalysis, "psychopathology," or "mental illness") was used by Freud—and by most of his followers—as a means for classifying certain forms of human behavior as falling within the scope of medicine, and hence (by *fiat*) outside that of ethics!

psychotherapy may revolve around nothing other than the elucidation and weighing of goals and values—many of which may be mutually contradictory—and the means whereby they might best be harmonized, realized, or relinquished.

The diversity of human values and the methods by means of which they may be realized is so vast, and many of them remain so unacknowledged, that they cannot fail but lead to conflicts in human relations. Indeed, to say that human relations at all levels—from mother to child, through husband and wife, to nation and nation—are fraught with stress, strain, and disharmony is, once again, making the obvious explicit. Yet, what may be obvious may be also poorly understood. This I think is the case here. For it seems to me that—at least in our scientific theories of behavior—we have failed to *accept* the simple fact that human relations are inherently fraught with difficulties and that to make them even relatively harmonious requires much patience and hard work. I submit that the idea of mental illness is now being put to work to obscure certain difficulties which at present may be inherent—not that they need be unmodifiable—in the social intercourse of persons. If this is true, the concept functions as a disguise; for instead of calling attention to conflicting human needs, aspirations, and values, the notion of mental illness provides an amoral and impersonal "thing" (an "illness") as an explanation for *problems in living* (Szasz, 1959). We may recall in this connection that not so long ago it was devils and witches who were held responsible for men's problems in social living. The belief in mental illness, as something other than man's trouble in getting along with his fellow man, is the proper heir to the belief in demonology and witchcraft. Mental illness exists or is "real" in exactly the same sense in which witches existed or were "real."

## Choice, Responsibility, and Psychiatry

While I have argued that mental illnesses do not exist, I obviously did not imply that the social and psychological occurrences to which this label is currently being attached also do not exist. Like

21

the personal and social troubles which people had in the Middle Ages, they are real enough. It is the labels we give them that concerns us and, having labelled them, what we do about them. While I cannot go into the ramified implications of this problem here, it is worth noting that a demonologic conception of problems in living gave rise to therapy along theological lines. Today, a belief in mental illness implies—nay, requires—therapy along medical or psychotherapeutic lines.

What is implied in the line of thought set forth here is something quite different. I do not intend to offer a new conception of "psychiatric illness" nor a new form of "therapy." My aim is more modest and yet also more ambitious. It is to suggest that the phenomena now called mental illnesses be looked at afresh and more simply, that they be removed from the category of illnesses, and that they be regarded as the expressions of man's struggle with the problem of *how* he should live. The last mentioned problem is obviously a vast one, its enormity reflecting not only man's inability to cope with his environment, but even more his increasing self-reflectiveness.

By problems in living, then, I refer to that truly explosive chain reaction which began with man's fall from divine grace by partaking of the fruit of the tree of knowledge. Man's awareness of himself and of the world about him seems to be a steadily expanding one, bringing in its wake an ever larger *burden of understanding* (an expression borrowed from Susanne Langer, 1953). *This burden, then, is to be expected and must not be misinterpreted.* Our only *rational* means for lightening it is *more understanding,* and appropriate *action* based on such understanding. The main alternative lies in acting as though the burden were not what in fact we perceive it to be and taking refuge in an outmoded theological view of man. In the latter view, man does not fashion his life and much of his world about him, but merely lives out his fate in a world created by superior beings. This may logically lead to pleading nonresponsibility in the face of seemingly unfathomable problems and difficulties. Yet, if man fails to take increasing responsibility for his actions, individually as well as collectively, it seems unlikely that some higher power or being would assume this task and carry this burden for him. Moreover, this seems hardly the proper time in human history for obscuring the issue of man's responsibility for his actions by hiding it behind the skirt of an all-explaining conception of mental illness.

### CONCLUSIONS

I have tried to show that the notion of mental illness has outlived whatever usefulness it might have had and that it now functions merely as a convenient myth. As such, it is a true heir to religious myths in general, and to the belief in witchcraft in particular; the role of all these belief-systems was to act as *social tranquilizers*, thus encouraging the hope that mastery of certain specific problems may be achieved by means of substitutive (symbolic-magical) operations. The notion of mental illness thus serves mainly to obscure the everyday fact that life for most people is a continuous struggle, not for biological survival, but for a "place in the sun," "peace of mind," or some other human value. For man aware of himself and of the world about him, once the needs for preserving the body (and perhaps the race) are more or less satisfied, the problem arises as to what he should do with himself. Sustained adherence to the myth of mental illness allows people to avoid facing this problem, believing that mental health, conceived as the absence of mental illness, automatically insures the making of right and safe choices in one's conduct of life. But the facts are all the other way. It is the making of good choices in life that others regard, retrospectively, as good mental health!

The myth of mental illness encourages us, moreover, to believe in its logical corollary: that social intercourse would be harmonious, satisfying, and the secure basis of a "good life" were it not for the disrupting influences of mental illness or "psychopathology." The potentiality for universal human happiness, in this form at least, seems to me but another example of the I-wish-it-were-true type of fantasy. I do not believe that human happiness or well-being on a hitherto unimaginably large scale, and not just for a select few, is possible. This goal could be achieved, however, only at the cost of many men, and not just a few being willing and able to tackle their personal, social, and ethical conflicts. This means having the courage and integrity to forego waging battles on false fronts, finding solutions for substitute problems—for instance, fighting the battle of stomach acid and chronic fatigue instead of facing up to a marital conflict.

Our adversaries are not demons, witches, fate, or mental illness. We have no enemy whom we can fight, exorcise, or dispel by "cure." What we do have are *problems in living*—whether these be biologic, economic, political, or sociopsychological. In this essay I was concerned only with problems belonging in the last mentioned category, and within this group mainly with those pertaining to moral values. The field to which modern psychiatry addresses itself is vast, and I made no effort to encompass it all. My argument was limited to the proposition that mental illness is a myth, whose function it is to disguise and thus render more palatable the bitter pill of moral conflicts in human relations.

## REFERENCES

HOLLINGSHEAD, A. B., & REDLICH, F. C. *Social class and mental illness.* New York: Wiley, 1958.

JONES, E. *The life and work of Sigmund Freud.* Vol. III. New York: Basic Books, 1957.

LANGER, S. K. *Philosophy in a new key.* New York: Mentor Books, 1953.

PETERS, R. S. *The concept of motivation.* London: Routledge & Kegan Paul, 1958.

SZASZ, T. S. Malingering: "Diagnosis" or social condemnation? *AMA Arch Neurol. Psychiat.,* 1956, 76, 432–443.

SZASZ, T. S. *Pain and pleasure: A study of bodily feelings.* New York: Basic Books, 1957. (a)

SZASZ, T. S. The problem of psychiatric nosology: A contribution to a situational analysis of psychiatric operations. *Amer. J. Psychiat.,* 1957, 114, 405–413. (b)

SZASZ, T. S. On the theory of psychoanalytic treatment. *Int. J. Psycho-Anal.,* 1957, 38, 166–182. (c)

SZASZ, T. S. Psychiatry, ethics and the criminal law. *Columbia law Rev.,* 1958, 58, 183–198.

SZASZ, T. S. Moral conflict and psychiatry, *Yale Rev.,* 1959, in press.

# HUMANS AS REINFORCING STIMULI IN
## SCHIZOPHRENIC PERFORMANCE

A. SHELDON GELBURD AND JAMES M. ANKER

Virtually every reference made to the performance of schizophrenics in the scientific literature alludes to their relative ineffectiveness when compared with normal Ss. Deficit behaviors of the schizophrenic have been thought to be due to underlying central nervous system pathology (e.g., Goldstein & Scheerer, 1941;Hanfmann & Kasanin, 1942) or motivational deficits of unknown origin (e.g., Hunt & Cofer, 1944; Huston & Shakow, 1948, 1949; Rodnick & Shakow, 1940). More recently, it has been shown that performance levels of schizophrenics can be dramatically improved or impaired by manipulating the aversive or appetitive qualities of reinforcing stimuli. Rodnick and Garmezy (1957), among others, suggested that schizophrenics, given proper appetitive or reward conditions, could perform almost as well as normal controls, but the presence of even mild censure tended to disrupt performance markedly. Other studies also found that schizophrenics were especially sensitive to aversive stimuli, but, additionally, found that this sensitivity led to significant facilitation of performance when efficient behavior provided the only possible avoidance of mildly noxious conditions (e.g., Anker, 1967; Atkinson & Robinson, 1961; Cavanaugh, Cohen, & Lang, 1960; Johannsen, 1961; Lang, 1959; Losen, 1961; Rosenbaum, Grisell, & Mackavey, 1957).

Several theorists have suggested that the behavior pattern associated with the syndrome is a direct manifestation of the schizophrenic's sensitivity to, and avoidance of, noxious stimuli, and that the origin of this sensitivity is persuasively interpersonal or social (Cameron, 1947; Sullivan, 1953). Distinctly human stimuli and social concepts have been found to be associated with decrements in the performance of schizophrenics (e.g., Harris, 1957; Turbiner, 1961). It has also been found that the effects of the presence of others in the experimental situation can have a marked influence on the performance of schizophrenics (Fischer, 1963; Hunter, 1961; Johannsen, 1961).

The purpose of this study was to establish the "negative" or aversive properties of humans as reinforcing stimuli for schizophrenics and to demonstrate this effect by contingent increments and decrements in psychomotor performance.

## METHOD

Ninety-one male, diagnosed schizophrenic patients, hospitalized for 1 yr. or more, without known brain damage or other confounding diagnoses, and with a clear record of a thinking disorder, were randomly assigned to seven groups of 13 Ss each. Ages ranged 20–55 yr. ($\bar{X} = 34.62$, $s = 8.24$), and education level 1–15 yr. (skewed, $mdn. = 3.08$). Between-group differences on these control variables were non-significant.

The task consisted of cancelling by pencil 90 "a's," interspersed every third to sixth letter with other letters on double-spaced lines. Five alternate forms allowed five different trials for each S. All Ss received the forms in the same order, with intervening rest periods of approximately the same duration as required by the task trials.

The effects of two independent variables were studied: (a) the amount of human stimulation impinging on S, and (b) when, relative to the

JOURNAL OF ABNORMAL PSYCHOLOGY, 1970, Vol. 75, pp. 195-198.

25

## TABLE 1
### ANALYSES OF VARIANCE

| Source of variation | df | $\Sigma x^2$ | $M^2$ | F | P |
|---|---|---|---|---|---|
| *Absence and intense groups* | | | | | |
| Method | 3 | 2 772.5 | 924.2 | 4.30 | <.01 |
| Within | 48 | 10 319.9 | 214.9 | | |
| Total | 51 | 13 092.4 | | | |
| *Absence and moderate groups* | | | | | |
| Method | 3 | 1 893.5 | 631.2 | 3.20 | <.05 |
| Within | 48 | 9 451.3 | 196.9 | | |
| Total | 51 | 11 344.8 | | | |
| *Absence and combined moderate and intense conditions* | | | | | |
| Method | 3 | 3 878.7 | 1292.90 | 6.23 | <.01 |
| Within | 87 | 18 067.3 | 207.67 | | |
| Total | 90 | 21 946.0 | | | |

period of task performance, these stimuli were presented.

Amount of human stimulation was varied at three levels: (a) none, S alone and E out of the room; (b) moderate, E sitting approximately 4 ft. in front and 10 ft. to the side of S, reading, looking away; and (c) intense, E at the side of S's table facing him.

The presence of E relative to task and rest periods was varied in four ways: (a) E with S during both task and rest periods (task-rest group); (b) E present during task but absent during rest periods (task group); (c) E absent during task but present during rest periods (rest group); and (d) E absent during both task and rest periods (absence group).

The first author served as E and was not familiar with the Ss before the study began. The dependent variable, increments in psychomotor speed, was measured by time in seconds to complete the first letter cancellation trial minus time on the fifth trial.

If schizophrenics are motivated to avoid the presence of humans, then Ss in the task group, especially in the intense category, should perform the letter cancellation task more efficiently because by doing so they reduce the proportionate amount of time E spends with them. Conversely, Ss in the rest group, especially in the intense category, should show relative decrements in performing the letter cancellation task because this inefficient performance proportionately would lengthen the amount of time away from E. The standard for both of these comparisons would be performance levels of the absence group which functioned without any interpersonal contingencies. The task-rest group, where the presence of E was not contingent upon performance, should show a relative inefficiency in performance because of the continuing interfering effects of an aversive stimulus.

The Ss were observed through a one-way screen by an assistant who timed trials and operated a 1-sec. warning light, followed 3 sec. later by a 1-sec. starting buzzer. Testing was done individually. The Ss were acclimated to the experimental room by E and given general instructions regarding the nature of the experiment and their participation in it. The letter cancellation task was explained in detail, illustrated, and the functions of the warning light and starting buzzer described. The Ss were told to finish the page as fast as they could and to signal their completion by banging the pencil down on the table.

All groups received identical instructions and treatments on the first trial. The E was absent during the first task period for all groups to establish an initial level of performance. Differential treatment began with the onset of the first rest period. Brief instructions were given at that time, setting conditions of the presence of E, for example, for the task group, "You can rest now. I'll go out while you rest. In a little while I'll have a new page of letters for you to do and I'll sit here while you do them [The E then indicated the chair by the desk, then left the room]."

Instructions were modified appropriately for the several treatment combinations. At the beginning of Trial 2, instructions were again given for each treatment combination. Trials (task and rest periods) followed without interruption through Trial 5.

### RESULTS

Some Ss completed the trials without cancelling all of the a's and some cancelled letters other than a. These omissions and errors were not remarkably frequent and there were no significant differences among treatment groups on either, for Trial 1 or Trial 5.

There were no indications that Ss were aware of the several contingencies of E's presence or of the nature of the study in that regard.

The data were analyzed in three steps. The three treatment groups in the intense category were evaluated with the standard, the absence group. The three treatment groups in the moderate category were evaluated with the standard, the absence group. Finally, the three treatment groups, summed over the intense and moderate conditions, were evaluated. In each analysis, dependent data were increments in letter cancellation speed between the first and fifth trial.

Results of the analysis of variance for the absence and the intense groups are presented in the first part of Table 1. Figure 1 presents the mean speed increments between the first and the last trial of these groups. Consistent with expectations, relative to the absence group, speed increments were better for the task group and slower for the rest and task-rest groups. The $F$ was significant at less than the .01 level, and Duncan's new multiple-range test established differences at the .01 level between the task and rest groups and the task and task-rest groups.

A similar, although less extreme, pattern was found among the absence and the moderate groups. The $F$ was significant at less than the .05 level, and Duncan's new multiple-range test established a difference at the .01 level between the task and rest groups. These results are presented in the second portion of Table 1. Figure 2 illustrates the similarity of pattern between the moderate and intense conditions. Interestingly enough, the relative retardation of learning in the task-rest group is less pronounced under the moderate condition.

The data for the task, rest, and task-rest groups were summed over the moderate and intense conditions and analyzed with absence group data, adjusting for unequal $n$'s, to allow a more precise statement of the general effect. These results are presented in the last

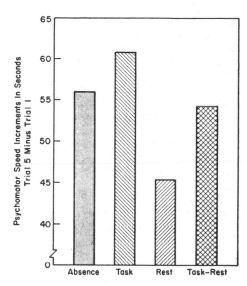

FIG. 2. Mean increments for absence and moderate groups.

portion of Table 1. As expected, the $F$ was significant at less than the .01 level. Duncan's test established differences at the .01 level between the task and rest groups and at the .05 level between the task and task-rest groups.

## DISCUSSION

The performance levels of the absence group, which were not contingent on the presence or absence of $E$, uniformly were midway between the faster speeds of the task groups and the slower speeds of the rest and task-rest groups. Presumably, when reducing the time spent by $E$ with $S$ was contingent on efficient performance, such improvement occurred. On the other hand, when the return of $E$ during the rest period could be delayed by responding less efficiently on the task, this too occurred. These data suggest that the presence of an unfamiliar person is an aversive stimulus for schizophrenic patients. The similarity of the results for the rest and task-rest groups makes this clear. If patients performed the task more efficiently in the presence of $E$ because of the desire to please him or to do well for him, then the data for the task-rest groups, with $E$ present during both task and

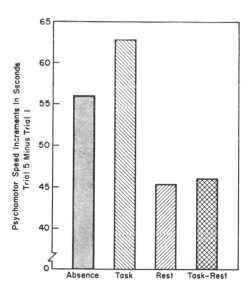

FIG. 1. Mean increments for absence and intense groups.

27

rest periods, should be similar to the data for the task group. This clearly is not the case. Escape from the presence of $E$ appears to have had definite reinforcing properties, and surprisingly consistent and strong ones at that. When a reduction in human stimulation was not contingent on performance, the continuous presence of $E$ tended to lower performance efficiency generally.

While the results support initial predictions, the scope and applicability of this study are obviously limited. Data were gathered with only one $E$, and such human variables as age, sex, degree of familiarity, physiognomy, and body type were not studied. Also the possibility of changing reinforcement values of particular persons by exposure over time and under proper conditions was not studied.

## REFERENCES

ANKER, J. M. Toward the therapeutic modification of schizophrenic behavior. *British Journal of Social Psychiatry*, 1967, 1, 304–312.

ATKINSON, R. L., & ROBINSON, N. M. Paired-associate learning by schizophrenic and normal subjects under conditions of personal and impersonal reward and punishment. *Journal of Abnormal and Social Psychology*, 1961, 62, 322–326.

CAMERON, N. *The psychology of behavior disorders: A biosocial approach.* Boston: Houghton Mifflin, 1947.

CAVANAUGH, D. K., COHEN, W., & LANG, P. J. The effect of "social censure" and "social approval" on the psychomotor performance of schizophrenics. *Journal of Abnormal and Social Psychology*, 1960, 60, 213–218.

FISCHER, E. H. Task performance of chronic schizophrenics as a function of verbal evaluation and social proximity. *Journal of Clinical Psychology*, 1963, 19, 176–178.

GOLDSTEIN, D., & SHEERER, M. Abstract and concrete behavior: An experimental study with special tests. *Psychological Monographs*, 1941, 53(2, Whole No. 239).

HANFMANN, E., & KASANIN, J. Conceptual thinking in schizophrenia. *Nervous and Mental Disorder Monographs*, 1942, No. 67.

HARRIS, J. G., JR. Size estimation of pictures as a function of thematic content for schizophrenic and normal subjects. *Journal of Personality*, 1957, 25, 651–671.

HUNT, J. McV., & COFER, C. N. Psychological deficit. In J. McV. Hunt (Ed.), *Personality and the behavior disorders.* New York: Ronald Press, 1944.

HUNTER, M. The effects of interpersonal interaction upon the task performance of chronic schizophrenics. *Dissertation Abstracts*, 1961, 21, 2004.

HUSTON, P. E., & SHAKOW, D. Learning in schizophrenia: I. Pursuit learning. *Journal of Personality*, 1948, 17, 52–74.

HUSTON, P. E., & SHAKOW, D. Learning capacity in schizophrenia. *American Journal of Psychiatry*, 1949, 105, 881–888.

JOHANNSEN, W. J. Responsiveness of chronic schizophrenics and normals to social and nonsocial feedback. *Journal of Abnormal and Social Psychology*, 1961, 62, 106–113.

LANG, P. J. The effect of aversive stimuli on reaction time in schizophrenia. *Journal of Abnormal and Social Psychology*, 1959, 59, 263–268.

LOSEN, S. M. The differential effects of censure on the problem-solving behavior of schizophrenic and normal subjects. *Journal of Personality*, 1961, 29, 258–272.

RODNICK, E. H., & SHAKOW, D. Set in the schizophrenic as measured by a composite reaction time index. *American Journal of Psychiatry*, 1940, 97, 214–225.

RODNICK, E. H., & GARMEZY, N. An experimental approach to the study of motivation in schizophrenia. *Nebraska Symposium on Motivation*, 1957, 5, 109–184.

ROSENBAUM, G., GRISELL, J. L., & MACKAVEY, W. R. Effects of biological and social motivation on schizophrenic reaction time. *Journal of Abnormal and Social Psychology*, 1957, 54, 364–368.

SULLIVAN, H. S. *The interpersonal theory of psychiatry.* New York: Norton, 1953.

TURBINER, M. Choice discrimination in schizophrenics and normal subjects for positive, negative, and neutral affective stimuli. *Journal of Consulting Psychology*, 1961, 25, 92.

# MENTAL ILLNESS AND THE IMPACT OF BELIEVING OTHERS KNOW ABOUT IT [1]

AMERIGO FARINA, DONALD GLIHA, LOUIS A. BOUDREAU,
JON G. ALLEN, AND MARK SHERMAN

It seems intuitively obvious that an interaction between two people will not go smoothly when one of them has a deeply degrading stigma such as having been mentally ill. There is ample research which leads one to hold such an expectation. The mentally ill are disliked and degraded to a surprising degree, as has convincingly been demonstrated by numerous investigators (Cohen & Struening, 1962; Cumming & Cumming, 1957; Ellsworth, 1965; Jones & Kahn, 1964; Manis, Houts, & Blake, 1963; Lamy, 1966; Lawner, 1966; Nunnally, 1961; Sherman, 1967; Struening & Cohen, 1963). For instance, insane people are less acceptable as friends and neighbors than dope addicts or ex-convicts and are described as more worthless than those who are blind or have leprosy. We would expect, then, that such highly unfavorable attitudes would influence the perceptions and behaviors of an individual toward someone he believes to have been mentally ill. Both laboratory and field studies have been done which quite clearly indicate this to be the case (Cohen & Struening, 1964; Farina, Holland, & Ring, 1966; Farina & Ring, 1965; Jones, Hester, Farina, & Davis, 1959). A person thought to have had a mental illness is not only evaluated less favorably and blamed for nonexistent shortcomings, but people also behave differently and generally more harshly toward him. In the Farina et al. (1966) study,

[1] The present studies were financed by research grants from the National Science Foundation (GS-848 and GS-2646). The authors' thanks are due to the staffs of the Norwich Hospital, Norwich, Connecticut, and the Providence Veterans Administration Hospital, Providence, Rhode Island.

JOURNAL OF ABNORMAL PSYCHOLOGY, 1971, Vol. 77, pp. 1-5.

for example, a confederate revealed to random groups of $S$s either that he had been hospitalized for mental illness or was reasonably well adjusted. The $S$s then had to shock him in order to guide him to the correct solution of a problem. Although the confederate behaved identically in the two conditions, his behavior was judged less adequate, he was liked less, he was given more painful shocks, and $S$s desired no further interaction with him when he reported a deviant personal history.

These studies substantiate the commonsense expectation that the "normal" is a contributor to the difficulty in the interaction between himself and a stigmatized person. They also suggest how this difficulty in the relationship is brought about. But the normal is not the only one involved in the interaction, of course, and he may not be the only one responsible for the problems a stigmatized person encounters in his dealings with others. Possibly a stigma is as important and salient for the afflicted as for the observer, and the blemished individual's perceptions and actions toward another person in an interaction may be greatly influenced by his stigma independently of the behavior of others. In fact, there is a study by Farina, Allen, and Saul (1968) which suggests this is exactly what happens. In that study, male undergraduate students who were unacquainted with each other were run in pairs. For some pairs, one of the $S$s was led to believe he had revealed he was a homosexual or had been mentally ill, whereas in fact the other $S$ always received the same neutral information. The results were that merely believing they were viewed as stigmatized influenced the $S$s' behaviors and caused them to be rejected by the other person. This study suggests the intriguing possibility that the rejection stigmatized people expect and fear is, in part, caused by themselves. However, the $S$s were ordinary college students and it remains to be determined if truly blemished people behave this way. That was the purpose of the two experiments being reported here.

# STUDY I

*Method*

A total of 30 Caucasian male psychiatric patients, none of whom had been in the hospital for more than 6 mo., were the *S*s of this study. They were contacted on their wards and asked to volunteer for an experiment which would in no way influence their status in the hospital. The study was described to them as concerned with finding out how well college students worked with patients in comparison to nonpatients. It was pointed out that such knowledge might be of aid in selecting students who wanted to do volunteer work in the hospital. They were further told that to do the study college students were brought to the hospital to work with patients, but only half of the students would be told the person with whom they were working was a patient. The remainder would be told the patient was a hospital employee, a maintenance worker. Half of the patients, selected at random, were then told that in their case the student believed them to be a maintenance worker and the remainder were informed that the student knew they were patients. They were then brought to a room where they met a college student, a confederate, who behaved in the same way with all *S*s and who was unaware of any *S*'s group membership. The groups of *S*s were seemingly representative of relatively acute state hospital patients, being, on the average, 30.9 yr. of age and having a mean of 11.6 yr. of education. Those assigned to the patient and worker groups were quite comparable for these two characteristics as well as all others examined, such as occupation, marital status, and diagnosis.

Patient and confederate were then told they would be working on a task as a cooperative team and that they were to do their best. The patient would first get 30 trials on a maze-like game sold commercially under the name "Labyrintspel" and the student would then get 15 trials. The game involves manipulating two knobs which can make the top of the box assume any angle and thus, by skillful manipulation, a steel ball can be made to move along a line toward the goal without falling into the holes which border the line. The Labyrintspel is described more fully elsewhere (Farina et al., 1968). It was explained to them that a single team score, consisting of the sum of the scores of each member, would be obtained. Cooperation was further required in that each person was not only to do his best, but one was also to make his partner profit from his experience. To accomplish this, the first performer (always the patient) was to describe verbally what the task was like while doing it. He was then given three practice trials followed by 30 trials with a 1-min. rest period after Trial 15. Following this, the confederate was given 15 trials while the patient was asked to verbally guide his performance. Their permission to tape-record all the verbal material was requested and obtained. This task was selected because it seemed particularly suited to revealing the effects of the manipulation, such as how

31

esteemed or stigmatized the patient felt and how much he thought someone would listen to his advice and take it seriously. A postexperimental questionnaire was finally administered to each person. The confederate's copy was primarily concerned with determining the impression the patients made on him, whether they appeared friendly, introverted, likable, etc. He was also asked to guess in which group they were. The patient's copy focused on how enjoyable he found the task, how helpful he thought he had been, and how he was evaluated by the other person. The questionnaires contained 8 and 11 items, respectively.

## RESULTS AND DISCUSSION

Analyses of the dependent measures revealed that none was significantly different for the two groups of $S$s. Virtually all of the measures were in the expected direction, and some of the differences were substantial. Most especially, patients spoke less to the confederate, manifested more anxiety in their speech according to a silence ratio score (Farina & Holzberg, 1970), and were less willing to work with the confederate in the future when they thought their status as patient was known by him. Nevertheless, none of the differences was significant, which suggests that it is not important to the patient whether someone knows about his history or not. At any rate, his belief about this does not influence the behaviors measured in the present study.

However, this conclusion does not appear wholly justifiable. There were, first of all, the directional trends described. Also, during the course of the study, we became aware of a number of factors which could have interfered with an adequate test of the hypothesis. Some of the patients appeared to be disturbed to an extent that the manipulation meant rather little to them. When only the seven most intact[2] patients in each group were considered, the difference between the groups in anxiety manifested in speech became much more marked. Moreover, many of the patients spontaneously indicated the students would not believe they were hospital employees because

---

[2] The selection was based on the score of the Hospital Adjustment Scale which was completed for each patient by an aide (Ferguson, McReynolds, & Ballachy, 1953).

of their clothes, which, in fact, were frequently slovenly and not of a type a maintenance man might be expected to wear. Finally, these were patients who were institutionalized at the time of the study. Ordinarily, they have little hope of hiding from anyone the fact that they were patients. Possibly it was difficult for them, given their circumstances and the setting in which they were seen, to really believe they could be seen in any way but as mental patients. Therefore, it was decided to make another test of this hypothesis using procedures which these considerations suggest.

## Study II

*Method*

Formerly hospitalized Caucasion males were the subjects of this study. All were undergoing psychotherapy at a Veterans Administration hospital outpatient clinic at the time of the study but were residing in the community. The patients' psychiatrists asked each to volunteer as an *S* after screening out those who might conceivably be upset by the experience. Those who volunteered—virtually all who were asked—subsequently met an *E* who explained more fully the nature of the study and arranged a time for the patient to participate. The explanation given was that the research was concerned with the problems faced by ex-mental patients in finding a job. Specifically, they were told, we would attempt to determine if potential employers were less likely to hire someone if he had a history of mental illness. Interestingly, many of the *S*s spontaneously reported that this had certainly been their experience and that it was only possible to get a job if one hid his history of mental illness from an employer. The person they were to meet was described as one of a number of trainees in hiring and personnel who were recruited from business establishments. It was further said that some of the trainees would know they were meeting a mental patient, whereas others would be told they were meeting a medical-surgical patient. This was quite believable since the large Veterans Administration hospital where the study was done treats nonmental patients principally. As in Study I, half of the patients were told that the trainee knew their true status and the remainder were told they were perceived as medical-surgical patients. Also as in Study I, the confederate remained ignorant of the group to which the *S*s were assigned. Table 1 presents descriptive data for the total group of 29 *S*s. Fifteen were assigned to the medical-surgical group and 14 to the mental patient group. There were no statistically significant differences between the two groups for any of the characteristics shown in the table. The sample appears similar to that

33

## TABLE 1

DESCRIPTIVE CHARACTERISTICS OF THE 29
SUBJECTS OF STUDY 2

| Item | No. |
|------|-----|
| Mean age | 39.3 |
| Mean grades completed | 11.7 |
| Warner index of occupational status | 5.0 |
| Percent diagnosed as schizophrenic | 54 |

of Study I except the *S*s are about 10 yr. older as might be expected in view of the different criteria they had to meet. As in Study I, they are of lower socioeconomic class. This is shown by the average education and the type of jobs held which average out to 5 in a 7-category (Category 1 being highest) rating system devised by Warner, Meeker, and Eells (1960).

The procedure employed was in essence the same as that of Study I. However, the patient was given only 20 trials after 3 practice trials and the confederate was then given 20 trials. Also, the patient was asked to talk at four points in the task; after he completed each block of 10 trials, after the confederate's practice trials, and after the confederate's first block of 10 trials. This change was instituted in the hope of reducing the marked individual differences found in Study I in willingness to talk. All speech was recorded and both participants were asked to complete questionnaires similar to those of Study I. The confederate's questionnaire contained eight items while the patient's contained nine plus a check of the manipulation.

## RESULTS

The speech and task performance dependent measures are shown in Table 2. As in Study I, patients spoke more when under the impression their co-worker was unaware they were mental patients. However, the difference was not statistically reliable. The anxiety score difference is quantitatively trivial although the

## TABLE 2

MEAN SPEECH AND LABYRINTSPEL SCORES OF
THE SUBJECTS IN THE TWO CONDITIONS

| S | Total time talked (in sec.) | Silence ratio | Labyrintspel score (20 trials) |
|---|---|---|---|
| Medical patient | 127.7 | .3122 | 65.0 |
| Mental patient | 108.8 | .3153 | 54.1 |

Note.—For the silence ratio, higher scores suggest greater anxiety.

direction of the difference is the same as before, that is, belief that the other knows about the stigma is associated with greater anxiety. The last score in Table 2 shows that Ss in the medical patient condition performed better on the Labyrintspel than those in the mental patient condition. The significance level of the difference is between the .05 and .10 level according to an analysis of variance.

The Ss' questionnaire responses revealed several interesting patterns. One of the items asked S to indicate how helpful he thought he had been and another to evaluate how helpful the trainee had judged him. By comparing these two items, it is possible to determine how many Ss in each group felt their contribution was underestimated and how many thought it was overvalued. The results were that six of the medical group Ss thought their contribution was overestimated by the trainee, whereas none of the Ss in the other group thought that. This difference is statistically significant at the .05 level. The only other difference was for the difficulty of the task, which was rated as more difficult by the mental patient Ss ($p < .10$). As for the confederate, he was not able to guess the group membership of the Ss beyond chance level. However, he rated the mental patient Ss as significantly more tense and anxious than those of the other group ($p < .05$). Also, he rated them as more poorly adjusted ($p < .10$). No other item reached a probability level of less than .10 (two-tailed).

## DISCUSSION

Study II presents a fairly coherent picture of what happens to a mental patient when he meets others he believes to be aware of his psychiatric history. He perceives those others as less appreciative of his efforts, he finds at least certain kinds of tasks more difficult, he tends to perform them less adequately, and (perhaps because of this) he is seen as more tense, anxious, and more poorly adjusted by a neutral observer. Study I lends some support to this conclusion since the direction of the differences was generally consistent with those of Study II. This conclusion holds numerous implications, some of which follow quite directly. Clearly, in an initial interaction with new people, and perhaps particularly on a job situation, former patients are better off if they believe those about them are unaware they once were patients. Perhaps patients should simply be advised not to reveal their history to co-workers. Whether to inform an employment interviewer is more of a problem. Patients frequently report being in a dilemma since if they inform him not only will they feel discomfort but may be refused work, while if they say nothing their history may later come to light and the situation be worse.

A much more general, if more tentative, implication is based on the assumption, almost certainly true, that all people have stigmatizing characteristics that are not obvious to others. These may differ in degree only from a history of mental illness. The present research suggests that, rather than disclosing these characteristics, there are some advantages in remaining very quiet about our moral lapses, shortcomings, and other facts viewed as unsavory. Not only does this study suggest that our own composure and behavior will be disrupted as a consequence of disclosure, but other research indicates that we will be treated more harshly. Thus in a study by Mosher, Farina, and Gliha (1970) a confederate was administered much more painful shocks when she let it be known she had been a prostitute than when she did not. Of course, further research may reveal this conclusion to hold only under certain types of conditions.

While belief that their psychiatric history was known influenced some of the patients' behaviors, other behaviors appeared unaffected. In particular, none of the speech measures in either study was (significantly) influenced although the studies were designed on the assumption that these were most likely to respond to the manipulation. Since evidence indicates that speech patterns do reflect changes in anxiety (Geer, 1966), it may be that patients learn to control certain behaviors such as speech, whereas a new task such as the

Labyrintspel reveals their underlying anxiety. Of course, it may not be very traumatic to meet someone known to be aware of one's mental illness and that would explain the limited changes in behavior which were found. All of the *S*s must have had such experiences many times prior to serving in the present study and they may have adapted to the situation. This is in contrast to the procedure of the Farina et al. (1968) study where college students for the first time believed themselves viewed as severely stigmatized and displayed numerous behavioral changes. But surely who it is that becomes aware and the circumstances under which it happens are bound to make an important difference. In both the studies reported the patient was told the other person was the focus of the research's interests, which may have served to reduce self-consciousness. Also, the patient was anticipating no further interaction following the experiment and, despite our efforts, the other person may not have appeared very important to the patient. Hence, the studies may only approximate the situation in which the former patient is facing a number of people who are very important to his future since they are neighbors, peers, and co-workers. If such people became aware of a history of mental illness, the impact upon a former patient's behavior might be much more evident. Further research along these lines would be relevant to mental illness, and, for the reasons considered, it might also be relevant to much day-to-day interpersonal behavior.

## REFERENCES

COHEN, J., & STRUENING, E. L. Opinions about mental illness in the personnel of two large mental hospitals. *Journal of Abnormal and Social Psychology*, 1962, 64, 349–360.

COHEN, J., & STRUENING, E. L. Opinions about mental health: Hospital social atmosphere profiles and their relevance to effectiveness. *Journal of Consulting Psychology*, 1964, 28, 291–298.

CUMMING, E., & CUMMING, J. *Closed ranks. An experiment in mental health education.* Cambridge, Mass.: Harvard University Press, 1957.

ELLSWORTH, R. B. A behavioral study of staff attitudes toward mental illness. *Journal of Abnormal Psychology*, 1965, 70, 194–200.

FARINA, A., ALLEN, J. G. & SAUL. B. B. B. The role of the stigmatized in affecting social relationships. *Journal of Personality*, 1968, **36**, 169–182,

FARINA, A., HOLLAND, C. H., & RING, K. The role of stigma and set in interpersonal interaction. *Journal of Abnormal Psychology*, 1966, **71**, 421–428.

FARINA, A., & HOLZBERG, J. D. Anxiety level of schizophrenic and control patients and their parents. *Journal of Abnormal Psychology*, 1970, **73**, 157–163.

FARINA, A., & RING, K. The influence of perceived mental illness on interpersonal relations. *Journal of Abnormal Psychology*, 1965, **70**, 47–51.

FERGUSON, J. T., McREYNOLDS, P., & BALLACHY, E. L. *Hospital Adjustment Scale*. Palo Alto, Calif.: Leland Stanford Junior University, 1953.

GEER, J. H. Effect of fear arousal upon task performance and verbal behavior. *Journal of Abnormal Psychology*, 1966, **71**, 119–123.

JONES, E. E., HESTER, S. L., FARINA, A., & DAVIS, K. E. Reactions to unfavorable personal evaluations as a function of the evaluator's perceived adjustment. *Journal of Abnormal and Social Psychology*, 1959, **59**, 363–370.

JONES, N. F., & KAHN, M. W. Patient attitudes as related to social class and other variables concerned with hospitalization. *Journal of Consulting Psychology*, 1964, **28**, 403–408.

LAMY, R. E. Social consequences of mental illness. *Journal of Consulting Psychology*, 1966, **30**, 450–455.

LAWNER, P. Unfavorable attitudes and behavior toward those bearing mental illness stigmas. Unpublished master's thesis. Storrs: University of Connecticut, 1966.

MANIS, M., HOUTS, P. S., & BLAKE, J. B. Beliefs about mental illness as a function of psychiatric status and psychiatric hospitalization. *Journal of Abnormal and Social Psychology*, 1963, **67**, 226–233.

MOSHER, D. L., FARINA, A., & GLIHA, D. F. Moral stigma punishment and guilt. Unpublished manuscript. Storrs: University of Connecticut, 1970.

NUNNALLY, J. C., JR. *Popular conceptions of mental health*. New York: Holt, Rinehart, & Winston, 1961.

SHERMAN, M. The influence of perceived mental illness and competence of performance on interpersonal impressions. Unpublished master's thesis. Storrs: University of Connecticut, 1967.

STRUENING, E. L., & COHEN, J. Factorial invariance and other psychometric characteristics of five opinions about mental illness factors. *Educational and Psychological Measurement*, 1963, **23**, 289–298.

WARNER, W. L., MEEKER, M., & Eells, K. *Social class in America*. New York: Harper & Row, 1960.

38

# THE MEDICAL MODEL IN SPECIAL EDUCATION

ROGER REGER

Today one finds occasional references in the literature, at seminars and conferences, and in professional discussions to the "medical model" or the "psychodynamic disease model," but there seems to be little or no general understanding of what the medical model is or how it is defined. This lack of understanding frequently can lead to muddled attempts at communication. Perhaps the question is not one of understanding, but rather of agreement. When two persons talk about the medical model and each has in mind a different conception of this model, it is very difficult to get together on any matters that follow in the ensuing stages of that particular communication. If the two persons can refer to a common definition, at least they can continue in their chain of communication.

## DEFINITION

There are many ways to view differences in human behavior. Valentine (1971) has outlined three models that deal with variations in groups within our society: deficit, differences, and bicultural. I have reviewed the use of the medical model in therapeutic efforts to change behavior (Reger, 1966). The medical model can be

PSYCHOLOGY IN THE SCHOOLS, 1972, Vol. 9, pp. 8-12.

discussed in a variety of contexts and situations: education, medicine, psychology, social work, and so on. This paper will focus only on the medical model in special education.

Two basic assumptions are inherent in the conception of the medical model in special education:

1. Behavior that deviates in a negative direction from normative standards is a reflection of a personal disease (or illness, disturbance, disorder, dysfunction).

2. Behavior that has been classified as deviant must be changed within the individual by a curative process.

Personal experience has suggested that many who discuss the medical model seem to be able to agree on these two major components. But when these two broad components are developed into practical workaday applications, there is no common agreement. For example, in a recent panel discussion led by the author the two basic assumptions seemed to be acceptable to everybody, but a psychiatrist in the group insisted that he worked outside the conceptual framework of the medical model, a logical impossibility unless he changed roles and did not work as a psychiatrist.

Now to elaborate on the first assumption, that deviant behavior is the reflection of a personal or inner disease. This assumption implies that children who cannot maintain themselves, or be maintained by the school, in the typical educational program have something wrong with them. The term "disease" itself seldom is used; other terms such as dysfunction, disorder, disturbance, or maladaptation are used instead.

Typically, after workups by psychologists and others, children whose behavior is deviant on the negative end of the frequency curve are "diagnosed." The categories into which the children are placed include mental retardation (with such nonsensical adjectives as "educable" and "trainable"), brain injury, brain damage, neurological dysfunction, emotional disturbance, and related labels.

When the medical model is used, it is the child who is mentally retarded or emotionally disturbed. Once the school has produced its diagnosis, it has relieved itself of any real responsibility for the child. It is not recognized that a child is "mentally retarded" or "emotionally disturbed" only because of the demands made upon him by school and society as reflected by the school. While an argument could be made that it is not the child who is retarded or disturbed, but rather the school, this argument simply would focus the medical-model spotlight on the other side of the coin.

The other assumption, that diseased behavior (or behavior that reflects a disease) must be cured, also has practical implications that influence special educational programs. After all, what does one do with a "mentally retarded" child other than to offer him education or training? What happens to the "emotionally disturbed" child? Does he simply cease to be emotionally disturbed for some unknown reason after an unspecifiable time? Or, in fact, is it the assumption of the medical model that this child has been "cured" of his emotional disturbance if his behavior changes from negatively deviant to somewhere within the normal or acceptable range?

Within the medical model some children, for instance the mentally retarded, are not "cured" but only receive continuous "care" or "treatment." The same applies to deaf, blind, and orthopedically disabled children. For emotionally disturbed children there are deliberate attempts to remove (cure, treat, alleviate) the emotional disturbance; if this fails, they fall into the care or rehabilitation category. No attempts are made to repair or cure the damaged brains of children classified as "brain injured," rather it is assumed that "other pathways" are developed or alternate forms of behavior are programmed into these children.

## TECHNIQUES

Many assume that they can maintain a professional "attitude" or "set" in adherence to the medical model, but actually perform their work outside the medical model. For example, a child can be "diagnosed" as emotionally disturbed, but his subsequent "treatment" will be based on a non-medically-modelled educational program. The assumption of the agent who produced the diagnosis is that education is a method of cure. If the educational program is operated on the same assumption, then obviously the program has a conceptual underpinning that is consistent with the medical model.

Sometimes a child may be classified as emotionally disturbed by a psychiatric agency, but the school may be independent of the conceptual or practical influence of the psychiatric group. In such a case, where the school does not consider the child to be emotionally disturbed and thus in need of a cure, the child has been classified in two different ways by two different agencies. Many find this possibility very disturbing; the feeling is that the outside agency and the school are operating at cross purposes or that they are not working together. But in fact the psychiatric agency can retain its conceptual viewpoint of the child and his living experiences without having to assume that there will be damage if the school insists on operating its programs within an "educational model" rather than a medical model. If any damage should occur, it is most likely to be as a result of an attempt to operate an educational program with an alien and impractical set of assumptions.

The techniques used to *diagnose* and then *cure* deviant children do not have a bearing on whether the process is related to the medical model. Many feel that if a psychiatrist works in a public school setting he therefore is not working within the medical model—simply because he has stepped outside his office or hospital. Or, at a slightly higher level of sophistication, many feel that if psychiatrists should work directly with teachers rather than with individual children, they therefore are not operating within the medical model framework. But if a child with problems is viewed within the framework of the medical model and his needs are defined within the framework of a "cure," then it does not matter whether individual psychotherapy or total environment is employed as a strategy.

## PERSONNEL

The most heat can be generated in discussions of the application of the medical model to special education when personnel are mentioned: *who* are the people who adhere to the medical model?

For some reason many of those who work within the framework of the medical model deny this relationship. "Yes," they will admit, "I believe it is conceptually proper for a child to be diagnosed as emotionally disturbed and then placed into a special class for the treatment of this condition." Then the speaker will add, "But I don't believe in the medical model." In fact it is interesting to note that many persons who practice within a medical-model context, but for some reason do not care to admit this, usually terminate a discussion about the matter with, "What difference does it make! I am concerned about *kids*!" This is a rather mindless admission that one does not have a guiding philosophy or is not aware of the determinants of one's actions.

With the exception of medical personnel themselves, whether or not an individual professional person follows the concepts of the medical model is determined ultimately by his actions as well as by his ideas (under the perhaps naive assumption that ideas determine action). Thus, school psychologists, teachers, social workers, administrators, and speech correctionists (but not speech therapists) may or may not work under the umbrella of the medical model. The school psychologist who administers intellectual and "personality" tests and classifies students as mentally retarded, etc., is a medical-model psychologist. The teacher who uses a "psycho-educational" approach or a "clinical" approach is a medical-model teacher. The administrator who employs "clinical personnel" in his programs thereby at least approaches the medical-model framework.

### DISCUSSION

What is "wrong" with the medical model? There is nothing wrong except to use the model in an alien context or to use the model and then deny doing so. It certainly makes sense for physicians to practice medicine within the conceptual framework of the medical model.

An attorney who tried to practice law within the context of a religious model probably would experience difficulty. A minister who tried to work with his congregation within the framework of a legal context probably would experience problems. A physician who did not believe in the prevention, diagnosis, and cure of disease undoubtedly would find his life somewhat confusing.

A teacher who believes his task is to diagnose and then cure children is not working within an appropriate conceptual context. A teacher's task is to help children learn, to guide them in growth toward established objectives in whatever areas are determined to be important by the profession and the community. The differences that exist among children should be recognized as legitimate, as normal, and as part of the human condition, rather than as "disease," "deficits," "deviations," and similar notions of a negative cast. Difference is not abnormal; difference is normal.

In the educational context there is no "mentally retarded child," and there is no "emotionally disturbed child." Children may have labels applied to them by others, just as some children are classified as "rural," as "teenagers," or as "tall." When a child enters a hospital for a heart condition he is treated as a child heart patient, not as a third grader. The hospital staff is concerned with definition and treatment of the child's medical condition, not his progress in reading.

When a child is seen as a "patient" in school, when he is looked at as a carrier of a medical-model illness (or deviation, etc.), then the teacher and the school are relieved of much of the responsibility for the child. If he makes little or no progress, it is because of him and his condition rather than the school teacher. If he makes too much of a problem for the school, the administration can say, "We're not set up here to handle that kind of child."

To add a note of positive philosophy, the school is responsible for *all* children, not just those who fit into the "normal range." The medical model has been a compromising agent between the school's view of itself as not having responsibility for problem (or deviant) children and parental demands for educational programs. Special education has served as the vehicle for attempts to mediate between the school and parent.

Eventually it will be necessary to avoid attempts to define educational problems, such as behavioral/performance differences in children, in non-educational terms. If a child cannot read, it is a learning problem; to relegate this problem to limbo through the use of such pseudo-medical jargon as "dyslexia" to classify the problem is an evasion of responsibility.

### REFERENCES

REGER, R. Behavior therapy, psychoanalysis, and the "medical model." *Psychology in the Schools,* 1966, *3,* 129-131.
VALENTINE, C. A. Deficit, difference, and bicultural models of Afro-American behavior. *Harvard Educational Review,* 1971, *41,* 137-157.

# Sociocultural Factors in Labeling Mental Retardates

JANE R. MERCER

## Problem

Field surveys,[2] studies using informants,[3] and educational surveys[4] consistently show a disproportionately large number of persons from ethnic minorities among those labeled as retarded by clinical measures. Such disproportions are especially noticeable in school populations. For example, the ethnic survey conducted annually since 1966 by the California State Department of Education has consistently shown

[1] Most of the data presented in this paper is adapted from a forthcoming volume by Jane R. Mercer entitled *The Eligibles and the Labeled*. This investigation was supported by Public Health Service Research Grant No. MH-08667 from the National Institute of Mental Health, Department of Health, Education, and Welfare, and Public Service General Research Support Grant No. 1-S01-FR-05632-02 from the Department of Health, Education, and Welfare.

[2] J. F. Jastak. H. M. MacPhee, and M. Whiteman, *Mental Retardation: Its Nature and Incidence* (Newark, Delaware, 1963); P. Lemkau, C. Tietze, and M. Cooper, "Mental-hygiene Problems in an Urban District," *Mental Hygiene*, XXV (January 1941), 624-646; W. P. Richardson, A. C. Higgins, and R. G. Ames, *The Handicapped Children of Alamance County, North Carolina: A Medical and Sociological Study*. (Wilmington, 1965).

[3] R. G. Ferguson, *A Study of the Problem of Mental Retardation in the City of Philadelphia*, Report of the Philadelphia Commission on the Mentally Retarded (Philadelphia, 1956); E. Gruenberg, *A Special Census of Suspected Referred Mental Retardation in Onondaga County*, Technical Report of the Mental Health Unit (New York, 1955).

[4] G. Brockopp, "The Significance of Selected Variables on the Prevalence of Suspected-mental Retardates in the Public Schools of Indiana," unpublished dissertation, Indiana University (Bloomington, 1958); F. A. Mullen and M. M. Nee, "Distribution of Mental Retardation in an Urban School Population," *American Journal of Mental Deficiency*, LVI (April 1952), 777-790.

PEABODY JOURNAL OF EDUCATION, 1971, Vol. 48, pp. 188-203.

rates of placement for Mexican-American and Negro children in special education classes that were two to three times higher per 1,000 than rates for children from English-speaking, Caucasian homes, hereafter called *Anglos*.[5]

In the epidemiology of mental retardation which we conducted in Riverside, California, disproportions by socioeconomic level and ethnic group appeared in the case register of retardates labeled by community organizations. Forty-one percent of the 812 persons on the case register who were nominated as retarded by 241 formal organizations in the community were living on census blocks for which the median value of housing was under $10,720.[6] Only 22.7 percent of the general population of the community lived on such blocks. Disproportions were even greater for those labeled by the public schools. Fifty-three percent of the retardates labeled by the public schools lived on blocks with a median housing value of under $10,720.

Anglos, who comprise 82 percent of the population of the community, made up only 54 percent of the labeled retardates. Mexican-Americans, who comprised only 9.5 percent of the community population, contributed 32 percent to the register of labeled retardates, three times more than would be expected from their proportion in the population. Negroes, who constituted 7 percent of the population of the community, contributed 11 percent to the register of labeled retardates. Ethnic disproportions were especially marked in the public schools. Only 37 percent of the labeled retardates in special education classes were Anglo children while 45 percent were Mexican-American and 16 percent were Negro. When socioeconomic differences were controlled by comparing only low-status Anglos with low-status Mexican-Americans and Negroes, disproportions for Negroes were eliminated but Anglos were still significantly underrepresented and Mexican-Americans significantly over-represented among the labeled retardates.

Why are there disproportionately large numbers of persons from low socioeconomic status and from ethnic minority backgrounds among those persons labeled as mentally retarded?

## Two Explanatory Frameworks

*The clinical perspective.* Persons who view mental retardation from a clinical, medical perspective tend to explain socioeconomic and ethnic differences in rates for labeled retardation in biological terms. They tend to view mental retardation as individual pathology which exists regardless of whether it has been diagnosed. Using either a pathological-medical model or a statistical model for identifying symptoms of

---

[5]*Racial and Ethnic Survey of California Public Schools,* Part 1: Distribution of Pupils, Fall, 1966, 1967, (Sacramento, 1967).

[6]*U.S. Censuses of Population and Housing: 1960,* Final Report PHC (1)-135, Census Tracts, San Bernardino-Riverside-Ontario, California, Standard Metropolitan Statistical Area, (Washington, 1962).

subnormality, they see mental retardation as a characteristic of the individual which transcends any particular social or cultural system. They believe that mental retardation can be discovered and diagnosed by the trained professional using the medical and psychological measures at his disposal. Within the framework of the clinical perspective, there are two types of explanations which are commonly given for disproportionately high rates of labeled retardation among the socioeconomically disadvantaged and ethnic minorities.

One school of thought, Zigler calls exponents of this school defect theorists, contends that all retardates suffer from specific physiological and cognitive defects over and above their slower rate of development. They argue that failure to detect the exact nature of the defect in those cases which appear to have no physiological defects is probably due to the relatively primitive nature of present diagnostic techniques. The overrepresentation of lower status persons results from the lower level of prenatal and postnatal care given to children reared in socioeconomically disadvantaged circumstances. Such children are exposed to a greater risk of organic damage because of poor diet, less adequate medical care, and other health hazards which are more prevalent in such environments than in more advantaged homes.[7] Because a large percentage of ethnic minority families in American society are socioeconomically disadvantaged, rates of defect tend to be higher for ethnic minorities. Considerable research evidence has accumulated to support this argument and differential exposure to biological hazards undoubtedly does account for some of the differences between groups.[8]

A second explanatory framework is that of the genetic theorists. They are prone to view higher rates among the disadvantaged and among ethnic minorities as the result of the polygenic distribution of the curve of intelligence in the population. They theorize that familial deficiencies in intelligence place those with lower intelligence at a competitive disadvantage which produces downward social mobility. Consequently, the families of the genetically retarded tend to gravitate to lower socioeconomic levels over several generations. The predominance of mental retardation among lower socioeconomic levels is explained as the result of the downward drift from higher social statuses. Such persons fall, genetically, in the lowest portion of the polygenic distribution of intelligence. Their performance is as much a part of the normal distribution of intelligence as the performance of persons who score in the upper ranges of the normal curve.

Research on sociocultural factors in mental retardation conducted from a clinical perspective tends to investigate hypotheses generated either by the defect theorists or the genetic theorists.

[7]E. Zigler, "Familial Mental Retardation: A Continuing Dilemma," *Science*, CLV (January 1967), 292-298.

[8]B. Pasamanick and H. Knobloch, "The Contributions of Some Organic Factors to School Retardation in Negro Children," *Journal of Negro Education*, XXVII (Winter 1958), 4-9.

*Social system perspective.* The social system perspective defines mental retardation as an achieved social status which some persons hold in some social systems. The role of retardate consists of the behavior expected of persons occupying the status of mental retardate. It is possible to study how a person achieves the status of mental retardate just as it is possible to study how a person achieves the status of doctor, banker, or engineer. Within the social system perspective, the overrepresentation of socioeconomically disadvantaged persons and persons from ethnic minorities in the devalued status of mental retardate can be studied as a status assignment phenomenon similar to other comparable social processes. From this perspective, the research question becomes, "Why are persons from lower socioeconomic statuses and/or ethnic minorities more likely to be assigned the status of mental retardate by formal organizations in the community than persons from higher socioeconomic statuses and/or the Anglo majority?"[9]

This paper, written from a social system perspective, explores two general hypotheses: (1) the high rate of assignment of persons from lower socioeconomic status and/or ethnic minorities to the status of mental retardate is related to an interaction between sociocultural factors and the clinical referral and labeling process which makes persons from these backgrounds more vulnerable to the labeling process than persons from the Anglo middle-class majority, and (2) that high rates of assignment of lower status and/or ethnic minorities is related to interaction between sociocultural factors and the nature of clinical measurement instruments. Each hypothesis will be explored separately.

## Interaction Between Sociocultural Factors and the Labeling Process

In the data files of the Riverside epidemiology of mental retardation, we have information on three different groups of labeled retardates in the City of Riverside, California. One data file contains information on persons who were nominated as mental retardates by formal organizations in the community. The other two files contain information on persons labeled by the public schools. Each of these data files was used to test the hypothesis that persons from lower socioeconomic levels and/or ethnic minorities are more vulnerable to the clinical labeling process.

[9] Jane R. Mercer, "The Epidemiology of Mental Retardation in an American City," presentation for the Staff Development Conference of the President's Committee on Mental Retardation, Airlie Conference Center, June 4-5, 1970; _____ , "The Meaning of Mental Retardation," forthcoming in Richard Koch and James Dobson, eds., *The Mentally Retarded Living in the Community*, (Seattle, 1970); _____ , "Sociological Perspectives on Mild Mental Retardation," in H. C. Haywood, ed., *Socio-Cultural Aspects of Mental Retardation: Proceedings of the Peabody-NIMH Conference* (New York, 1970);_____, "Institutionalized Anglocentrism: Labeling Mental Retardates in the Public Schools," forthcoming in Peter Orleans and Eilliam Russell, Jr., eds., *Race, Change, and Urban Society* (New York, 1971);_____, "Who Is Normal? Two Perspectives on Mild Mental Retardation," in E. G. Jaco, ed., *Patients, Physicians, and Illness,* 2nd ed. (Glencoe, 1971, in press).

*Analysis of the labeling process in the community.* There were 361 Anglos, 221 Mexican-Americans, and 79 Negroes nominated as mental retardates by those formal organizations in Riverside which employed psychologists or medical professionals to make diagnoses of mental retardation. We have called them the clinical organizations because they were staffed by professionals trained in the clinical tradition who presumably used standard clinical procedures in making evaluations. The persons on the clinical case register were those who had been assigned the status of mental retardate as a result of decisions made by these clinically trained professionals who selected, evaluated, and labeled clients in many different social organizations. It is not possible to know, in retrospect, exactly what factors were weighed in each case. However, we can gain some insight into the overall labeling process by a careful study of the end result of these interlocking, multiple decisions.

If labeled retardates from low-status homes and ethnic minorities are less clinically subnormal or less physically disabled than persons labeled as retarded from high-status homes and the Anglo majority, this difference would support the hypothesis that the former are more vulnerable to being labeled and that higher vulnerability tends to inflate rates for labeled retardation among low-status and minority groups. There are two questions to be answered. Do persons labeled as retardates from low-status homes and from ethnic minorities deviate as far from the statistical average on clinical measures as those from high-status homes and the Anglo majority? Are persons from low social status and ethnic minorities who are assigned to the status of mental retardate less physically disabled than high-status persons or persons from the Anglo majority?

Approximately 90 percent of the files of persons nominated by clinical organizations included direct or indirect information on six major trends of physical disabilities: speech, ambulation, hearing, arm-hand use in self care, vision, and seizures. Disability ratings using file information could not be based strictly on medical definitions because of the restricted nature of information in most dossiers, but it was possible to make global ratings for arm-hand use, speech, vision, ambulation, and hearing using four-point rating scales ranging from no difficulty to extreme difficulty. If a person was reported as having "no difficulty," he received a score of 0; "some difficulty," a score of 1; "much difficulty," a score of 2; and "extreme difficulty," a score of 3. If no seizures were mentioned, he received a 0 on that item. If seizures had occurred in the past but were no longer present or their infrequency was not given, he received a score of 1. If he currently had seizures less than once a year, or a few times a year, he received a score of 2. If he currently had seizures once a month or more, he received a score of 3. An individual received 0 if there was no mention of an illness, accident, or operation involving the central nervous system; and a score of 1 for each involvement mentioned. An individual's physical disability index score was the sum of his ratings on these items. Theoretically, scores could range from 0 through 21, however, actual scores ranged between 0 and 13.

## TABLE 1

### Mean IQ and Mean Number of Physical Disabilities for Persons Holding the Status of Mental Retardate in the Community by Socioeconomic Status and Ethnic Group

| | Socioeconomic Status | | | Ethnic Group | | | |
|---|---|---|---|---|---|---|---|
| | Low Status Housing Under $10,750 (N=365) | High Status Housing Over $10,750 (N=323) | Significance Level[a] | Anglo (N=361) | Mexican-American (N=221) | Negro (N=79) | Significance Level[a] |
| **Clinical Case Register** | | | | | | | |
| Mean IQ | 63.6 | 63.0 | NS | 61.5 | 64.3 | 61.2 | NS |
| Mean Physical Disabilities | 1.2 | 2.1 | ⟨.001 | 2.2 | 1.0 | .8 | ⟨.001 |
| **Educable Mental Retardates** | SES Index 0.29[b] (N=162) | SES Index 30+ (N=93) | | (N=144) | (N=63) | (N=61) | NS |
| Mean IQ | 70.0 | 68.9 | NS | 68.8 | 71.4 | 69.3 | |
| Mean Physical Disabilities[c] | 1.3 | 1.6 | NS | 1.8 | .9 | 1.0 | ⟨.001[c] |
| Mean Adaptive Behavior Failures[b] | 9.5 | 9.8 | NS | 10.3 | 9.9 | 7.2 | ⟨.001[c] |

[a]One-way analysis of variance was used for ethnic comparisons and a test for socioeconomic comparisons.

[b]Duncan Socioeconomic Index for head of household's occupation was used. There were 13 cases for whom occupation of household could not be coded.

[c]The mean number of Physical Disabilities for the general population of the community 6-15 years of age was .2 and the mean Adaptive Behavior Failures was 2.7 on these scales.

Table 1 presents the mean IQ and the mean number of physical disabilities, by social status and by ethnic group, for the persons on the clinical case register. Median value of housing on the census block was used as the measure of socioeconomic status for analyzing the clinical case register. There were 365 of the persons on the clinical case register who were living on blocks for which the housing was valued at $10,750 or less and 323 living on blocks valued above that figure. There were no significant differences in mean IQ between socioeconomic levels as measured by housing value nor between the three ethnic groups. Low-status persons had a mean IQ of 63.6 and high-status persons a mean of 63.0. The average Anglo on the clinical case register had an IQ of 61.5, the average Mexican-American had a mean IQ of 64.3, and the average Negro had a mean IQ of 61.2.

Low-status persons and those from ethnic minorities were found to be significantly less physically disabled. High-status labeled retardates had significantly more physical disabilities, mean 2.1, than low-status labeled retardates, mean 1.2 (p⟨.001). Anglos had an average disability score of 2.2 while that for Mexican-Americans was 1.0 and for Negroes .8 (p⟨.001). Only 32 percent of the labeled Anglos had no disabilities

49

while 61 percent of the labeled Mexican-Americans, and 71 percent of the labeled Negroes were without reported physical disabilities. Ethnic differences persisted when social status was controlled, although they were slightly reduced ($p < .001$).

However, there was a pattern in the distribution of IQ's within ethnic group, not shown in Table 1, which is worthy of note. Anglos had a higher percentage of persons with very low and very high IQ's, while the scores for Mexican-Americans and Negroes were concentrated in the middle ranges, IQ's between 40 and 79 ($X^2 = 44.6$, 8df, $p < .001$). This pattern persisted even when social status was held constant. Labeled retardates with IQ's above 80 were not only more likely to be Anglo but had more physical disabilities and were significantly more likely to have been nominated by a medical professional. Apparently, the medical doctor, using a medical pathological diagnostic model, diagnoses some physically disabled referrals as mentally retarded on the basis of physical anomalies when, in fact, they have IQ's which are in the normal range statistically. This produces a disproportionate number of disabled Anglos with high IQ's on the clinical case register because almost no Mexican-Americans or Negroes were nominated from medical sources. Most Mexican-American and Negro labeled retardates were normal-bodied and were labeled by the schools rather than their family doctor. Because the school used a strictly statistical rather than medical definition of normal, there were very few persons labeled as mental retardates by the school who had an IQ over 80. Consequently, labeled retardation is more closely tied to the statistical model of normal and to performance on an IQ test for Mexican-Americans and Negroes than for Anglos. Simply comparing mean IQ's obscures these complexities. Physical disabilities appear to be the intervening variable. Anglos labeled as mentally retarded had more physical disabilities, hence, were more visibly different from the general population.

The comparison of the clinical characteristics of persons from different social statuses and ethnic groups nominated for the clinical case register supports the hypothesis that there is an interaction between sociocultural factors and the labeling process. Labeled low-status persons were less physically disabled than labeled high-status persons. Labeled Mexican-Americans and Negroes were less physically disabled than labeled Anglos. Overall, their mean IQ's were similar to the mean for Anglos but labeled Anglos had significantly more physical disabilities and were, presumably, more visibly different than either Mexican-American or Negro labeled retardates. This finding tends to support the hypothesis that less physically disabled members of minorities are labeled as retarded while labeled Anglos are more visibly different.


*Analysis of children holding the status of educable mental retardate in the public schools.* During the academic year 1969-70, the Pupil Personnel Departments of the Riverside and Alvord Unified School Districts re-evaluated all 268 children in their

50

classes for the educable mentally retarded.[10] Students ranged from 7 through 19 years of age. Fifty-four percent were Anglos, 23 percent were Mexican-Americans, and 23 percent were Negroes. Approximately 80 percent of the children in these school districts were Anglos, 13 percent were Mexican-American, and 7 percent Negro. Thus, Mexican-American and Negro children were overrepresented and Anglo children underrepresented among those holding the status of mental retardate in the public school. Seventy-seven percent of the children in classes for the educable mentally retarded were from homes in which the head of household had a blue-collar job and 60.4 percent were from homes in which the head of household had a job rated between 0 and 29 on the Duncan Socioeconomic Index.[11]

A school psychologist retested each child using the Wechsler Intelligence Scale for Children. Interviewers, employed by the research project, interviewed the parents of each child. Interviewer and parent were matched for ethnic group and a Spanish version of the interview was used when the parent preferred being interviewed in Spanish. Information on the adaptive behavior and physical disabilities of each child and the sociocultural characteristics of his family were secured. The Adaptive Behavior and Physical Disability Scales used in this study were those developed for the field survey of the Riverside epidemiology.[12] The Adaptive Behavior Scales are age-graded measures which contain questions about the child's social-role performance in his family, neighborhood, community, and school. During the interview, the interviewer also secured information about the child's physical disabilities, any illnesses involving the central nervous system, and whether he had ever had seizures. Both the Adaptive Behavior and Physical Disability Scales were scored by counting the number of items failed by each child.

Table 1 presents the mean IQ, the mean number of physical disabilities, and the mean number of adaptive behavior failures for those labeled educable mental retardates by social status and ethnic group. As with the clinical case register, differences between the mean IQ's of the children of differing socioeconomic statuses and ethnic groups could be accounted for by chance. Differences in physical disabilities by socioeconomic status could also be accounted for by chance but this finding did not hold true for ethnic group. The average Anglo child failed 1.8 items on the Physical Disability Scales while the average Mexican-American labeled retardate had .9 physical disabilities and the average Negro had one physical disability ($p < .001$). When social status was held constant, ethnic differences persisted but were slightly

[10] I wish to thank Albert Marley, of the Riverside Unified School District, and Robert W. Hocker and J. Martin Koeppel, of the Alvord School District, and their staffs for their support, advice, and cooperation in collecting the data for this analysis. I also wish to thank Rosa McGrath and Lillian Redmond who served as interviewers in the reevaluation study.

[11] A. J. Reiss, Jr., *Occupations and Social Status* (Glencoe, 1961).

[12] Mercer, *The Eligibles and the Labeled.*

reduced. The findings for adaptive behavior were identical to those for physical disability. Differences by socioeconomic status could be accounted for by chance but ethnic differences were statistically significant. The average Anglo labeled retardate in these school districts had 10.3 adaptive behavior failures compared to 9.9 for Mexican-American and 7.2 for Negro retardates (p ⟨.001).

The mean number of physical disabilities for a representative sample of the general population of the community 6 through 15 years of age in the field survey of the epidemiology (N=1875) was .2, and the mean number of adaptive failures was 2.7. Both averages are significantly less than the average number of failures for the labeled children. Thus, children labeled as educable mental retardates by the public schools in these two school districts were significantly more physically disabled and had more adaptive behavior failures than children in the general population; but, within the labeled population, Anglos had significantly more physical disabilities and more adaptive behavior failures than Mexican-Americans and Negroes. Findings from the study of children holding the status of educable mental retardate in the public schools paralleled those for the clinical case register. Even though these were two completely different populations of labeled mental retardates, the average IQ's of persons in the three ethnic groups were, essentially, identical, but persons from ethnic minorities had fewer physical disabilities and adaptive behavior failures.

*Analysis of the labeling process in the public schools.* The labeling process in the public schools was investigated by studying the characteristics of all 1,234 children referred, for any reason, to the Pupil Personnel Department of the Riverside Unified School District during a single school year.[13] Approximately 31 percent of the children were referred as possible candidates for classes for the gifted; 30 percent were referred primarily because of behavior and disciplinary problems; 20 percent were referred because of academic difficulty with no mention of special education; and 8 percent were referred specifically for evaluation and possible placement in special education classes for the mentally retarded. At the time of the study, approximately 81 percent of the children of the school district were Anglo, 11 percent Mexican-American, and 8 percent Negro. Thirty-six percent lived on census blocks for which the housing was valued below $12,000.[14] The distribution by social status and by ethnic group of all the children referred to the Pupil Personnel Department was almost identical to the distributions in the school district itself. Low-status and /or minority children were not referred at a higher rate than their percentage in the population nor were they tested by the psychologist at a higher rate.

[13] I wish to thank the following persons in the Riverside Unified School District who made this study possible: Superintendent Bruce Miller; Richard Robbins, director of pupil personnel; Donald Ashurst, director of special education.

[14] *U.S. Censuses of Population and Housing: 1960.*

TABLE 2

ETHNIC CHARACTERISTICS OF A COHORT OF CHILDREN AT VARIOUS
STAGES IN THE LABELING PROCESS IN THE PUBLIC SCHOOLS

| Ethnic Group | Tested by Psychologist (N=865) Percentage | Found Eligible for Placement—IQ 79- (N=134) Percentage | Recommended for Placement (N=81) Percentage | Placed in Status of MR (N=71) Percentage |
|---|---|---|---|---|
| Anglo | 82.9 | 47.4 | 37.9 | 32.1 |
| Mexican-American | 7.6 | 32.7 | 40.9 | 45.3 |
| Negro | 9.5 | 19.8 | 21.2 | 22.6 |
| Median Value Under $12,000 | 38.8 | 70.7 | 72.7 | 74.6 |

Table 2 presents the ethnic characteristics of the 865 children who were tested by a psychologist from the 1,234 children in the original cohort referred for psychological evaluation; 82.9 percent were Anglo, 7.6 percent Mexican-American, and 9.5 percent were Negro. These percentages closely approximate the ethnic distribution of the school population. Among the children tested, there were 134 children who received an IQ of 79 or below. They were eligible for placement in a special education class on the basis of their test performance. It was at this stage in the referral process that the ethnic percentages shifted dramatically. Only 47.4 percent of the children failing the test were Anglo while 32.7 percent were Mexican-American and 19.8 percent were Negro. In other words, there were four times more Mexican-American children among those who failed the test than would be expected from their percentage in the population tested. There were twice as many Negro children as would be expected, and only about half as many Anglo children.

Although the IQ test was the major factor producing ethnic disproportions, the differential vulnerability of Mexican-American and Negro children to the labeling process persisted into the next two stages of the labeling. Eighty-one of the 134 children eligible for placement in classes for the mentally retarded were recommended by the psychologist for placement. Only 37.9 percent of those recommended for placement were Anglo while 40.9 percent were Mexican-American and 21.2 percent were Negro. Thus, there were disproportionately more of the eligible Mexican-American and Negro children recommended for placement and disproportionately fewer of the eligible Anglo children recommended for placement by the psychologist.

There were 71 children who were actually placed in the status of mental retardate in this school district. The ethnic distribution for the children who were placed is even more disproportionate than that for the children recommended for placement or children found eligible for placement. Less than a third of the children who achieved the status of mental retardate in this particular year were Anglos while 45.3 percent were Mexican-American and 22.6 percent were Negro. Six times more Mexican-American children and two and a half times more Negro children were placed than would be expected from their proportion in the school district population. Children from ethnic minority groups were not only failing IQ tests at a higher rate but selective factors operating in the labeling process resulted in disproportionately more minority children being recommended and placed in the status of mental retardate from among those who were eligible for placement.

The same pattern also appeared for socioeconomic status as measured by the value of housing on the block on which each child lived. About 39 percent of the children tested by the psychologists came from homes located on blocks with a median housing value of under $12,000 but 70.7 percent of those failing the IQ test came from homes on such blocks. The percentage increased for the final two stages of the labeling process, so that, ultimately, three-fourths of the children placed in the status of mental retardate in the year of the referral study were from homes located in blocks with low housing values.

The analysis of the characteristics of labeled retardates on the clinical case register, of labeled retardates in the program for educable mental retardates in the public schools, and of children referred for psychological evaluation in the public schools all showed a similar pattern. Persons from low socioeconomic level and ethnic minority groups were more vulnerable to the labeling process. Those who were labeled from ethnic minority groups had significantly fewer physical disabilities than their Anglo counterparts and had fewer adaptive behavior failures. Persons from minority groups assigned the status of mental retardate were not only less deviant physically and behaviorally than Anglo labeled retardates, but the analysis of the labeling process in the public schools indicated that children from minority groups were more likely to be recommended for placement and placed in the status of mental retardate than Anglo children once they failed an IQ test. An identical pattern was found for children from low socioeconomic levels. This interaction between referral and labeling processes and the sociocultural characteristics of the person being evaluated could account for some of the socioeconomic and ethnic differences in prevalence rates found in studies of labeled retardation.

*Interaction Between Sociocultural Factors and Clinical Measures*

The second hypothesis to be explored in this paper is that overrepresentation of persons from ethnic minorities in the status of mental retardate may be related to interaction between sociocultural factors and clinical measures. Because the primary clinical measure used in the diagnosis of mental retardation is an intelligence test, the discussion will concentrate on this particular clinical measure.

In the field survey which was conducted in Riverside, a representative sample of persons living in that city was selected for study. As part of the survey, intelligence measures were secured on a subsample of 556 Anglos, 100 Mexican-Americans, and 47 Negroes from 7 months through 49 years of age. In order to determine the amount of the variance in IQ accounted for by ethnic group and socioeconomic status, a regression analysis was computed using IQ as the dependent variable and ethnic group (dichotomized Anglo vs Mexican-American and Negro) and socioeconomic status (dichotomized Duncan Socioeconomic Index score of occupation of head of the household 0-29 vs 30 or higher) as the independent variables. Table 3 presents the findings from that analysis.

## TABLE 3

CORRELATIONS BETWEEN ETHNIC GROUP, SOCIOECONOMIC STATUS, AND IQ
IN THE RIVERSIDE FIELD SURVEY

| | Children 7 Months–15 Years | Adults 16–49 Years | Entire Sample (N-703) 7 Months–49 Years |
|---|---|---|---|
| | Percentage Variance | Percentage Variance | Percentage Variance |
| Ethnic Group Only | r = .45   20.3 | r = .62   38.4 | r = .53   28.1 |
| SES Only | r = .27   7.3 | r = .40   16.0 | r = .33   10.9 |
| Ethnic Group Plus SES | R = .46   21.2 | R = .65   42.3 | R = .55   30.3 |

For children 7 months through 15 years of age, ethnic group alone was correlated .45 with IQ, accounting for 20.3 percent of the variance in IQ. The correlation was higher for adults 16-49 years of age, .62, accounting for 38.4 percent of the variance in IQ. When all ages were combined, the correlation was .53, accounting for 28.1 percent of the variance in IQ. All correlations are significant beyond the .001 level of significance.

Socioeconomic status, alone, was not as highly predictive of IQ as ethnic group. It accounted for only 7.3 percent of the variance in the IQ's of children, 16 percent of the variance in the IQ's of adults, and 10.9 percent of the variance in the IQ's for the entire sample.

When ethnic group and socioeconomic status were both used in a stepwise multiple regression to predict IQ, the correlation was only slightly higher than for ethnic group alone. This indicates that knowledge of socioeconomic status adds relatively little predictability beyond ethnic group because most of the variance accounted for by socioeconomic status is shared with ethnic group. The most important finding, however, is that between 20 percent and 40 percent of the variance in IQ of the persons in this sample could be accounted for by ethnic group alone, depending upon the age of the persons being studied. Sociocultural factors were more highly correlated with IQ for adults than children.

In order to determine how much of the variance in IQ within each ethnic group could be accounted for by sociocultural factors, the sociocultural characteristics of the families of the persons in the sample were used as independent variables and a regression analysis was done for each ethnic group separately. Each sociocultural characteristic was dichotomized so that one category corresponded to the community mode on that characteristic and the other category was nonmodal. All sociocultural variables described characteristics of the family or family members and were not characteristics of the person himself, except as we infer that he may have acquired certain characteristics because of the environment in which he lives.

TABLE 4

CORRELATIONS BETWEEN FAMILY BACKGROUND CHARACTERISTICS AND IQ

| | *R* | *Variance Accounted For* |
| --- | --- | --- |
| | | *Percentage* |
| Mexican-American (N=100) | .61 | 37.2 |
| Negro (N=47) | .52 | 27.0 |
| Anglos (N=556) | .31 | 9.6 |
| All Ethnic Groups (N=703) | .50 | 25.0 |

The first set of data in Table 4 presents the findings for Mexican-Americans. Eighteen sociocultural characteristics of the family were correlated .61 with IQ. They accounted for 37.2 percent of the variance in the measured intelligence of this group of Mexican-Americans (p ⟨.01). The six sociocultural characteristics which best predicted high IQ were: living in a household in which the head of household had a white-collar position; living in a family with five or fewer members; living in a family in which the Duncan socioeconomic index score for the head of household's occupation was 30 or higher; living in a family in which the head of household was reared in an urban environment; living in a family in which the head of household was reared in the United States; and living in a family in which the head of household was male. These six variables, combined, produced a multiple correlation coefficient of .57 and accounted for 32.5 percent of the variance in IQ.

The multiple correlation coeffecient for the small number of Negroes in the sample, .52, did not quite reach the .05 level of significance. However, the pattern of relationships is similar to that for Mexican-Americans. The variables studied were identical to those used in the analysis of Mexican-Americans except that an item on use of English in the home was omitted. For Negroes, living in a family in which the spouse of the head of household was reared in a nonsouthern state was the best single predictor. The five other family variables which, together, predicted the most variance were: male head of household; head of household having a white-collar job; a family consisting of biological parents and their chidren; a family living in a home they own or are buying; and a family in which the spouse of the head of household has had an eighth grade education or more.

The multiple correlation coefficient for Anglos was .31 (p ⟨.01), accounting for 9.6 percent of the variance in IQ. Independent variables used in the regression analysis were identical to those used for Negroes except that segregated vs desegregated minority neighborhood was omitted for Anglos because all Anglos lived in nonminority neighborhoods. For Anglos, two socioeconomic variables were among the six best predictors: living in a household in which the socioeconomic index score of the head of household's occupation was 30 or higher and a household in which the head of household had a white-collar occupation. Anglos with higher IQ's also tended to come from nuclear families that had not been broken by divorce or separation; families in which the spouse of the head of household had been reared in an urban environment and had had a high school education or more.

When all three ethnic groups were combined, sociocultural characteristics of the family backgrounds were correlated .50 with IQ, accounting for 25 percent of the variance.

*Summary.* It is clear from the preceeding analysis that the correlation between sociocultural factors and standard measures of intelligence are significant. Ethnic group, alone, accounted for 28 percent of the variance in IQ's between Anglos, Mexican-Americans, and Negroes in this particular sample, while socioeconomic status, alone, accounted for only 10.9 percent of the variance. The two, together, accounted for 30.3 percent of the variance. Studying each ethnic group, separately, we found that more than 25 percent of the variance in IQ's within the Mexican-American and Negro populations could be accounted for by characteristics of the individual's family background. However, family background characteristics accounted for only 9.6 percent of the variance in Anglo IQ's. The relatively small amount of the variability in the IQ's of the Anglos in this sample which could be accounted for by family background characteristics may be due, in part, to the homogeneity of the Anglo population of Riverside, which is mainly middle- and upper middle-class in status.

It is not possible with our data to compare the clinical and social system perspectives, directly, as explanatory frameworks for interpreting higher rates of labeled mental retardation among ethnic minorities. Undoubtedly, medical care is poorer and health hazards greater among the economically and educationally disadvantaged. To the extent that ethnic minorities are economically and educationally disadvantaged, we would expect higher rates of organic damage and higher rates of mental retardation among them. However, this argument does not explain why rates for labeled retardation among ethnic minorities are three to five times higher than those for Anglos, even when socioeconomic status is held constant? Neither does it explain, if there is more biological damage among persons from lower socioeconomic levels and ethnic minorities, why labeled retardates from lower socioeconomic levels and ethnic minorities have fewer physical disabilities reported in organizational records and by parents than persons from higher socioeconomic levels and the Anglo majority?

Genetic theorists would argue that the biological differences are genetic and not manifest in visible physical disabilities and that downward drift of the genetically inferior accounts for differentials by socioeconomic level. If one assumes relatively equal access to the opportunity structure for all Anglos, the downward drift hypothesis could have some validity when applied to the Anglo population. However, that hypothesis cannot explain the surplus of Mexican-Americans and Negroes among the labeled retarded. They have never had equal access to the opportunity structure of American society nor have they ever held higher social statuses from which the poorly endowed could drift downward.

We have proposed a third hypothesis—that differential vulnerability to the labeling process may account for a large part of the unexplained difference in rates for labeled retardation. We have seen that persons from ethnic minorities who are labeled as retarded have fewer physical disabilities and fewer adaptive behavior failures than labeled retardates from the Anglo majority. Clinical measures, such as the standard intelligence test, are correlated with sociocultural characteristics so that persons from nonmodal sociocultural backgrounds are systematically handicapped. In these circumstances, higher rates of labeled mental retardation for ethnic minorities and persons from socioculturally nonmodal backgrounds are inevitable. However, these higher rates may have little or no relationship to the biological or genetic characteristics of the persons being labeled. Instead, they may be the result of the culture-bound perspective with which clinical measures are being interpreted.

It is time to analyze more carefully the assumptions of the clinical perspective and to assess critically whether these assumptions are warranted in identifying mentally retarded persons in America's multi-cultural society. A diagnostic nomenclature and evaluation system which treats persons from diverse cultural backgrounds as if they were culturally homogeneous cannot provide an adequate framework for comprehending the complexities of a pluralistic world.

What is needed is an evaluation system that is as multifaceted as American society. One way this goal could be achieved is by developing pluralistic norms for clinical measures. With such norms, an individual's performance could be evaluated in relation to the distribution of scores of others who have had comparable opportunities to learn the cognitive and verbal skills measured by the test. Only if a person rates as subnormal in the distribution of scores for his own sociocultural group would he be regarded as subnormal. However, such pluralistic norms could not be developed for an entire ethnic group because there is little homogeneity within ethnic group. We have seen that 27 percent to 37 percent of the variance in IQ within ethnic group can be accounted for by sociocultural factors. There are individuals in each ethnic group who come from socioculturally modal backgrounds. For them, standard norms based on the modal population of the United States are appropriate. For those from nonmodal backgrounds, the standard norms are not appropriate.

One possibility is to classify each person within ethnic group by the sociocultural modality of his family background using those sociocultural characteristics most highly correlated with clinical measures for his ethnic group as the basis for classification. Norms could then be developed for each category of sociocultural modality. The *meaning* of a particular clinical score could then be evaluated against two normative frameworks:

(1) The person's position relative to the standard norms for the test would indicate where he stands in relationship to the general population of the United States. For a child, this score would indicate his probability of succeeding in American public schools as now constituted. For an adult, this score would indicate his probability of participating fully in the mainstream of American life.

(2) The person's location on the norms for his own sociocultural modality group would reveal the amount of knowledge he has acquired about the language and culture of the dominant society compared to others who have had comparable opportunities to learn. This comparison would provide insight into his potential for learning, if he were given further opportunities to acquire the knowledge and skills needed to participate fully in American life. In other words, the person's placement on the standard norms would indicate how far he has to go to participate in American urban, industrial society. His placement on the sociocultural norms appropriate for his sociocultural background would indicate the probability that he will get there, if given adequate educational experiences.

PART II

WILLIAM C. RHODES

# The Disturbing Child: A Problem of Ecological Management

*Abstract: The suggestion is made that some of our critical child problems relate to reciprocal or complementary conditions residing not only in the child, but in the transactions between the child and the reciprocating environment. New educative arrangements, structures, and organizations are proposed which might reflect such an ecological view of child problems.*

I AM going to suggest an alternative way of looking at the problem we call emotional disturbance in children. From this point of view I will draw some suggestions of modified measures for handling the problem.

In this alternative view of disturbance it is suggested that the nucleus of the problem lies in the content of behavioral prohibitions and sanctions in the culture. Any behavior which departs significantly from this lore upsets those who have carefully patterned their behavior according to cultural specifications. The subsequent agitated exchange between *culture violator* and *culture bearer* creates a disturbance in the environment. It is this reciprocal product which engages attention and leads to subsequent action.

The child judged to be the most disturbed is the one who uniformly arouses disturbed reactions in those around him. The less disturbed child does not produce such uniform reactions. All of us have known children who were judged disturbed under the tutelage of one teacher, while appearing fairly normal under another teacher. This is an example of the reciprocity involved in the condition called disturbance.

Generally, we assume that emotional disturbance is the exclusive property of the child. This approach has borrowed from the physiological model and applied it to psychological disturbance. For a long time we have probed, analyzed, and dissected the psychic structure, the chemical structure, the neurological substrate, the glandular constituents, and the genetic history of the organism in a search for the essence of disturbance. We have carefully reviewed the developmental history of the organism and studied the influence of the environment upon it. In all of these attempts the starting point has been the assumption that a flaw within the child was responsible for the disturbance.

## An Ecological View

If we could temporarily put aside the physiological or host organism point of view and substitute an ecological point of view, it might provide us with a fresh start. A view of emotional disturbance as a reciprocal condition might suggest new approaches and new measures for management.

With the problem thus restated, conditions such as pathology, divergence, or discordance become environmental products of the emotive exchange between excitor and responder instead of a simple property of the excitor himself. We can then address ourselves to the agitated environmental product, in which both sides bear relationship to the problem, rather than the child alone. The "dis-ease" would be considered as much a condition in the responder as in the elicitor.

In this bilateral statement of the problem, the

EXCEPTIONAL CHILDREN, March 1967, pp. 449-455.

child becomes an excitor whose behavior or life style elicits reciprocating emotive reactions from a community of responders. The reaction may contain varied mixtures of anxiety, frustration, anger, eroticism, etc., depending upon the cultural prohibitions or sanctions which the reactor has incorporated into himself. Culture violating behavior becomes upsetting to surrounding individuals when its message is received and recognized under the overlay of sanctions and prohibitions which the responding individuals have acquired from the storehouse of the culture. The child judged most disturbed is the one who violates a large number of behavioral codes, and/or some of the most central codes. The intensity of observer reaction may be related to the observer's degree of difficulty in controlling and accepting comparable tendencies in himself.

This restatement could be compared to the old question about the relationship of noise to a falling tree and the human ear. If a tree crashes in the forest, but there is no human receptor apparatus to be activated by the subsequent sound waves, is there a noise? Does the sound reside in the crashing tree which sets up the sound wave, does it reside in the receptor mechanism, or is it a product of both? We might ask the same thing about emotional disturbance. When an individual lives or behaves in a disturbing fashion, does the disturbance exist without a reactor group to register the condition? Does the disturbance reside in the child, the reactor, or is it a product of both?

**Diagnosis—by Whom?**

Let us try still another tack with this baffling puzzle. Why is a specific kind of excitor behavior or human condition diagnosed differentially only after there are overt rejoinders from the environment? Can a human behavior or human condition have a defined defective quality before community response gives it a name? For instance, physical assault may be interpreted as crime, as sickness, or as sin, depending upon which societal institution at a particular period of time in a particular culture is allowed to make the judgment and provide the enjoining response. If convention in the prevailing culture sets up judge and jury as the official recording instruments, the behavior may be considered criminal. If the medical establishment is backed by cultural authority, it may be called sickness. If the church is the official spokesman of the community, it may be called sin.

The definition and subsequent handling depend upon which societal system is allowed to represent the public in the transaction between the precipitating individual and the responding community. Thus, it is only after the fact, after the action has provoked an enjoining reaction, that we "know" what we are dealing with. In a way, then, it is the overt engagement operations of society which define the state of the subject.

The question is not, "What is it really?" The question is, "What is the predominant purpose of the society in the actions it pursues with the subject after society's response has been triggered?" My answer is that in all of these cases society's unspoken and unrecognized purpose is much more to lower its own stress level than to solve the problem facing it. By a peculiar twist of logic, however, it reserves its subsequent operations for the subject, and only the subject. Society fails to recognize pathology, divergence, or disturbance as a product of the reciprocity between activator and resonator. Therefore, it fails to apply itself to study and solution of all terms of the problem. It concentrates upon the activator, temporarily relieves the tension of the reciprocator, and never quite comes to grips with the whole problem.

Our zealous search for the causes and cures of emotional disturbance in children is particularly disquieting to me when I look back at other excitors in history. For instance, suppose we had set up a National Institute of Witchery in Salem to study the cause and cures of witchcraft? Here was a condition which had developed to epidemic proportions in the culture of that time. Unfortunately, there existed no science of psychology and no science of testing at that particular time. Therefore we will never know the personality trait characteristics of witches, nor the family constellations which produced them. Or what if Spain had set up a National Scientific Foundation of Inquisition to study heresy, with the avowed aim of developing measures of early identification of heretics, effective treatment of heretics, and heresy control programs?

I am not using these comparisons to equate our modern concern for emotional disturbance with the thirteenth century concern with heresy. However, I am saying that we should consider the cultural relativity of the condition we call emotional disturbance. I am saying, let us be cautious that our concern over baffling individuals in our own society does not deteriorate into the same implacable cultural convictions that existed in other eras.

Although it is probably true that the condition of disturbance can be attributed to the excitor as well as the respondent, we do not know how much to attribute to the excitor, how much to the respondent, and how much to the stirred up environmental conditions which result from their interaction. We do know that the condition of emotional disturbance does produce strain within the community of responders, and that this strain is one of the definers of the child as the problem.

### The Behavioral Codes of the Culture

In the particular view of disturbance which I have outlined, the nucleus of the problem lies in the content of behavioral prohibitions and sanctions in the culture. The purpose of these prohibitions is to transform individual behavior into forms which make collective existence possible. No matter how you look at it, the individual and the collective are not one single process. The individual has his own unique birth and death, his time span and history, which, in the ultimate sense, are not really shared with anyone. He is transformed into a collective member only by the accumulation of human experiences preserved in the repository of culture. The way in which he lives, thinks, and responds in society is to a large extent extracted from this cultural bank.

One of the problems is that these guides are frequently discrepant with the natural behavioral propensities in the individual. Under such circumstances, he must learn to renounce or hide those tendencies which do not conform to cultural dictates. Concealing or denying such tendencies is accomplished at some expense to the individual as he tries to abide by cultural codes. Whether such tendencies are ever truly extinguished, we do not know.

When an individual violates any of these codes, we recognize it as the overt manifestation of a potential which lurks within us. We are therefore aroused by what it triggers off within us and react toward it somewhat as we would if we ourselves were performing or experiencing the behavior.

The problem is multiplied by the fact that behavioral prohibitions and sanctions have accumulated over many centuries. It is very difficult to eliminate any of them from the culture, even though they may be pure legends with no real basis in the facts of how most individuals behave under the particular circumstances associated with the legend.

With such an accumulation hanging over us, there are limitless forms of behavior which can disturb us. The range of children's behaviors to which we respond with upset is extensive. In our tendency to refer such upset within ourself to the child who stimulates the upset, we blanket a large proportion of children under the category of disturbance. We must recognize the strain of the responder as a contributor to the disturbance.

### Management of the Problem

If we concede that the disturbance lies not only in the child, but also in the reactive environment, what change must we make in managing the problem?

To begin with, the goals would no longer be exclusively concerned with changing the child. Instead we would substitute two new goals, a short term and a longer term goal. The short term goal is to enter into a disturbed situation and change it. The long term goal is to modify the process by which an individual becomes a culture bearer.

The bilateral view of disturbance as an agitated exchange between culture violator and culture bearer requires that we consider the reciprocal condition within the environmental context that links the two together. The immediate management of a disturbed condition requires that we address ourselves not only to the child, but to his living units and the individuals within his living units who are disturbed by his behavior or his life style.

Furthermore, if the nucleus of the problem lies in the behavioral prohibitions and sanctions in the culture, then a new way of education must be found so that the culture bearer can gain some freedom or distance from the aspects of culture which are oppressive.

*Short Term Management.* In the matter of short term management, consideration must be given to the total situation, the relevant circumstances of the reciprocity between the child excitor and the culture bearing responders. We reeducate not only the child but also his relevant human environment, including such living units as family, classroom, play groups, and residential cottages. They must be modified to engage the child as a human being, to respond to him without the intervention of cultural prohibitions.

As an example, I will describe a research project which, although aimed at culturally disadvantaged rather than emotionally disturbed children, illustrates the same principles and procedures.

Children between 18 months and 3 years of age are tutored in their homes one hour a day, five days a week. The aim of the project is to prevent the usual IQ deficiency which occurs in the lowest socioeconomic group after 3 years of age. The child is the intended target. In order to concentrate upon language development, the tutor goes into the home to work with the child. The work of the tutor has led to a very interesting development which relates directly to the type of role I am prescribing for the special teacher of disturbing children.

After a few months experience, it became evident that although the teacher had intended to tutor only the child, the mother was also involved in the teaching-learning transaction. The tutor was teaching the mother how to relate differently to the child and how to participate in his development. The mother was learning to view the child in a different light. The effort, concern, and importance given to the child seemed to impress upon the mother that this was an important human being, deserving of considerable time and attention. The siblings also became part of the teaching situation. In the home setting, the teacher could not avoid teaching the family as a whole and producing changes in its interactions with the child.

The teacher has interrupted and intervened in the process of transmission of a particular culture which was coming from the mother's own learnings and experiences. A new cul-

tural frame of reference is being established which is not only changing this family, but in turn will probably change the culture of the progeny of these children. The teacher has literally stepped into the stream of cultural transmission and altered its quality and flow. She is a teacher to the living culture, the living unit in which the child is embedded.

## Project ReEd

As another example of the alternative view that disturbance is an ecological condition rather than an individual pathology, I will describe the original conception and operations of Project ReEd, a project for disturbed children at Peabody College. The project included a degree training program for special teachers of disturbing children, a research arm, and two residential schools staffed by the specially trained teachers with consultation from the traditional mental health professionals. One school is under the Mental Health Department of Tennessee, and the other is under the Mental Health Department of North Carolina.

The project did not begin with the idea of curing the child. Rather, it started out with the idea of interrupting a pathological process which was progressively affecting the child. Therefore, there was no plan for long term, residential treatment, isolated from the normal developmental forces in the child's life. The major societal systems or ecological units of the child's life, his home, his school, and his neighborhood were considered the important factors. The child was given respite by placing him for four to six months in a specially designed, constructive field of forces—the ReEd schools. A liaison teacher in the ReEd school worked with the child's special school to keep the lines to the child open, and also to feed back to the regular school the different way in which the child was handled and was responding. The child's community was expected to mobilize family counseling services and its array of constructive paraphernalia and developmental forces, such as recreational and character building agencies, in behalf of the child's return to the care of the community.

## The Teacher's Role

In view of the definition of emotional disturbance as an ecological condition, involving an excitor and a responder in a particular setting, I believe the approach of Project ReEd should be carried a few steps further. A great burden is placed upon the special teacher, and for this reason, we will have to be more creative in producing a special breed for this role, a special strain of human yeast in the role of teacher. The special teacher must be freed, to a greater extent than most of us are now free, from the biases and unwitting oppressions of the culture, in order to be able to recognize that even the most indulgent society can err in providing the conditions for the right relationship between the self and the culture.

This teacher would become educator not only to the stressor but also to the strained members of the disturbed transaction which we now call pathology. This teacher would have to cool out the overheated situation created between the excitor child and his community of receptors. She would be a modulator of cultural shock. She would recognize that the disturbed environmental product is a bilateral effect of the interaction between the culture violator and the overconditioned culture bearer.

Specifically, this difficult role would require the teacher to enter into the living units in which the child functions. She would address him in the context of family, class, neighborhood, and become a teacher to this total context. Instead of separating him out into a special class, she would follow him and several like him into the regular class, entering into a team teaching relationship with his regular teacher. In school, she would not only act as a buffer, but would teach by example how to respond to the child without the deleterious intervention of culture conditioned emotions such as anger, fear, eroticism, frustration. This should not be a full day's job. She should be free to follow him into his own home for an hour or so a week to teach the mother and the family through demonstration, example, and interpretation, how to respond in ways that reduce turbulence between the excitor or stressor child and his immediate community of responders. She would, in many cases, move with him into his neighborhood life, particularly if he comes from the lower socioeconomic segment where life is lived on the streets to a major extent. She would have to move onto his turf, his quarters, in order to become a transitive force between

the conditionings of his life and the reactors to him and their conditionings. In short, she would become a teacher to his living units, modifying not only the child, but the crucial units which contain the child.

Involved in fluid movement in and out of various living units, the teacher would become an ecological preceptor—a modulator of both sides of the transaction which is involved in emotional disturbance. In a limited way, the crisis teacher advocated by Bill Morse of the University of Michigan and others plays such a role in the school setting. She is available to the regular classroom teacher to intervene in crises or erupting classroom situations, either to handle the particular child on the spot, or remove him to a special resources room.

Unfortunately, I think that our special classes are limiting themselves in what they can accomplish by removing the child from the setting of his difficulty and trying to produce all of the change in him alone. This approach is based upon the traditional view of a host organism with a disease. Modification procedures in the educative setting thus consist of educational treatment of the child and make it difficult to engage the ecology of the child. We are confined to a classroom, to a set of traditional teacher/pupil, pupil/pupil, educator/administrator relationships. These have little to do with some of the most crucial environing circumstances of the child's life, little to do with his living culture.

*Long Term Management.* From the short term goal of modifying the environing circumstances of a particular child's life, we move on to the long term goal of changing the way in which we transmit culture and the way we teach the child how to relate to the culture. I claimed that the nucleus of the problem of disturbance lay in the behavioral codes of the culture. If this is so, the haphazard way in which culture is transmitted and the haphazard or chance way in which individuals learn to live with it and incorporate it, should be looked at very carefully. Let me move directly into some of the operational aspects of what I am talking about.

To better prepare the child to be both an individual and a societal animal, and to teach him how to evaluate the culture and its relationship to his life, we will probably have to develop new types of educative institutions which concentrate on teaching the child not only how to incorporate and relate to the burgeoning body of knowledge and fact, but also how to live in a complex society.

The schools, as educational instruments, do not carry on this task of setting up and guiding the dialogue between the individual and the society. In a sense they do not support his need to maintain his sense of independent being, with the right to be just as he is, or become all that his own nature has blueprinted for him without regard to culture. Before education can serve as the balance wheel between man and his world, it will be necessary to alter its concentration upon subject matter instruction and upon the single classroom teacher as the purveyor of all knowledge needed by the child.

If the school would take on the more important role of developing the child as a member of society and as an individual in his own right, it will have to take advantage of the resources at hand. The resources include all the paraphernalia of counseling and guidance, school social work, school psychology, special education, pupil personnel services, and child development specialists, which I think are presently being misused.

These resources currently play a very peripheral role in support of the schools' mission of instruction. All of this apparatus is used only to back up the classroom teacher's instructional role. This seems to be a wasteful use of these resources. Furthermore, they compete among themselves for the small segments of time allowed to their very tangential roles. Their insights into the culture and knowledge of the interactions between societal systems and individuals are not being capitalized upon. They are not being used to give the child an understanding of himself in relationship to the culture and to his society. These educative functions should be systematized and provided as a continuing force in the developmental stages of child life. They are not. Instead, they are largely errand boys of education and society.

I suggest that we have now reached the stage in our behavioral science, mental science, and social science knowledge and technology at which a dramatically different kind of schooling should be provided for the child as a systematic part of his educative environment.

The school could be organized into two new major divisions. One division would carry on the present form of instruction; the other would be the psychosocial division, whose purpose would be to educate the child toward a reasonable relationship between self and society. This second division would have equal status with the first, with its own director to meld all of the various personnel, methods, content, and atmospheres of the various peripheral services devoted to life chance education of the child.

Under this reorganization, school would have two functions, with two staffs, each playing a bilateral role in child development. The curriculum of the child would be divided into these complementary functions: instruction on the one hand and life cultivation on the other. Each child would be scheduled into both areas according to his life needs.

The curriculum in the psychosocial or life cultivating area would draw heavily upon the unused reserves of the social, behavioral and mental health sciences. These reserves would move into a central role in education for life, out into the world by entering into the child's real living units of home, neighborhood, and leisure time organizations. It would help him look at the relationship between his self and his society. It would teach him to examine critically the demands of the society upon the self. It would help him develop the internal means of social and cultural criticism so that he could intelligently assess the independence of the self from the impositions of the culture. He would be taught to increase his range of freedom from the culture.

This part of the child's education would be considered as central to his life and to the viability of our society as the current conception of subject matter education. It would be considered basic and necessary, rather than a luxury to be supported only if there is extra money in the school budget, or if there are so many problem children that it is upsetting to us and the school.

Considerable thought would have to be given to the reorganization and reconsolidation of existing resources. It would involve not only the personnel currently attached to schools but also personnel deployed in the community in other settings. It would call for devising a total curriculum of psychosocial education which would meld all of these splintered school efforts together and patch and shore up its deficiencies. It would call for bringing all of these together in a coordinate and interrelated form, and apportioning out parts of the life education task to each of them.

Such a planned melding of the diverse mental health and social service forces into an educative instrument would be less palliative and less crises oriented, and more a long term continued influence upon the lives of children. It would benefit not only the children who disturb us, but also the children who do not now disturb us.

We have a critical need for a societal instrument which is constantly dealing with the right relationship between self and society. This approach would be one type of instrument that could be forged in the long term goal of modifying the relationship between the individual and the culture and of keeping the culture open to social changes.

# PSYCHOTHERAPY WITH CHILDREN: A FURTHER EVALUATION

E. E. Levitt

## PRELIMINARY CONSIDERATIONS

In 1957, the author reviewed articles involving the evaluation of the results of psychotherapy with children for the period 1929–1955 (Levitt, 1957a). A total of 18 reports of evaluations at close and 17 at follow-up were found. Of the total of nearly 8000 child patients, two-thirds were rated as improved at close and three-quarters at follow-up. Using 'defectors' from treatment (i.e. children who had been accepted for treatment but who never began treatment) as a control baseline, approximately the same percentages were found for respective control groups. It was concluded that the results failed to support the contention that psychotherapy with children is effective.

This conclusion was supported by the results of a long-range, follow-up study at the Institute for Juvenile Research in Chicago (Levitt, 1959), one of the largest community child guidance clinics in the United States. Treated groups were compared with defector controls from the same clinic population on 26 variables, and no differences were found.

The review has been criticized by Eisenberg and Gruenberg (1961), Heinicke (1960) and Hood-Williams (1960).* The major point is that defectors (alternatively 'terminators' or 'discontinuers') constitute an inappropriate control group because they may be less disturbed individuals who are able to respond favourably to the diagnostic procedure alone. The hypothesis certainly appears reasonable, though none of the critiques actually cite experimental findings which bear directly on it. There are, however, a number of investigations which do have direct bearing.

* By restricting his analysis of data to only two studies, Heinicke was able to arrive at the conclusion that treated children at least showed a greater degree of 'successful adjustments', while the control cases showed a greater percentage of 'partial improvements'. In addition to the obvious potential effect of selecting two investigations from many, those who are experienced psychotherapists cannot help but be struck by the greater difficulty in distinguishing among degrees of improvement, as opposed to distinguishing between any improvement and no improvement whatsoever. This suggests that the distinction between 'successful' and 'partial' will usually be relatively unreliable. Eisenberg classified neurosis in children as a "disorder for which there is reasonable likelihood of response to treatment", but admits that no definite conclusion concerning the efficacy of psychotherapy can be ventured at present. Despite his criticisms, Hood-Williams accepts the defectors as a control group, "albeit with reservations, whose very nature demands that conclusions drawn from them should be highly tentative". A detailed rebuttal of his critique has already appeared (Levitt, 1960).

BEHAVIOR RESEARCH AND THERAPY, 1963, Vol. 1, pp. 45-51.

One study (Levitt, 1957b) shows that defector cases and those who have had some treatment do not differ on 61 factors, including two clinical estimates of severity of symptoms, and eight other factors relating to symptoms. Another study (Levitt, 1958a) found that experienced mental health professionals were unable to detect a difference in severity of symptoms between treated and defector child cases, based on case records. On a 5-point scale, the mean severity ratings were 3·02 for the defector children and 2·98 for the treated cases. Judgments of motivation for treatment also did not distinguish the two groups.

Ross and Lacey (1961) found that the defector cases had fewer histories of developmental difficulties, fewer 'unusual behaviours' (confusion, disorientation, panic reactions, unpredictable, meaningless and self-destructive acts), a lower incidence of specific somatic complaints, and less parental 'marital disharmony' (not including divorce and separation). The defectors also tended to have had shorter waiting periods between application and intake interview. There was no relationship to socio-economic status. Lake and Levinger (1960) did find a relationship with socio-economic status, with the defectors tending to come from lower strata, but they found no relationship between continuing into therapy and the length of the waiting period. They report positive correlations between continuing into treatment and motivation of the parent for treatment.

A follow-up study of 142 defectors (Levitt, 1958b) disclosed that a family member was clearly resistant to treatment in 24 per cent of the cases, but 52 per cent attributed defection to deficiencies of the clinic, or to environmental circumstances.

Overall, the findings seem to be in conflict. Some of the studies appear to indicate that the defectors are less disturbed, but some appear to show no differences. One study shows a relationship to the socio-economic status, while another does not. The waiting period and parental motivation were found to be associated with termination in one study, but not in another.

The problem in attempting to reconcile these conflicting findings is that the definitions of 'treated' and 'defector' vary among studies. In the Levitt (1957b, 1958a) studies, a treated case was one which had at least 5 treatment interviews; in the Ross and Lacey study (1961) a minimum of 16 interviews. The term is not defined specifically in the Lake and Levinger investigation (1960). A defector in the Levitt studies is a case which had had a complete diagnostic work-up, had been accepted for therapy, and had failed the appropriate appointment when it was offered. For Ross and Lacey, a defector is one who had less than 5 treatment interviews, and terminated against clinic advice. In the Lake and Levinger study, a defector is a case which broke contact with the clinic after a complete application procedure, including an interview, but no diagnostic work-up. It is entirely possible that these differences in definition lie at the root of the discrepancies in findings.

Ideally, the defector should be an individual who has been procedurally identical with the treated case except for the factor of formal treatment itself. In the Ross-Lacey investigation, the defectors could have had as many as 4 treatment interviews. In the Lake-Levinger study, the defectors had not been subjected to diagnostic evaluation, and had evidently, therefore, not actually been accepted for treatment. Only in the Levitt investigations does the handling of the defector case appear to satisfy the criterion. If we accept the results of these studies (Levitt, 1957b; Levitt, 1958a) then the conclusion is that there does not seem to be any basis for the view that the defector cases were more or less seriously disturbed than treated cases, at the time of diagnostic evaluation.

It is probably true that a defector group contains a percentage of cases which have noticeably improved in the interim between the diagnostic evaluation and the offer of therapy.* The critics of the 1957 review speculate that the defector group may be a poor control because it is likely to contain substantially more of such cases than will the group which eventually goes on to formal treatment.

There are several arguments against this contention. It has been pointed out (Levitt, 1960) that follow-up interviews with parents of defector cases suggest that about 18 per cent terminated contact with the clinic because of the interim symptomatic improvement. Only about 12 per cent offered this as the sole explanation for termination. This percentage could, of course, affect an inter-group comparison, but it hardly seems sufficient to account for an overall improvement rate of some 65 per cent.

The second point is simply that the treated group might also have an interim improvement rate, which would balance, or partly offset, this phenomenon in the defector group.

Interim improvement is usually a corollary of the hypothesis that the defectors are less seriously disturbed initially, since such a child is more apt to be improved by a brief contact. Another argument against the idea of interim improvement as a bias follows from the evidence which appears to suggest that the defectors are not, in fact, less seriously disturbed.

Summing up, we can say that the defectors may be a biased control group, though the available evidence appears to indicate otherwise. The need for such a control is undeniable and no one has yet suggested a superior method of establishing the baseline of spontaneous remission.

Eisenberg and Gruenberg (1961) and Eisenberg, Gilbert et al. (1961) believe that failure to distinguish among diagnostic categories tends to obfuscate an evaluation of outcome. They argue that it would be more revealing to match treated and defector control groups by diagnosis. The contention appears reasonable; spontaneous remission is usually variable among illnesses. Unfortunately, data on defector groups by diagnostic categories are not available. It is possible, however, to determine whether outcome varies by diagnosis among treated cases, which is the logical first step. The present review of evaluation studies will attempt to accomplish this.

## THE PRESENT REVIEW

The present review is based on 22 publications in which evaluative data are presented.[†] More than half of these are evaluations at follow-up rather than at close, but no distinction is made in this review. Some of the follow-up intervals are very short, and the interval is not stated in some studies. Furthermore, the combined breakdowns into diagnostic categories and into follow-up and close studies would fractionate the data to the point where comparisons would be unfeasible.

* It is a common belief among clinic workers that this improvement is a function of therapeutic properties of the diagnostic procedure. If this is indeed true, then the amount of such improvement is likely to vary considerably from clinic to clinic, as the evidence (Filmer-Bennett and Hillson, 1959; Phillips, 1957) indicates that the diagnostic procedure varies. However, the etiology of the improvement is not relevant to the argument.

† As in the earlier review, several studies have been excluded because of overlapping, and other reasons. Eisenberg's data (1958b) are included in the later study of Rodriguez et al. (1959). A second publication by O'Neal and Robins (1958b) includes data of an original publication (1958a). The latter is used because of its more complete presentation. The general improvement–nonimprovement findings are similar. Most of the results of the study by Cytryn et al. (1960) are included in the subsequent paper by Eisenberg et al. (1961). The article by Cunningham et al. (1956) appeared in the earlier review as an unpublished paper. The study of Michael et al. (1957) is inappropriate since only 25 of 606 treated cases were located at follow-up

Data from the investigations are divided into five groups according to diagnostic criteria. Two groups are reasonably clearcut; psychotic children (Annesley, 1961; Bender and Gurevitz, 1955; Hamilton *et al.*, 1961; Kane and Chambers, 1961; Kaufman *et al.*, 1962), and those with special symptoms such as enuresis, tics, and school phobia (Hersov, 1960; Lazarus and Abramovitz, 1962; Phillips, 1961; Rodriguez *et al.*, 1959; Zausmer, 1954). A third group deals with cases of delinquency, aggressive behaviours, anti-social acting-out, etc. (Annesley, 1961; Cytryn *et al.*, 1960; Eisenberg *et al.*, 1958a; Morris *et al.*, 1956; Rexford *et al.*, 1956). The fourth group is roughly analogous to the adult neurotic (Annesley, 1961; Dorfman, 1958; Eisenberg, Gilbert *et al.*, 1961). The fifth group, which is by far the largest, is a mixed one in which a number of different diagnostic categories are represented, and includes accounts of general or unclassified child guidance clinic samples (Chess, 1957; La Vietes *et al.*, 1960; Miller, 1957: O'Neal and Robins, 1958a; Phillips, 1960; Seidman, 1957). The groupings are not entirely pure, but there is little overlap. By and large, cases of organicity have been excluded.

The establishment of a separate category for children with special symptoms does not imply that such a symptom may not be pathognomic of a more extensive psychological disorder. The distinction is required by the fact that the evaluation of therapy in these cases is based solely on outcome of treatment of the special symptom.

The therapy procedures which are represented in the studies cover a fairly broad range, including counselling with parents, environmental manipulation, techniques based on learning theory, nondirective counselling of children, and the use of adjunctive drugs. Shock therapies, chemotherapy as the exclusive approach, and other somatic treatments have been excluded. Several recent innovations in therapeutic methods are also excluded, largely because the numbers of cases are small, or because a systematic evaluation procedure does not appear in the study. Included in this category are Charny's 'isolation treatment' (Charny, 1961), and the operant conditioning techniques of Ferster and DeMyer (1961).

## RESULTS

The data from the 22 evaluation studies are summarized in Table 1. The customary trichotomous breakdown is employed: Much Improved includes any classification indicating great improvement, or 'cured'; any classification indicating lesser degree of improvement, such as 'partly', 'moderately', or 'slightly', is subsumed under Partly Improved; the No Improvement class also takes in 'worse'.

TABLE 1. SUMMARY OF EVALUATION DATA FROM TWENTY-TWO STUDIES

| Type of disorder | Number of studies | Much improved | | Partly improved | | Unimproved | | Total | Overall (%) improved |
|---|---|---|---|---|---|---|---|---|---|
| | | (N) | (%) | (N) | (%) | (N) | (%) | (N) | |
| Neurosis | 3 | 34 | 15 | 107 | 46 | 89 | 39 | 230 | 61 |
| Acting-out | 5 | 108 | 31 | 84 | 24 | 157 | 45 | 349 | 55 |
| Special symptoms | 5 | 114 | 54 | 49 | 23 | 50 | 23 | 213 | 77 |
| Psychosis | 5 | 62 | 25 | 102 | 40 | 88 | 35 | 252 | 65 |
| Mixed | 6 | 138 | 20 | 337 | 48 | 222 | 32 | 697 | 68 |
| Total | 24* | 456 | 26·2 | 679 | 39·0 | 606 | 34·8 | 1741 | 65·2 |

* The study of Annesley (1961) contributed data to three classifications.

The overall improvement rate for the 1741 cases in the present review is 65·2 per cent. Since evaluations at close and follow-up are not separated, the pooled defector rate of 72·5 per cent must be used as the baseline (Levitt, 1957a). This rate is significantly greater than the 65·2 per cent rate found in the present study. However, if we eliminate the psychotic and acting-out children (an attempt was made to do this in the earlier review) the adjusted figure becomes 68·3 per cent which does not differ significantly from the defector rate of 72·5 per cent.

If we pool all evaluation studies in the 1957 review, we find that 73·3 per cent of the cases show improvement. This is significantly higher than the improvement rate for studies in the present review. Again, an elimination of the psychotic and acting-out children from the present group makes the comparability more exact. We find, nonetheless, that the adjusted improvement rate of 68·3 per cent in the present study is still significantly lower than the rate for studies in the 1957 review. However, a difference of 5 per cent could easily be due to differences in sampling, treatment procedures, evaluation methods, and other sources of variation. Its clinical significance is certainly negligible.

The $3 \times 5$ matrix of frequencies of Table 1 yields a chi-square which is significant far beyond the 0·1 per cent level. It appears that much of the variation among diagnostic categories is a function of differences between the Much Improved and Partly Improved classifications. However, even if we aggregate the data for the two classifications of improvements, the $2 \times 5$ matrix still results in a chi-square which is significant beyond the 0·1 per cent level. If the two groups which seem to provide the greatest variation, the acting-out children and those with special symptoms, are eliminated, the resulting $2 \times 3$ matrix yields a nonsignificant chi-square.

## DISCUSSION

The results of this second review of evaluations of outcome of therapy with children are similar to those of the earlier review, and like those earlier findings, do not differ markedly from results obtained with defector cases. And again, the inescapable conclusion is that available evaluation studies do not furnish a reasonable basis for the hypothesis that psychotherapy facilitates recovery from emotional illness in children.

Apart from this global inference, the data suggest that there is merit in Eisenberg's contention that comparisons of treated and defector cases ought to be made within diagnostic categories. It appears that the improvement rate with therapy is lowest for cases of delinquency and anti-social acting-out, and highest for identifiable behavioural symptoms, like enuresis and school phobia. However, until the required comparisons are actually made, it would be incautious to conclude that therapy is more or less successful with any diagnostic group. It is perfectly possible that the spontaneous remission rate, as indicated by appropriate defector control groups, is also lower for the delinquents and higher for the special symptoms, and that the differences which are found in Table 1 simply reflect these facts.

Strupp's statement (1962) that we have not yet arrived at the appropriate time for a definitive outcome study is probably quite true. It also appears true that in recent years, research attention has turned away from the evaluation of outcome *per se* and has taken up the therapist and the therapy process as phenomena for investigation. However, the study of therapeutic dyad or of the personality of the therapist as a variable, or other process phenomena, does not obviate the need for precise measurement of outcome. To find the personality or the process which makes for successful treatment, we must still have an appropriate evaluation of that treatment. As Strupp (1962) says, "Concerted effort is needed to develop meaningful and measurable criteria of therapeutic outcome." It is hard to see how this can be done without continuing to evaluate the outcome of therapy itself.

Indeed, the definitive investigation may already be in process. An evaluation study sponsored by the Jewish Board of Guardians in New York City (Bloch and Rosenfeld, 1962) is now entering its eighth year and will continue for at least two more years. The enormous care and attention to detail of this investigation makes it possible that it may evolve into Strupp's 'missing link' of psychotherapy with children.

## REFERENCES

ANNESLEY, P. T. (1961) Psychiatric illness in adolescence: Presentation and prognosis. *J. ment. Sci.* **107** 268–278.

BENDER, L. and GUREVITZ, S. (1955) The results of psychotherapy with young schizophrenic children. *Amer. J. Orthopsychiat.* **25**, 162–170.

BLOCH, D. A. and ROSENFELD, E. (1962) *Evaluation (process-outcome) studies of the psychiatric treatment of children.* Progress report and research plans for the years 1962–1964. Unpublished memorandum, Jewish Board of Guardians, New York.

CHARNY, I. W. (1961) *Regression and reorganization in the "isolation treatment" of children: A clinical contribution to sensory deprivation research.* Paper presented at the meeting of the American Psychological Association, New York.

CHESS, S. (1957) *Evaluation of the effectiveness of an interracial child guidance clinic: diagnosis and treatment.* Unpublished paper, New York.

CUNNINGHAM, J. M., WESTERMAN, H. H. and FISCHHOFF, J. (1956) A follow-up study of patients seen in a psychiatric clinic for children. *Amer. J. Orthopsychiat.* **26**, 602–611.

CYTRYN, L., GILBERT, A. and EISENBERG, L. (1960) The effectiveness of tranquilizing drugs plus supportive psychotherapy in treating behaviour disorders of children: A double blind study of 80 outpatients. *Amer. J. Orthopsychiat.* **30**, 113–128.

DORFMAN, E. (1958) Personality outcomes of client-centered child therapy. *Psychol. Monogr.* **72**, No. 456.

EISENBERG, L., MARLOWE, B. and HASTINGS, M. (1958a) Diagnostic services of maladjusted foster children: An orientation toward an acute need. *Amer. J. Orthopsychiat.* **28**, 750–763.

EISENBERG, L. (1958b) School phobia: A study in the communication of anxiety. *Amer. J. Psychiat.* **114**, 712–718.

EISENBERG, L. and GRUENBERG, E. M. (1961) The current status of secondary prevention in child psychiatry. *Amer. J. Orthopsychiat.* **31**, 355–367.

EISENBERG, L., GILBERT, A., CYTRYN, L. and MOLLING, P. A. (1961) The effectiveness of psychotherapy alone and in conjunction with perphenazine or placebo in the treatment of neurotic and hyperkinetic children. *Amer. J. Psychiat.* **117**, 1088–1093.

FERSTER, C. B. and DeMYER, M. K. (1961) The development of performances in autistic children in an automatically controlled environment. *J. chron. Dis.* **13**, 312–345.

FILMER-BENNETT, G. and HILLSON, J. S. (1959) Some child therapy practices. *J. clin. Psychol.* **15**, 105–106.

HAMILTON, D. M., McKINLEY, R. A., MOORHEAD, H. H. and WALL, J. H. (1961) Results of mental hospital treatment of troubled youth. *Amer. J. Psychiat.* **117**, 811–816.

HEINICKE, C. M. (1960) Research on psychotherapy with children: A review and suggestions for further study. *Amer. J. Orthopsychiat.* **30**, 483–493.

HERSOV, L. A. (1960) Refusal to go to school. *J. child Psychol. Psychiat.* **1**, 137–145.

HOOD-WILLIAMS, J. (1960) The results of psychotherapy with children: A revaluation. *J. cons. Psychol.* **24**, 84–88.

KANE, R. P. and CHAMBERS, G. S. (1961) Improvement: Real or apparent? A seven year follow-up of children hospitalized and discharged from a residential setting. *Amer. J. Psychiat.* **117**, 1023–1026.

KAUFMAN, I., FRANK, T., FRIEND, J., HEIMS, L. W. and WEISS, R. (1962) Success and failure in the treatment of childhood schizophrenia. *Amer. J. Psychiat.* **118**, 909–913.

LAKE, M. and LEVINGER, G. (1960) Continuance beyond application interviews in a child guidance clinic. *Soc. Casewk.* **91**, 303–309.

LAVIETES, R. L., HULSE, W. and BLAU, A. (1960) A psychiatric day treatment center and school for young children and their parents. *Amer. J. Orthopsychiat.* **30**, 468–482.

LAZARUS, A. A. and ABRAMOVITZ, A. (1962) The use of "emotive imagery" in the treatment of children's phobias. *J. ment. Sci.* **108**, 191–195.

LEVITT, E. E. (1957a) Results of psychotherapy with children: An evaluation. *J. cons. Psychol.* **21**, 189–196.

LEVITT, E. E. (1957b) A comparison of "remainers" and "defectors" among child clinic patients. *J. cons. Psychol.* **21**, 316.

LEVITT, E. E. (1958a) A comparative judgmental study of "defection" from treatment at a child guidance clinic. *J. clin. Psychol.* **14**, 429–432.

LEVITT, E. E. (1958b) Parents' reasons for defection from treatment at a child guidance clinic. *Ment. Hyg. N.Y.* **42**, 521–524.

LEVITT, E. E., BEISER, H. R. and ROBERTSON, R. E. (1959) A follow-up evaluation of cases treated at a community child guidance clinic. *Amer. J. Orthopsychiat.* **29**, 337–347.

LEVITT, E. E. (1960) Reply to Hood-Williams. *J. cons. Psychol.* **24**, 89–91.

MICHAEL, C. M., MORRIS, H. H. and SOROKER, E. (1957) Follow-up studies of shy, withdrawn children—II. Relative incidence of schizophrenia. *Amer. J. Orthopsychiat.* **27**, 331–337.

MILLER, D. H. (1957) The treatment of adolescents in an adult hospital: A preliminary report. *Bull. Menninger Clin.* **21**, 189–198.

MORRIS, H. H., ESCOLI, P. J. and WEXLER, R. (1956) Aggressive behavior disorders of childhood: A follow-up study. *Amer. J. Psychiat.* **112**, 991–997.

O'NEAL, P. and ROBINS, L. N. (1958a) The relation of childhood behavior problems to adult psychiatric status. *Amer. J. Psychiat.* **114**, 961–969.

O'NEAL, P. and ROBINS, L. N. (1958b) Childhood patterns predictive of adult schizophrenia. *Amer. J. Psychiat.* **115**, 385–391.

PHILLIPS, E. L. (1957) Some features of child guidance clinic practice in the U.S.A. *J. clin. Psychol.* **13**, 42–44.

PHILLIPS, E. L. (1960) Parent-child psychotherapy: A follow-up study comparing two techniques. *J. Psychol.* **49**, 195–202.

PHILLIPS, E. L. (1961) Logical analysis of childhood behavior problems and their treatment. *Psychol. Rep.* **9**, 705–712.

REXFORD, E. N., SCHLEIFER, M. and VAN AMERONGEN, S. T. (1956) A follow-up of a psychiatric study of 57 antisocial young children. *Ment. Hyg. N.Y.* **40**, 196–214.

RODRIGUEZ, A., RODRIGUEZ, M. and EISENBERG, L. (1959) The outcome of school phobia: A follow-up study based on 41 cases. *Amer. J. Psychiat.* **116**, 540–544.

ROSS, A. O. and LACEY, H. M. (1961) Characteristics of terminators and remainers in child guidance treatment. *J. cons. Psychol.* **25**, 420–424.

SEIDMAN, F. (1957) A study of some evaluation variables in a child guidance center. Paper presented at the meeting of the American Association of Psychiatric Clinics for Children.

STRUPP, H. (1962) Psychotherapy. *Annu. Rev. Psychol.* **13**, 445–478.

ZAUSMER, D. M. (1954) The treatment of tics in childhood. *Arch. Dis. Childh.* **29**, 537–542.

75

RONALD H. COMBS

JERRY L. HARPER

# Effects of Labels on Attitudes of Educators toward Handicapped Children

*Abstract: Effects of clinical labels on attitudes of experienced and inexperienced educators toward exceptional children were explored. Labeled and unlabeled descriptions of mentally deficient, psychopathic, schizophrenic, and cerebral palsied children were distributed to 160 educators. Attitudes toward the children, and the labels, were measured on a 25 item rating scale. Results were interpreted to mean that labeling does affect the educator's perception of exceptional children. The effects were not consistent for different labels. For the mentally deficient, the child was seen more negatively when the description was unlabeled than when labeled. Labeled descriptions of psychopathic, schizophrenic, and cerebral palsied children were rated more negatively than were unlabeled versions. Experience did not seem to affect educators' perceptions of exceptional children.*

A LACK of experimental data appears in the literature concerning the effects of labels on teachers' perceptions of children. Clinical observations have led some professionals to the conclusion that labels influence the view taken toward an exceptionality. Menninger (1964) states that ". . . the label applied to the illness becomes about as damaging as the illness itself" (p. 12). He points out that, once applied, labels tend to mark a person as being different, even after recovery. Addressing himself to the general reactions of the family in learning that a child is handicapped, McDonald (1962) implies that part of the reaction is a result of confusion and misinformation on the part of the parents. A portion of this confusion and misinformation may be a result of negative attitudes toward the label.

If labels do elicit negative attitudes, it would appear that they may be extended to children so labeled. That is, significant members of the environment may respond to the exceptional child in accordance with attitudes toward the label, rather than factual information and understanding. If these attitudes are negative, the behavior of others toward the child may serve to foster and extend the exceptionality, rather than to help the child adjust.

The school is but one factor in the total environment that affects development and adjustment of the exceptional child. It is, however, a highly significant factor. Haring (1957) indicates that the attitudes and understanding teachers have about exceptional children are influential in determining the intellectual, social, and emotional adjustment of the child. Since teacher attitudes are important in determining the adjustment of the child, it would be significant to learn what factors lie behind the development of positive attitudes toward the exceptional child.

Want (1952) reports that teachers' attitudes toward school, children, and teaching did not seem to be affected by teaching experience. Attitudes of teachers became more homogeneous with experience, while the degree of negativeness or positiveness appeared to remain constant.

Major (1961) implies that experience may actually increase some teachers' rejections of

EXCEPTIONAL CHILDREN, February 1967, pp. 399-403.

the exceptional child. She points out that while the preparation of teachers is extensive, it does not always include adequate techniques for handling the unusual child. Major suggests that ". . . these teachers may feel that their enterprise is being disrupted by a seeming misfit" (p. 328). It may be that experience results in a personal involvement in the perception of exceptional children. That is, negative perceptions of educators toward labels may be magnified by classroom experience, since they tend to see the exceptional child in terms of a disturbance to their regular classes and therefore, a personal problem to themselves.

## Purpose of Study

Investigation of effects of labels on attitudes of educators toward exceptional children was conducted in regard to the terms: schizophrenia, psychopathy, mental deficiency, and cerebral palsy. Effects of experience were examined by comparing attitudes of inexperienced educators with attitudes of educators who had professional experience in schools.

The following hypotheses were tested:

1. Educators presented with behavioral descriptions of exceptional children will make significantly more negative responses to labeled than to unlabeled descriptions.
2. Educators with experience will make significantly more negative responses to descriptions of exceptional children than will inexperienced educators.

## Method

*Subjects.* The subjects were 70 male and 90 female students at Fort Hays Kansas State College selected on the basis of courses in which they were enrolled. Eighty of the subjects came from courses in the professional education sequence and represented the inexperienced professional group. These students had declared intention to enter the field of teaching and had recently completed a nine week directed teaching assignment in a public school.

A second group of 80 subjects representing experienced professional personnel was obtained by selection from graduate level courses during the summer session at the college. These subjects had completed three or more years of teaching experience in secondary, junior high,

or elementary schools. The mean years of experience was 9.9.

*Instruments.* All materials presented to the subjects were included in test booklets. Each booklet consisted of personal data, instructions, and four check lists. The first two pages were the personal data and instruction sheets. Following these, each booklet contained descriptions of schizophrenic, cerebral palsied, psychopathic, and mentally deficient children.

The order of the exceptionalities within the booklets was determined by randomization. Each exceptionality appeared only once in each booklet. Randomization was used to determine whether each description was labeled or unlabeled. This randomization was limited in that an equal number of labeled and unlabeled descriptions for each exceptionality was included. Eighty booklets were prepared for administration to the inexperienced group. A second set of 80 booklets arranged in the same order was prepared for the experienced group.

Check lists were developed to present descriptions of exceptional children and record subjects' responses. Each check list consisted of a behavioral description of an exceptional child, a list of 25 adjectives, and a four point response scale. Check lists were developed for each exceptionality differing only in the inclusion or exclusion of the label. The alphabetically arranged adjectives and the response scale remained constant.

Behavioral descriptions and labels were developed on four female exceptional children from actual case reports by Strauss and Lehtinen (1947), Shoobs (1942), and Berkowitz and Rothman (1960). Descriptions were derived for schizophrenic, psychopathic, mentally deficient, and cerebral palsied children.

Each description, without label, was presented to three clinical psychologists in Hays, Kansas. This board of experts was asked to apply a label to each description. Agreement among all members of the board and the author of the original case report was obtained on all but one description, schizophrenic, and this was resolved by discussion.

The 25 adjectives selected for the check list included 20 negative and 5 positive terms. The negative terms selected were: aggravating, annoying, defiant, demanding, depressing, destructive, disgusting, disobedient, disorganized, disrespectful, exasperating, frustrating, inattentive, quarrelsome, spoiled, ungrateful, unpleasant, unpredictable, unresponsive, and unrewarding. Positive terms selected were: considerate, dependable, merry, stable, and well mannered.

The negative adjectives for the check list were obtained by asking 15 full time public school teachers to rank a list of 40 terms as to negativeness when used to describe behavior, and frequency with which the terms were encountered in the school. The 20 adjectives selected were those rated most negative and most frequently encountered in the school after summing the two ratings.

The positive adjectives were selected from Worchel and Worchel (1961). These terms were included in the check list to provide a break in the response set which had seemed to occur in a pilot study when only negative terms were used. These terms were excluded in determining subjects' scores.

Reliability of the check list was determined by test retest technique. Test booklets were administered to a class of 20 undergraduate education students at the college, followed by a retest of the same class after a period of two weeks. A Pearson product moment correlation of .71 was obtained.

Presentation of material was accomplished with groups of from 20 to 50 subjects. Data were collected from the inexperienced professional group during the spring semester at the college. The experienced professional group was tested during the succeeding summer session.

For each of the four exceptionalities, subjects rated the applicability of each of the 20 negative and 5 positive terms on a four point scale. Yes was scored as 4; probably yes, 3; probably no, 2; and no, 1. The sum of the ratings on each exceptionality, excluding the positive terms, was used as subject's score. By this method, four scores, one for each exceptionality, were obtained for each subject. These scores represented degrees of negative attitude.

*Experimental Design.* Four $2 \times 2$ factorial designs were used to test for differences in attitudes expressed by experienced and inexperienced educators toward exceptional children under labeled and unlabeled conditions.

Labeled and unlabeled descriptions of schizo-phrenic, psychopathic, mentally deficient, and cerebral palsied children were presented to subjects in booklets. Randomization was used to vary the order of exceptionalities and the labeled and unlabeled descriptions. Each of the 160 subjects received one booklet which determined the cell in each of the four designs in which his score would appear. This technique provided for 40 independent subjects in each cell of the four $2 \times 2$ designs.

*Treatment of Data.* Subjects' scores were computed by totaling the weighted ratings on the check list. Scores ranged from 20 to 80 on each exceptionality. Twenty terms were included on the check list, with a minimum of one and a maximum of four points for each item. The higher the score from the check list, the more negative the attitude. Analysis of variance was used to analyze the data.

## Results and Conclusions

The means and standard deviations for attitude scores obtained for each exceptionality are reported in Table 1. The results of the analysis of variance for each exceptionality are reported in Table 2. The main effects for each analysis of variance are population and presentation. A significant difference was found between labeled and unlabeled presentations for each exceptionality. No significant differences were found between populations or for the interaction of the main effects.

A significant difference was found between labeled and unlabeled presentations for the mentally deficient exceptionality ($F = 4.46$, $p = < .05$). This difference was in favor of the unlabeled group. No significant differences were found between experienced and inexperienced teachers, or for the interaction of the main effects for this exceptionality. Results failed to support either of the stated hypotheses; effect of the label mentally deficient was in direct contrast to the hypothesized effect.

Significant differences were also found between labeled and unlabeled presentations for the psychopathic child ($F = 7.01$, $p < .01$), the schizophrenic child ($F = 8.91$, $p < .005$), and the cerebral palsied child ($F = 10.98$, $p < .001$). These differences were in favor of the labeled groups, which supported hypothesis 1 for these exceptionalities. No significant differences were

78

found between experienced and inexperienced teachers in their responses to the descriptions of these children. Results failed to support hypothesis 2 for the psychopathic, the schizophrenic, and the cerebral palsied exceptionalities.

It may be concluded that labels do affect the attitudes of teachers toward exceptional children. The effects varied among exceptionalities. When the label mentally deficient was applied, the child was perceived less negatively than when the label was not used. Labels applied to psychopathic, schizophrenic, and cerebral palsied children resulted in more negative ratings than when the same children were unlabeled.

These findings suggest that professionals should be extremely careful, if not reluctant, to use clinical labels in describing a child to teachers. It is questionable what the effects of such information may be on the teacher's perception of the child, but it has been shown that varying effects do occur. For some labels it is possible that a neutral, or even a positive effect may result. For other labels, however, it is likely that the effect will be negative and result in the teacher behaving toward the child in a manner that will foster elements of his behavior that are making him exceptional.

No differences were found between the attitudes of experienced and inexperienced teachers toward exceptional children. These findings support Want's (1952) conclusion that teachers' attitudes toward children do not seem to be affected by teaching experience. Results also introduce some doubt into Major's (1961) suggestion that experience may actually increase some teachers' rejections of the exceptional child. However, Major was speaking in generalities and did not specifically imply that a majority of teachers were so affected by experience.

## TABLE 1
### Means and Standard Deviations of Subjects' Scores on Attitudes toward Exceptionalities

| Presentation | Subjects | Mental Deficiency | | Psychopathy | | Schizophrenia | | Cerebral Palsy | |
| | | Mean | SD | Mean | SD | Mean | SD | Mean | SD |
|---|---|---|---|---|---|---|---|---|---|
| Labeled | Experienced | 41.71 | 8.81 | 64.55 | 8.23 | 54.10 | 9.51 | 55.10 | 9.59 |
| | Inexperienced | 44.03 | 10.33 | 65.27 | 7.82 | 54.55 | 8.90 | 53.13 | 8.00 |
| Unlabeled | Experienced | 46.38 | 8.85 | 61.18 | 6.95 | 50.03 | 9.48 | 48.65 | 10.89 |
| | Inexperienced | 45.18 | 6.20 | 62.13 | 8.12 | 49.70 | 9.91 | 49.98 | 7.83 |

$N = 640$     $n = 40$

## TABLE 2
### Summary of Analyses of Variance of Scores on Attitudes toward Exceptionalities

| | Mental Deficiency | | | Psychopathy | | | Schizophrenia | | | Cerebral Palsy | | |
| Source of Variation | df | Mean Square | F | df | Mean Square | F | df | Mean Square | F | df | Mean Square | F |
|---|---|---|---|---|---|---|---|---|---|---|---|---|
| Between Presentations | 1 | 336.4 | 4.46[a] | 1 | 425.76 | 7.01[b] | 1 | 796.56 | 8.91[c] | 1 | 921.60 | 10.98[d] |
| Between Populations | 1 | 12.1 | .16 | 1 | 28.06 | .47 | 1 | .16 | .002 | 1 | 4.23 | .05 |
| Interaction: Presentation × Population | 1 | 122.5 | 1.62 | 1 | .51 | .01 | 1 | .32 | .07 | 1 | 108.88 | 1.30 |
| Within Cells | 156 | 75.5 | | 156 | 60.74 | | 156 | 89.42 | | 156 | 83.94 | |
| Total | 159 | | | 159 | | | 159 | | | 159 | | |

[a] $p < .05$
[b] $p < .01$
[c] $p < .005$
[d] $p < .001$

Although no effort was made to rank labels from most to least negative, a review of the means between exceptionalities would suggest that this would be appropriate in future studies. Labels for psychotic disorders elicited significantly more negative attitudes than did labels for neurotic, retardant, or neurological disorders. It could be hypothesized that retardation labels elicit significantly fewer negative attitudes than do labels for psychotic, neurotic, or neurological disorders.

It may be concluded that labels do affect the attitudes of teachers toward exceptional children. Additional research is needed to determine the degree to which this conclusion can be generalized to other populations. More information is needed on the varying effects of different labels.

## References

Berkowitz, Pearl, and Rothman, Esther. *The disturbed child: recognition and psychoeducational therapy in the classroom.* New York: New York University Press, 1960.

Haring, N. G. A study of classroom teachers' attitudes toward exceptional children. *Dissertation abstracts,* 1957, 17, 103-104.

McDonald, E. T. *Understand those feelings.* Pittsburgh: Stanwix House, Inc., 1962.

Major, Iris. How do we accept the handicapped? *Elementary School Journal,* 1961, 61, 328-330.

Menninger, K. Psychiatrists use dangerous words. *The Saturday Evening Post,* 1964, 237 (16), 12-14.

Shoobs, N. E. *Corrective treatment for unadjusted children.* New York: Harper and Brothers, 1942.

Strauss, A. A., and Lehtinen, Laura E. *Psychopathology and education of the brain injured child.* New York: Grune and Stratton, Inc., 1947.

Want, E. The measurement of teacher attitudes toward groups contacted in the school. *Journal of Educational Research,* 1952, 46, 113-122.

Worchel, T. L., and Worchel, P. The parental concept of the mentally retarded child. *American Journal of Mental Deficiency,* 1961, 65, 782-788.

RONALD H. COMBS *is School Psychologist, Department of Special Education, Public Schools of Topeka, Kansas; and* JERRY L. HARPER *is Associate Professor, Department of Psychology, Wisconsin State University, Eau Claire.*

REGINALD L. JONES

# Labels and Stigma in Special Education

THE problem of labels and stigma in special education was investigated in this study. The concerns are limited to those labeled "educable mentally retarded," "culturally disadvantaged," and "culturally deprived" who constitute the largest groups of exceptional children in the schools. There is some impressionistic evidence to suggest that other groups of exceptional children in the schools are stigmatized by the special class placement and feel the effects of the negative disability labels, i.e. those in classes for the mildly emotionally disturbed, neurologically impaired, learning disabled, and trainable mentally retarded. Thus, many of the findings of the present investigation may also apply to these groups.

Inclusion of the "culturally disadvantaged" and "culturally deprived" as special education categories can be debated. They have been included in one recent textbook on the psychology and education of exceptional children and do represent a deviation sufficient to suggest the need for special curriculum adaptations.

The central theme of this study was that deficiencies exist in the delivery of services to exceptional children in two important respects:

1. Insufficient attention has been given to the fact that some of the labels used imply deficiencies and shortcomings which generate attendant problems of lowered self concept and expectations which interfere with children's optimum growth and development.

2. No systematic inquiry has been conducted into children's perceptions of the labels and special services which are offered them.

There is growing recognition that these are problem areas as indicated by two recent national conferences on the labeling and categorizing issues in special educa-

EXCEPTIONAL CHILDREN, March 1972, pp. 553-564.

tion, by the growing number of local conferences and workshops for teachers and psychologists in which these topics are key issues, and by modified training patterns in institutions for the education of teachers and school psychologists to deal with these problems.

Unfortunately, this activity is characterized by a curious absence of empirical foundation. For example, there is no documentation of the extent of the problem of labels and stigma as perceived by teachers, pupils, school administrators, citizens, and parents. There is no documentation of strategies designed to deal with these problems—empirically based or otherwise. Insofar as this author has been able to determine, no empirical study has been reported in the literature dealing with labels and stigma in public school populations of exceptional children. Apparently, data are needed in these areas if we are to plan more effectively for the delivery of service to exceptional children. One purpose of this study is to provide some results from a program of research devoted to the above problems.

The concern about labels and stigma in special education has been stimulated by minority groups, particularly blacks and Mexican Americans (browns) who point to the disproportionate numbers of their members in special classes for the mentally retarded and to the stigma associated with such placement. Their argument is that the minority child is doubly penalized by placement in special classes, first because of race or national origin and secondly because of deficit labels leading to a stigmatizing placement. Data to support disproportionate placement of blacks and browns in special classes is well known. For example, blacks and browns comprised approximately 8 and 13 percent respectively of the pupils enrolled in the California public schools, but 26 and 26 percent respectively (or 52 percent) of those enrolled in special classes for the mildly retarded (California State Department of Education, 1971).

The concern about the excessive placement of minority children in special classes for the mildly retarded extends beyond the fact of mere disproportionate representation. Rather, the concern is with the consequences of such practices for the child—lowered self concept; rejection by teachers, parents, and peers; and poor prospects for postschool adjustment and employment. Some professional special educators would add that the absence of demonstrated validity for self contained special classes, combined with the points noted above, are ample reasons for the demise of self contained classes for the educable mentally retarded. Others have argued that this is a premature judgment, however, since there are several definable subgroups of minority children now being classified as educable mentally retarded; some students may well be most appropriately placed in the self contained special class (MacMillan, 1971). As these diverse points of view indicate, the appropriateness of various administrative plans for the educable mentally retarded remains an area of some controversy (Jones, 1971a).

### Labeling Children Culturally Deprived and Culturally Disadvantaged

The current descriptive term for the child of lower socioeconomic background, usually of black or other minority status, is culturally disadvantaged or culturally deprived. Many current textbooks and articles describe the "deprived" and "disadvantaged" child's presumed cognitive, motivational, effective, demographic, and background characteristics. Like other exceptional children he is characterized as missing something which is necessary for successful school performance. Seldom have the consequences of the labels used to describe the child been explored.

The present section takes up this task and deals with the following questions. Do children of certain socioeconomic backgrounds label themselves culturally deprived or culturally disadvantaged or do they accept such labels? What are the consequences in terms of school attitudes, motivation, and self concept associated with the acceptance of the labels? What are the affective responses to these labels? What are the cognitive understanding of the terms? What are the consequences in terms of teacher and counselor behavior and expectations and in terms of student performance? These questions must be dealt with in an exploration of the effects of labels on the child. While the present concern is with the terms culturally disadvantaged and culturally deprived, similar questions must be asked for the more conventional categories of exceptional children.

That these terms are keenly felt by blacks is indicated in a recent paper by Clark (1969), the first black president of the American Psychological Association, who wrote:

> Although I reveal a certain cynicism by this, I find myself constantly thanking God that when I was in the Harlem public schools nobody knew that I was culturally deprived. I'm afraid that if they did know I would not have been taught on the grounds that being culturally deprived I wouldn't be able to learn [p. 36].

Similarly Johnson (1969), a black special educator, has written:

> When we speak of inner city, or ghetto or core area and when we use euphemisms such as educationally disadvantaged, culturally deprived, and poverty-ridden, we are really talking about Black people or Afro-Americans. . . . I am suggesting that education has failed in its responsibilities to Black Americans. What then about special education which has long been involved in educational endeavors in the inner cities?

> Its Black clientele has been labeled delinquent and retarded, thus helping the general educational enterprise to avoid some of the responsibility for its failure to adapt to individual and collective needs. Basically this labeling process imputes a lack of ability or a lack of values which are acceptable to the schools.

> The rule of thumb for Black Children is: IQ below 75 = learning problem or stupidity; and IQ above 75 = behavior problem or crazy [p. 244].

## Children's Perceptions of Themselves as Culturally Disadvantaged and Culturally Deprived

A survey of one large metropolitan school district (Jones, 1970a) in the Midwest was undertaken in which some 7,252 children in grades 4, 6, 8, 9, 10, and 12 were requested to give a variety of self perceptions: Do you see yourself as culturally disadvantaged? Do you see yourself as middle class? Do you see yourself as lower

class? The subjects represented the entire school system and included 934 students in grade 4, 772 in grade 6, 1,339 in grade 8, 1,803 in grade 9, 1,028 in grade 10, and 1,376 in grade 12. Significant numbers of minority and lower socioeconomic students were represented permitting analyses on these dimensions. Such analyses were unnecessary, however, since most students at all grade and socioeconomic levels rejected the labels as descriptive of themselves. Thus in schools where excessive numbers of mothers were receiving Aid to Dependent Children and where virtually all children were lower socioeconomic status blacks, the label was rejected by as many students as was the case in predominantly white middle class schools. Most students of whatever social class perceived themselves as middle class. Insofar as the validity of responses was concerned, the subjects' self descriptions were unrelated to a measure of social desirability. Using biserial correlations, no significant relationships were found between social desirability scores and self descriptions at any grade level. Therefore, confidence in the validity of the responses is high.

A related methodological question concerns whether or not the respondents were familiar with certain of the terms used in the study, e.g. culturally deprived and culturally disadvantaged, among others. The concern is particularly relevant for our elementary school respondents.

A study involving 259 students in grades 5 and 6 was undertaken in which the children were requested to give definitions of some 20 terms including key items of interest in the present investigation. Prior to a content analysis of responses the subjects were grouped into high, average, and low ability groups based on group intelligence test scores recorded in school records and into low and middle class backgrounds based on teacher reports. Such measures proved unnecessary, however, since virtually none of these young subjects could give satisfactory responses to the key terms culturally deprived and culturally disadvantaged.

Content analyses of these terms, and others, were also carried out in 24 junior and senior high schools using 2,397 students in grades 9 and 12. The results were particularly interesting with respect to omissions and tangential remarks given by subjects in some schools. Many older subjects could give satisfactory responses to these terms. A curious finding, however, was the tendency for many omissions and irrelevant or defensive terms to be given in certain schools. A clinical interpretation would lead to the conclusion that there was more defensiveness among the students in these largely black schools in responding to the terms culturally disadvantaged and culturally deprived.

## Affective Responses

Although the younger respondents were unfamiliar with the terms culturally deprived and culturally disadvantaged, the terms could hold certain affective and attitudinal meanings for the children. In spite of their inability to give satisfactory conventional definitions, it was suspected that at some level young elementary children were familiar with the terms and did have feelings about them. This notion was tested with 49 black children in grades 3 to 6 in a small midwestern community. The subjects responded to a number of questions related to their affective perceptions of various labels, e.g., if someone called you culturally disadvantaged, would that be good or bad? The subjects responded to 19 different socioeconomic and class descriptive terms, the results of which are presented in Table 1. As data in the Table reveal, the respondents perceived the terms culturally disadvantaged and culturally deprived as essentially negative descriptions with 78 and 68 percent, respectively, of the respondents indicating "bad" if the terms were used as descriptive of themselves. Additional data in Table 1 confirm previous suspicions about affective responses to certain other special education terms. Thus it is good to be gifted (agreed to by 74 percent of the respondents) but bad to be a slow learner or mentally retarded (agreed to by 96 and 92 percent, respectively, of the respondents). Other data were confusing, e.g. the perception of the label black as bad, and the label colored as good. It has been assumed, based on current sloganeering (i.e. black is beautiful) and the changing times, that a more favorable affective meaning would be attached to the term black than has been the case

### TABLE 1

Student Reactions to Certain Socioeconomic and Class Descriptive Terms (N = 49)

| Term | Percent of subjects | |
| --- | --- | --- |
| | Responding good | Responding bad |
| Black | 22 | 76* |
| Culturally deprived | 30 | 68 |
| Culturally disadvantaged | 16 | 78 |
| Deprived area (lived in) | 16 | 82 |
| Colored | 74 | 24 |
| Head Start | 34 | 64 |
| Inner city (lived in) | 66 | 28 |
| Poverty | 32 | 64 |
| Lower class | 6 | 92 |
| Mentally retarded | 6 | 92 |
| Middle class | 66 | 30 |
| Negro | 76 | 22 |
| Poor | 4 | 94 |
| Rich | 94 | 4 |
| Slow learner | 2 | 96 |
| Slum school | 2 | 96 |
| Upper class | 94 | 4 |
| White | 10 | 88 |
| Gifted | 74 | 24 |

*Percentages do not add up to 100 because of omissions and rounding error.

heretofore. Evidence exists that this is the case with older blacks (Dansby, in press). Further exploration of the meaning of the findings for younger black populations should be the focus of additional work in this area.

## Acceptance of Deprivation Labels and School Attitudes

It is one thing to know that children reject the labels culturally deprived and culturally disadvantaged, but a more important question relates to the consequences of acceptance or rejection of the labels and school attitudes. Do children who label themselves culturally disadvantaged or culturally deprived hold lower school attitudes than those who see themselves, regardless of objective circumstances, as middle class? Using biserial correlations, one study of 1,706 children in grades 4 and 6 revealed reliably lower school attitudes (e.g. attitudes toward teacher-pupil relationships, other pupils, and the school plant, or general feelings about school) for those who labeled themselves culturally deprived or culturally disadvantaged as opposed to those who labeled themselves middle class. The finding held across schools of varying socioeconomic classes and was independent of social desirability response sets (Jones, 1970a).

It does not seem unreasonable to speculate that similar relationships will be found between acceptance of deficit labels in other areas of disability (e.g. educable mentally retarded and educational handicap) and the respondent's school and self attitudes. This area still needs additional investigation.

## Labels and Performance—Two Experiments

There has been no work which supports the belief that deficit labels actually affect the learning and performance of those so labeled. If labels have deleterious effects as hypothesized by many special educators, it should be possible to demonstrate that learning and performance proceeds more slowly or inefficiently under a deficit label than under a neutral or a positive label. The present section presents the results of explorations of this hypothesis using experimental methods (Jones, 1970b).

Two studies on the effects of having black college students perform a digit-symbol substitution task under various label conditions were undertaken. In the first, the students (who believed the digit-symbol task to be a measure of psychomotor intelligence) completed the forms with one of three labels at the bottom of each page: (a) study of culturally disadvantaged college students, (b) study of black college students, or (c) study of college students. No attention was called to the labels in the instructions, and students under the three conditions were randomly assigned to the treatments within classrooms. The selected students were 243 black college students in three predominantly black colleges—two in the South ($N$'s = 63 and 120) and one in the Midwest ($N$ = 60). The data from each school were treated separately. The hypothesis tested was that digit-symbol performance would be highest for the black college student condition and lowest for the culturally disadvantaged conditions.

One-way analyses of variance of total number of symbols correctly translated revealed no reliable differences ($p > .05$) in mean performance for students in the

three conditions at any of the three schools, thus providing no support for the hypothesis ($F = 2.63$, $df$ 2/57; $F = .54$, $df$ 2/117; and $F = .26$, $df$ 2/60). A small followup pilot study revealed that few subjects could actually recall the labels.

A second study using 100 different black students in two predominantly black midwestern colleges was a followup to the above studies. It was designed to mirror, in a rigorous experimental fashion, practices followed in present day schools—i.e., a student is identified as having an educationally related deficiency and he is placed in some special program to remediate the deficiency. The possibility that the fact of placement may itself lead to a decrement in rather than a stimulus to performance has not been the object of serious investigation. The subjects were first given the digit-symbol substitution test (a measure of learning ability) under a nonlabel condition. About 1 week later the subject was informed via a personal letter (a) that he had scored in the high group and would be given the advanced exercises to permit further improvement of his performance or (b) that he had scored in the low group and hence remedial exercises would be given. This would be followed by an immediate posttest to determine the effectiveness of the remedial or advanced exercises. To heighten awareness of the experimental variables the content of the letter, letterhead, and the signature line attempted to call attention to the treatments which were: (a) study of culturally disadvantaged college students ($N = 25$), (b) study of black college students ($N = 25$), (c) study of college students ($N = 25$), or (d) project accelerate ($N = 25$). These labels were also placed at the bottom of each page of the intermediate (remedial or advanced) tests which were identical for the four treatments but a more difficult form of the digit-symbol task than the pre- or posttest. A posttest (identical to the pretest) followed the intermediate exercises. Finally, the nature of all experimental manipulations was explained to the subjects and all questions about the study were answered.

No reliable differences ($p > .05$) in pretest performance were found. A one-way analysis of variance of posttest scores revealed no reliable differences in digit-sym-

85

bol performance as a function of exposure to the treatments ($p > .05$).

Several possibilities may account for failure to support the hypothesis: (a) dependent measures which were not sensitive to treatment effects, (b) a confirmed failure of subjects to attend to the labels, and (c) the fact that the subjects were college students, a somewhat homogeneous group who may have been impervious to the suggestion that they possessed learning deficiencies. There is a need to carry out similar investigations using more heterogeneous public school populations.

### Teacher Expectations and Labels

Teacher expectations about the performance of children can come to serve a self fulfilling prophecy. Such a possibility was brought to attention in a dramatic way by the research of Rosenthal and Jacobson (1968) who pretested a group of elementary school children with a standard nonverbal test of intelligence, the test being represented to the teachers as one that would predict intellectual blooming. Approximately 20 percent of the children in grades 1 through 6 were randomly identified as students with a potential to bloom intellectually. These children and others not so identified were retested with the same nonverbal IQ test after 1 semester and after 1 and 2 academic years. It was found that students in the control group made some significant gains in IQ, with 19 percent gaining 20 or more IQ points; 47 percent of the special children, however, gained 20 or more total IQ points.

The Rosenthal studies have been faulted on many methodological grounds (Barber & Silver, 1968a, 1968b; Thorndike, 1968). However, the results of related investigations have suggested that teachers do hold low expectations for certain classes of students and that such expectations do relate to the ways in which teachers interact with their pupils.

The Herriott and St. John study (1966), based on interviews with a national sample of teachers and pupils in urban public schools, reported that the lower the socioeconomic status of the schools the smaller the proportion of teachers who held favorable opinions about the motivation and behavior of their pupils. Moreover, these same teachers were less likely to report that they had personal loyalty to the principal, that they desired to remain at their present school, or that they enjoyed their work. The finding which concerned work satisfaction is particularly important since there is evidence that reported satisfaction in teaching is directly correlated with pupil school morale (Jones, 1968). Pearson product moment correlations between eight indices of school morale and reported teacher satisfaction for 34 randomly selected teachers and their fourth grade students in 34 urban classrooms revealed significant correlations between reported satisfaction with teaching and (a) attitudes toward other pupils ($p < .01$), (b) pupil-teacher relationships ($p < .05$), (c) general feelings about school ($p < .01$), and (d) general school morale ($p < .05$). Similar analyses were carried out with 28 sixth grade classrooms. However, no significant correlations were found between reported teacher satisfaction and any of the morale subscales.

For young children, teacher satisfaction appears to be related to pupil satisfaction. Unfortunately, it is not possible to know which group influenced which. Perhaps perceived poor pupil attitudes led to lowered satisfaction in teaching; or the situation could have been reversed with pupils responding to perceived poor teacher attitudes. Regardless of the order of development of the attitudes, lowered satisfaction in work with children in the early grades seems closely tied to pupil satisfaction with school.

### Mediation of Expectancy Effects

What happens to the "culturally disadvantaged" child in the classroom? If expectancy effects are at all operative, how are they mediated? Several studies have examined the mechanisms through which expectancy effects become translated into actual teacher behavior. The first was that of Beez (1968) which showed the effects of teacher expectation on pupil performance. Subjects were 60 teachers and 60 pupils in a Head Start program. Teachers taught each child the meaning of a symbol. Half the teachers had been given the expectancy that, based on a psychological appraisal of the child, good learning would occur; the remaining half were led to expect poor learning.

The results showed 77 percent of those alleged to have good intellectual prospects learned five or more symbols, whereas only 13 percent of those alleged to have poor prospects achieved at this level. Moreover, teachers who had been given favorable expectations about their pupils actually attempted to teach more symbols than those teachers who had been given unfavorable expectations about their pupils.

Expectations cover not only subjective forecasts of pupil ability and motivation but extend to school attitudes as well. Expectations regarding the school attitudes of a "culturally disadvantaged" child held by a group of college students were investigated in a social cognition experiment (Jones, 1970a). Subjects were 119 female undergraduate students who volunteered to participate in a psychology experiment as part of an introductory psychology course requirement. Approximately 75 percent of the participants were prospective teachers. Seventy-five of the subjects (experimental group) were given the following instructions:

This is a study to determine the way in which individuals make certain kinds of predictions about the responses of others.

Please fill out the enclosed inventory according to the instruction on the booklet. However instead of answering the questions as you normally would, answer as you think the person described below would respond.

A twelve year old culturally deprived boy in the 6th grade in an inner city school.

Remember, you are to answer as you feel this person would.

Please answer every question, even though you may sometimes find it difficult to make a decision.

A second group of 44 respondents (control group) received instructions, identical to those above except that the boy in the vignette was not described as inner city or culturally deprived. According to the instructions given above, all subjects completed the School Morale Inventory (Wrightsman, 1968), an inventory designed to measure student feelings about school in a number of important areas.

TABLE 2

School Attitudes Attributed to Culturally Deprived and Nondeprived School Children

| | Predicted attitudes | |
| Attitude subscale | Deprived $N = 75$ Mean | Nondeprived $N = 44$ Mean |
|---|---|---|
| School plant | 3.15 | 6.37* |
| Instruction | 2.36 | 4.77 |
| Community | 1.95 | 6.57 |
| Administration, regulations, and staff | 2.56 | 5.01 |
| Other students | 4.63 | 7.44 |
| Teacher-student relationships | 4.00 | 6.53 |
| General school morale | 3.31 | 5.50 |
| Total morale | 21.89 | 45.52 |

*All differences were significant at less than the .01 level. The maximum score for individual subscales is 12 and for total morale is 84.

The inventory was scored in the conventional manner and the subtest scores given under the set to simulate the culturally deprived child compared (using $t$ tests) with those given under the set to simulate the nondeprived child. The results were unequivocal; the deprived child was predicted to have reliably lower morale on all subscales of the School Morale Inventory (see Table 2).

The study was repeated with a group of experienced teachers and counselors who had completed a year of study in an institute devoted to preparing counselors of "culturally deprived" youth. The responses of these specialists were identical to those given by the undergraduate students: the school attitudes held by the "culturally deprived" were predicted to be reliably lower than those held by the "nondeprived." For both counselors and undergraduate subjects the cognitions given for the "deprived" child were considerably more discrepant than those actually given by children who could be so labeled.

No pretests of counselor cognitions were obtained. It is difficult therefore to know the extent to which any changes took place in counselor attitudes toward the "deprived" as a function of the year long institute. It is possible that counselor attitudes were even more negative than those found at the end of their training. Following a full year of training devoted to the "culturally deprived," counselors held negative and stereotyped views of this group. If this program for counselors is any good, it suggests that prospects for modifying negative attitudes toward the "deprived" through formal training (including considerable field work) are not bright.

The results of investigations reported here reveal that children do reject the labels culturally deprived and culturally disadvantaged as descriptive of themselves. Acceptance of such terms as self descriptive has been found to be associated with lowered attitudes toward school. Moreover, teachers and counselors hold clear stereotypes about the characteristics and attitudes of children so labeled. Unfortunately, most of these characterizations and stereotypes are negative, and the spectre of the self fulfilling prophecy is ever present.

The results suggest the need for modification of labeling practices in this area, for as Clark (1969) observed:

> . . . the most serious of all the obstacles which must be overcome is the tendency to label these youngsters, to name-call them, and to embark on the self-fulfilling prophecy of believing them to be uneducable by setting up social science and educational jargon which justifies this belief, setting up procedures and approaches which make education almost impossible, and then proving all of it by demonstrating that these children are retarded. If we are going to educate these children, this, I believe is the significant obstacle [p. 36].

Also, Mackler and Giddings (1967) stated:

> . . . We must purge ourselves of the concept of cultural deprivation and all its derogatory implications. If a concept is needed, then we must seek a more accurate, authentic, and honest term. If we conclude that no term is needed perhaps that will be all the better [p. 397].

### Stigma, Stigma Management, and the Educable Mentally Retarded

This discussion is divided into three parts. The first deals with the problem of stigma as perceived by the retarded themselves, while the second treats teacher perceptions of stigma and techniques for its management. The third section looks at special classes from the perspective of the former special education student.

*Retarded Students' Perceptions of Special Class Placement*

Aside from the pioneering study by Edgerton (1967) with former institutionalized retarded persons, no research on stigma and stigma management associated with the mentally retarded appears to have been reported in the literature. There is, however, ample evidence to suggest the existence of negative stereotypes of the retarded (Guskin, 1963; Wilson, 1970). The studies reported in the aforementioned reviews all dealt with reports of attitudes of the nondisabled toward the retarded. However, in planning school programs for the educable mentally retarded it seems important to have some knowledge of the retarded student's perceptions of his special class placement and of techniques which he uses to manage the fact of such placement. Heretofore, such information has not been available.

Research at the elementary school level (Meyerowitz, 1962) indicated that the young child's self concept drops following placement in a self contained special class for the educable mentally retarded. At the high school level, the self concept of the special class educable retarded student was found to be lower than that of nonretarded students in regular classes (Jones, 1968). It is not possible to establish cause and effect relationships between special education placement and lowered self concept because of methodological problems in the above studies. The presumptive evidence, however, is that this is the case. One high school educable retarded student noted:

> . . . I don't tell them [friends] I'm in special class. I didn't care last year [junior high school] but I do now because all these people make fun of me.

And another indicated:

> I don't like to see some of the [regular] students come in here [to visit special class] because they're my friends and I don't want them to know I'm here.

A small pilot study on stigma and stigma management by a group of high school boys enrolled in a special class for the educable mentally retarded in a large midwestern city was revealing (Jones, 1970a). Seventeen of the 23 respondents lied when asked about their school work.

Most said that they enrolled in regular, not special, courses, indicating that they were not proud of their special class placement or their academic success in general. Those elaborating on their responses indicated that they said regular work in order to avoid ridicule. Sixteen of the 23 respondents indicated that special education was disliked because they were made to feel different and made fun of. While most of the respondents expressed the view that visitors should be permitted to visit the classroom, there was an underlying reluctance to do so and some qualification of responses.

> "Yes and no." If they'd [special students] act right they'd [regular students] be allowed. Some of the people in here don't act right, and others don't want people to know its not like the regular classes.

Sixteen of the respondents indicated that they had received queries about being in special education. In these queries the retarded student was asked about the content and organization of special education classes or ridiculed for such placement. The subjects usually attempted to cover up by saying that the work was the same and that they were graded in the same manner as in regular classes.

Seven of the 23 respondents indicated that being in the special class had changed their friendships. The effect of special class placement on friendships was limited, however, because many respondents had friends outside the special class. Of the respondents expressing the view that special class placement had a negative effect on their friendships, the most frequent reason was that others (i.e. regular students) saw the special class as inferior. Here is an example:

> Yes it has very much [i.e. placement in a special class has affected friendships]. Some of my friends won't even talk to me because they think I'm too dumb and dilentary. I just tell them I don't give a damn about the other fellow. This is me and myself and I don't care what they think 'cause its not hurting me its hurting them.

For some boys, enrollment in a special class made it more difficult to keep a girlfriend:

> If you want a girlfriend, she won't like

you 'cause you're in the special class. She'll think you're stupid and kinda weird. They think you're retarded. Girls mostly, some boys.

Eleven respondents saw the special class placement as having a negative effect on opportunities for postschool job placement, although students in work-study programs were more optimistic in this regard. Fourteen of the 23 respondents were aware of techniques used to hide or cover the fact of special class placement. Eleven volunteered that they themselves practiced such strategies.

Thirteen of the respondents could think of nothing in school which made them happy with their special education placement, and 21 of the 23 respondents could think of no out-of-school event which led to satisfaction with such placement. Finally, not 1 of the 23 respondents indicated the special class as his preferred educational placement.

The results were followed up on 116 additional educable retarded students in self contained classrooms in three midwestern cities at both the junior and senior high school. The similar results suggest that for the populations under study and probably for others the phenomenon of stigma in the noninstitutionalized educable retarded is indeed real.

### Teacher Perception and Management of Stigma

If the problem of stigma is real as data from the retarded themselves indicate, the questions of how it was perceived by teachers and what, if anything, was being done about it seemed critical. Answers to these questions were dealt with in a questionnaire completed by a random sample of 317 Ohio elementary and secondary teachers of the educable retarded (Jones, 1971b). Key findings of this investigation are presented in Table 3, which summarizes evidence bearing on teacher awarenesss of stigma associated with special class placement and on teacher strategies for stigma management. Particularly noteworthy is the fact that, while evidence points to problems of stigma in up to 93 percent of the classes, few curriculum materials or strategies were used by teachers to deal with these problems.

According to teacher reports, terms such

TABLE 3

## Teacher Perception and Management of Stigma

| Question | Percentage of yes responses | | |
| --- | --- | --- | --- |
| | Senior high $N = 94$ | Junior high $N = 129$ | Elementary $N = 94$ |
| 1. Are you aware of any evidence which indicates that your pupils are ashamed of being in a class for slow learners?* | 83 | 82 | 51 |
| 2. Are you aware of any names or derogatory labels attached to your class or the pupils in it? | 80 | 90 | 81 |
| 3. Have you had discussions with your class about the attitudes of others toward them or the class? | 93 | 93 | 85 |
| 4. Do you ever discuss ways that the children can deal with those who ask about their grade or class placement or the subjects they are taking? | 71 | 74 | 78 |
| 5. Do you use any units or special materials to help your pupils adjust to the fact of their special class placement or to the attitudes of others toward them? | 46 | 43 | 41 |

*Slow learner is the Ohio term for educable mentally retarded which was in use in Spring 1969 when the study was conducted.

a dumb, dumb bunny, dum-dum, retard, Z, eddie, and dodo were among the derisive terms frequently used to describe the special class. The teacher's name, the room number, or the name of the local school for the retarded was also a basis for identifying special class students. The terms were used by regular students, by students of only slightly higher placement, and by the special education students themselves. There were also reports of the derisive terms being used by regular teachers.

As the data in Table 3 reveal, most teachers had held discussions with the students about the attitudes of others toward them or the class. Name calling and ridicule by other (regular) students was the most frequent stimulus for these discussions although incidents sparked by the special class students themselves was also a stimulus in some cases. Conclusions stemming from these teacher-led discussions included the following:

1. Students should accept themselves, i.e. adjust to others (do the best they can and get a better outlook).
2. Students should ignore (or tolerate) remarks.
3. Students should behave better ("act intelligent") as do regular students.
4. The student has many advantages and positive aspects (i.e., they can learn; they can excel in something; the special education program is good).
5. Students should note that other persons

are ignorant for calling names (also immature and inferior).

There were a number of additional reasons given by teachers which defy easy classification. Most striking in all their responses, however, is the uncertainty with which teachers approach this area and the paucity of validated techniques for dealing with the problem.

### Stigma and Postschool Adjustment

The student labeled educable mentally retarded while in school does not erase this experience from his consciousness following graduation or school termination. There is evidence that the individual is sensitive to the fact of his former special class placement and that such sensitivity does influence interaction with friends, acquaintances, and potential employers. The extent to which stigma was operating in the lives of former special class students was investigated in one followup study of 405 individuals. These students had been eligible for, though not all had been placed in, classes for the educable mentally retarded, and they had graduated or dropped out of a work-study or regular special education program. These individuals were interviewed in their homes by professionally trained interviewers and represented a sample from a pool of 2,213 subjects who had been identified as meeting the basic criteria of the study, i.e., they were (a) eligible for placement in a special class and (b) eligible for graduation between June 1964 and June 1968. Participants included students from one big city district, and semirural and suburban districts (Dyck & Jones, 1969).

One interview question was the following:

Since you left school, how many people have you told that you were in special classes or a work-study program in school?

Of 269 individuals responding to this question, 94 (35 percent) indicated "anyone who asks" while 98 (36 percent) indicated "no one." Seventy-eight (29 percent) of the respondents would confide in a few people. Thus 65 percent of the respondents would tell no one or only a few people of their former special class placement suggesting that it was not a fact of which they were proud. (The finding could also reflect, of course, the subjects' knowledge that because of potential ridicule and public misunderstanding the fact of former special class placement must be communicated judiciously.)

Several other perceptions of the school program reported by former special class students are noteworthy. Four questions were asked about the perceived value of special education in facilitating (or hindering) work and interpersonal adjustment. Responses to the questions are summarized in Table 4, which presents results for work-study graduates, work-study dropouts, special education graduates, and special education dropouts.

As can be seen from inspection of the data, when contrasted with special education graduates and dropouts, work-study graduates are more likely to report that having been in special education had been helpful. As would be anticipated, fewer special education graduates and dropouts, as contrasted with work-study graduates and dropouts, agreed that special class placement had caused problems. In addition, work-study graduates, in contrast to other categories of special education students, were more likely to agree that the schools could "help students get better jobs than they would get otherwise." In a somewhat related vein, work-study graduates were more likely to report that being in a special program helped "get along better with other people."

Overall, the findings revealed that the program was viewed most positively by work-study graduates and, as a rule, least positively by special education dropouts. However, no group embraced their program wholeheartedly as revealed by the fact that almost two-thirds of the respondents would tell no one or only a few people of their former special class placement and fewer than half of the respondents believed that the schools had helped to prepare them for effective interpersonal relationships. Moreover, interviewers judged that approximately one-fifth of the respondents showed slight or strong dislike, irritation, and/or embarrassment at being asked the questions about special education.

TABLE 4

Evaluation of School Program Helpfulness

| Question | Work-study graduates | | Work-study dropouts | | Special education graduates | | Special education dropouts | |
|---|---|---|---|---|---|---|---|---|
| | N | Percent | N | Percent | N | Percent | N | Percent |
| 1. Looking back, has being in special education or a work-study program been helpful to you? (Yes) | 125 | 58.6 | 37 | 49.3 | 11 | 44.0 | 14 | 34.1 |
| 2. Has being in special education or a work-study program caused any problems for you? (No) | 134 | 62.9 | 49 | 65.3 | 13 | 52.0 | 20 | 48.7 |
| 3. Can schools help students get better jobs than they would get otherwise? (Yes) | 143 | 67.1 | 46 | 61.3 | 13 | 52.0 | 22 | 53.6 |
| 4. Did being in special education help you get along better with other people? (Yes) | 103 | 48.3 | 33 | 44.0 | 8 | 32.0 | 10 | 24.3 |

## Final Note

It is apparent that considerable additional work needs to be undertaken in our explorations of the effects of labels and stigma on the special child. It is apparent also, in planning educational programs for exceptional children, that labels and stigma are only two variables among a host of factors to be considered in developing optimum educational placements for the exceptional child. Other variables include the quality of personnel and resources available in the classroom or school building, the child's history of acceptance or rejection, the degree of environmental support available to the child, the kinds of educational alternatives available to the child in the school district, and many other considerations as well. Nothing written here is meant to deny the importance of these considerations. Rather, the point of the paper has been to call attention to two important classes of variables that need to be considered in planning services for exceptional children but which have previously been neglected and to provide data which highlight the importance of these variables.

## References

Barber, T. X., & Silver, M. J. Facts, fiction, and the experimenter bias effect. *Psychological Bulletin Monograph*, 1968, **70**, 1-19. (a)

Barber, T. X., & Silver, M. J. Pitfalls in data analysis and interpretation: A reply to Rosenthal. *Psychological Bulletin Monograph*, 1968, **70**, 48-62. (b)

Beez, W. V. Influence of biased psychological reports on teacher behavior and pupil performance. *Proceedings of the 76th Annual Convention of the American Psychological Association*, 1968. Pp. 605-606.

California State Department of Education. *Placement of pupils in classes for the mentally retarded: A report to the legislature as required by House resolution 262.* Sacramento: California State Department of Education, 1971.

Clark, K. B. Learning obstacles among children. In A. L. Roaden (Ed.), *Problems of school men in depressed urban centers.* Columbus, Ohio: College of Education, The Ohio State University, 1969.

Dansby, M. P. Black pride in the 70's: Fact or fantasy? In R. L. Jones (Ed.), *Black psychology.* New York: Harper and Row, in press.

Dyck, D., & Jones, R. L. *A comprehensive followup of work study graduates of the Montgomery County schools.* Dayton, Ohio: Montgomery County Board of Education, 1969.

Edgerton, R. B. *The cloak of competence.* Berkeley: University of California Press, 1967.

Guskin, S. Social psychologies of mental deficiencies. In N. R. Ellis (Ed.), *Handbook of mental deficiency.* New York: McGraw-Hill, 1963.

Herriott, R., & St. John, N. H. *Social class and the urban school.* New York: John Wiley and Sons, 1966.

Johnson, J. J. Special education and the inner city: A challenge for the future or another means for cooling the mark out? *The Journal of Special Education*, 1969, **3**, 241-251.

Jones, R. L. Student attitudes and motivation. In Ohio State University Advisory Commission on Problems Facing the Columbus (Ohio) Public School (Eds.), *A report to the Columbus Board of Education.* Columbus, Ohio: The Ohio State University, 1968. Pp. 272-300, 313-332.

Jones, R. L. New labels in old bags: Research on labeling blacks culturally disadvantaged, culturally deprived, and mentally retarded. Unpublished paper presented at the Annual Convention of the Association of Black Psychologists, Miami Beach, September, 1970. (a)

Jones, R. L. Labeling black college students culturally disadvantaged: A search for behavioral correlates. Unpublished paper presented at the Annual Convention of The Western Psychological Association, Los Angeles, April, 1970. (b)

Jones, R. L. (Ed.) *Problems and issues in the education of exceptional children.* Boston: Houghton Mifflin, 1971. (a)

Jones, R. L. Teacher management of stigma in classes for the educable mentally retarded. Unpublished paper presented at the Annual Meeting of the California Educational Research Association, April, 1971. (b)

Mackler, B., & Giddings, M.-G. Cultural Deprivation: A study in mythology. In E. T. Keach, Jr., R. Fulton, & W. E. Gardner, *Education and social crisis.* New York: John Wiley and Sons, 1967.

MacMillan, D. L. Special Education for the mildly retarded: Servant or savant. *Focus on Exceptional Children*, 1971, **2**, 1-11.

Meyerowitz, J. H. Self derogations in young retardates and special class placement. *Child Development*, 1962, 33, 443-451.

Rosenthal, R., & Jacobson, L. *Pygmalion in the classroom.* New York: Holt, Rinehart, & Winston, 1968.

Thorndike, R. L. Review of Rosenthal, R. and Jacobson, L. Pygmalion in the classroom. *American Educational Research Journal*, 1968, **5**, 708-711.

Wilson, W. Social psychology and mental retardation. In N. R. Ellis (Ed.), *International review of research in special education.* Vol. 4. New York: Academic Press, 1970.

Wrightsman, L., Nelson, R. H., & Tranto, M. The construction and validation of a scale to measure children's school morale. Unpublished paper, George Peabody College for Teachers, 1968.

LLOYD M. DUNN

# Special Education for the Mildly Retarded— Is Much of It Justifiable?

A better education than special class placement is needed for socioculturally deprived children with mild learning problems who have been labeled educable mentally retarded. Over the years, the status of these pupils who come from poverty, broken and inadequate homes, and low status ethnic groups has been a checkered one. In the early days, these children were simply excluded from school. Then, as Hollingworth (1923) pointed out, with the advent of compulsory attendance laws, the schools and these children "were forced into a reluctant mutual recognition of each other." This resulted in the establishment of self contained special schools and classes as a method of transferring these "misfits" out of the regular grades. This practice continues to this day and, unless counterforces are set in motion now, it will probably become even more prevalent in the immediate future due in large measure to increased racial integration and militant teacher organizations. For example, a local affiliate of the National Education Association demanded of a local school board recently that more special classes be provided for disruptive and slow learning children (Nashville *Tennessean*, December 18, 1967).

The number of special day classes for the retarded has been increasing by leaps and bounds. The most recent 1967-

EXCEPTIONAL CHILDREN, September 1968, pp. 5-23.

1968 statistics compiled by the US Office of Education now indicate that there are approximately 32,000 teachers of the retarded employed by local school systems—over one-third of all special educators in the nation. In my best judgment, about 60 to 80 percent of the pupils taught by these teachers are children from low status backgrounds—including Afro-Americans, American Indians, Mexicans, and Puerto Rican Americans; those from nonstandard English speaking, broken, disorganized, and inadequate homes; and children from other nonmiddle class environments. This expensive proliferation of self contained special schools and classes raises serious educational and civil rights issues which must be squarely faced. It is my thesis that we must stop labeling these deprived children as mentally retarded. Furthermore we must stop segregating them by placing them into our allegedly special programs.

The purpose of this article is twofold: first, to provide reasons for taking the position that a large proportion of this so called special education in its present form is obsolete and unjustifiable from the point of view of the pupils so placed; and second, to outline a blueprint for changing this major segment of education for exceptional children to make it more acceptable. We are not arguing that we do away with our special education programs for the moderately and severely retarded, for other types of more handicapped children, or for the multiply handicapped. The emphasis is on doing something better for slow learning children who live in slum conditions, although much of what is said should also have relevance for those children we are labeling emotionally disturbed, perceptually impaired, brain injured, and learning disordered. Furthermore, the emphasis of the article is on children, in that no attempt is made to suggest an adequate high school environment for adolescents still functioning as slow learners.

## Reasons for Change

Regular teachers and administrators have sincerely felt they were doing these pupils a favor by removing them from the pressures of an unrealistic and inappropriate program of studies. Special educators have also fully believed that the children involved would make greater progress in special schools and classes. However, the overwhelming evidence is that our present and past practices have their major justification in removing pressures on regular teachers and pupils, at the expense of the socioculturally deprived slow learning pupils themselves. Some major arguments for this position are outlined below.

94

Homogeneous groupings tend to work to the disadvantage of the slow learners and underprivileged. Apparently such pupils learn much from being in the same class with children from white middle class homes. Also, teachers seem to concentrate on the slower children to bring them up to standard. This principle was dramatically applied in the Judge J. Skelly Wright decision in the District of Columbia concerning the track system. Judge Wright ordered that tracks be abolished, contending they discriminated against the racially and/or economically disadvantaged and therefore were in violation of the Fifth Amendment of the Constitution of the United States. One may object to the Judge's making educational decisions based on legal considerations. However, Passow (1967), upon the completion of a study of the same school system, reached the same conclusion concerning tracking. The recent national study by Coleman, et al. (1966), provides supporting evidence in finding that academically disadvantaged Negro children in racially segregated schools made less progress than those of comparable ability in integrated schools. Furthermore, racial integration appeared to deter school progress very little for Caucasian and more academically able students.

What are the implications of Judge Wright's rulings for special education? Clearly special schools and classes are a form of homogeneous grouping and tracking. This fact was demonstrated in September, 1967, when the District of Columbia (as a result of the Wright decision) abolished Track 5, into which had been routed the slowest learning pupils in the District of Columbia schools. These pupils and their teachers were returned to the regular classrooms. Complaints followed from the regular teachers that these children were taking an inordinate amount of their time. A few parents observed that their slow learning children were frustrated by the more academic program and were rejected by the other students. Thus, there are efforts afoot to develop a special education program in D.C. which cannot be labeled a track. Self contained special classes will probably not be tolerated under the present court ruling but perhaps itinerant and resource room programs would be. What if the Supreme Court ruled against tracks, and all self contained special classes across the nation which serve primarily ethnically and/or economically disadvantaged children were forced to close down? Make no mistake—this could happen! If I were a Negro from the slums or a disadvantaged parent who had heard of the Judge Wright decision and knew what I know now about special classes for the educable mentally retarded, other things being equal, I would then go to court before allowing the schools to label my child as "mentally retarded" and place him in a "self contained special school or class." Thus there is the real possibility that additional court actions will be forthcoming.*

### Efficacy Studies

The findings of studies on the efficacy of special classes for the educable mentally retarded constitute another argument for change. These results are well known (Kirk, 1964) and suggest consistently that retarded pupils make as much or more progress in the regular grades as they do in special education. Recent studies such as those by Hoelke (1966) and Smith and Kennedy (1967) continue to provide similar evidence. Johnson (1962) has summarized the situation well:

It is indeed paradoxical that mentally handicapped children having teachers especially trained, having more money (per capita) spent on their education, and being designed to provide for their unique needs, should be accomplishing the objectives of their education at the same or at a lower level than similar mentally handicapped children who have not had these advantages and have been forced to remain in the regular grades [p. 66].

Efficacy studies on special day classes for other mildly handicapped children, including the emotionally handicapped, reveal the same results. For example, Rubin, Senison, and Betwee (1966) found that disturbed children did as well in the regular grades as in special classes, concluding that there is little or no evidence that special class programing is generally beneficial to emotionally disturbed children as a specific method of intervention and correction. Evidence such as this is another reason to find better ways of serving children with mild learning disorders than placing them in self contained special schools and classes.

---

* Litigation has now occurred. According to an item in a June 8, 1968, issue of the *Los Angeles Times* received after this article was sent to the printer, the attorneys in the national office for the rights of the indigent filed a suit in behalf of the Mexican-American parents of the Santa Ana Unified School District asking for an injunction against the District's classes for the educable mentally retarded because the psychological examinations required prior to placement are unconstitutional since they have failed to use adequate evaluation techniques for children from different language and cultural backgrounds, and because parents have been denied the right of hearing to refute evidence for placement. Furthermore, the suit seeks to force the district to grant hearings on all children currently in such special classes to allow for the chance to remove the stigma of the label "mentally retaded" from school records of such pupils.

Our past and present diagnostic procedures comprise another reason for change. These procedures have probably been doing more harm than good in that they have resulted in disability labels and in that they have grouped children homogeneously in school on the basis of these labels. Generally, these diagnostic practices have been conducted by one of two procedures. In rare cases, the workup has been provided by a multidisciplinary team, usually consisting of physicians, social workers, psychologists, speech and hearing specialists, and occasionally educators. The avowed goal of this approach has been to look at the complete child, but the outcome has been merely to label him mentally retarded, perceptually impaired, emotionally disturbed, minimally brain injured, or some other such term depending on the predispositions, idiosyncracies, and backgrounds of the team members. Too, the team usually has looked for causation, and diagnosis tends to stop when something has been found wrong with the child, when the why has either been found or conjectured, and when some justification has been found for recommending placement in a special education class.

In the second and more common case, the assessment of educational potential has been left to the school psychologist who generally administers—in an hour or so—a psychometric battery, at best consisting of individual tests of intelligence, achievement, and social and personal adjustment. Again the purpose has been to find out what is wrong with the child in order to label him and thus make him eligible for special education services. In large measure this has resulted in digging the educational graves of many racially and/or economically disadvantaged children by using a WISC or Binet IQ score to justify the label "mentally retarded." This term then becomes a destructive, self fulfilling prophecy.

What is the evidence against the continued use of these diagnostic practices and disability labels?

First, we must examine the effects of these disability labels on the attitudes and expectancies of teachers. Here we can extrapolate from studies by Rosenthal and Jacobson (1966) who set out to determine whether or not the expectancies of teachers influenced pupil progress. Working with elementary school teachers across the first six grades, they obtained pretest measures on pupils by using intelligence and achievement tests. A sample of pupils was randomly drawn and labeled "rapid learners" with hidden potential. Teachers were told that these children would show unusual intellectual gains and school progress during the year. All pupils were retested late in the school year. Not all differences were statistically significant, but the gains of the children who had been arbitrarily labeled rapid learners were generally significantly greater than those of the other pupils, with especially dramatic changes in the first and second grades. To extrapolate from this study, we must expect that labeling a child "handicapped" reduces the teacher's expectancy for him to succeed.

Second, we must examine the effects of these disability labels on the pupils themselves. Certainly none of these labels are badges of distinction. Separating a child from other children in his neighborhood—or removing him from the regular classroom for therapy or special class placement—probably has a serious debilitating effect upon his self image. Here again our research is limited but supportive of this contention. Goffman (1961) has described the stripping and mortification process that takes place when an individual is placed in a residential facility. Meyerowitz (1965) demonstrated that a group of educable mentally retarded pupils increased in feelings of self derogation after one year in special classes. More recent results indicate that special class placement, instead of helping such a pupil adjust to his neighborhood peers, actually hinders him (Meyerowitz, 1967). While much more research is needed, we cannot ignore the evidence that removing a handicapped child from the regular grades for special education probably contributes significantly to his feelings of inferiority and problems of acceptance.

*Improvements in General Education*

Another reason self contained special classes are less justifiable today than in the past is that regular school programs are now better able to deal with individual differences in pupils. No longer is the choice just between a self contained special class and a self contained regular elementary classroom. Although the impact of the American Revolution in Education is just beginning to be felt and is still more an ideal than a reality, special education should begin moving now to fit into a changing general education program and to assist in achieving the program's goals. Because of increased support at the local, state, and federal levels, four powerful forces are at work:

*Changes in school organization.* In place of self contained regular classrooms, there is increasingly more team teaching, ungraded primary departments, and flexible groupings. Radical departures in school organization are projected—educational parks in place of neighborhood schools, metropolitan school districts cutting across our inner cities and wealthy suburbs, and, perhaps most revolutionary of all, competing public school systems. Furthermore, and of great significance to those of us who have focused our careers on slow learning children, public kindergartens and nurseries are becoming more available for children of the poor.

*Curricular changes.* Instead of the standard diet of Look and Say readers, many new and exciting options for teaching reading are evolving. Contemporary mathematics programs teach in the primary grades concepts formerly reserved for high school. More programed textbooks and other materials are finding their way into the classroom. Ingenious procedures, such as those by Bereiter and Engelmann (1966), are being developed to teach oral language and reasoning to preschool disadvantaged children.

*Changes in professional public school personnel.* More ancillary personnel are now employed by the schools—i.e., psychologists, guidance workers, physical educators, remedial educators, teacher aides, and technicians. Furthermore, some teachers are functioning in different ways, serving as teacher coordinators, or cluster teachers who provide released time for other teachers to prepare lessons, etc. Too, regular classroom teachers are increasingly better trained to deal with individual differences—although much still remains to be done.

*Hardware changes.* Computerized teaching, teaching machines, feedback typewriters, ETV, videotapes, and other materials are making autoinstruction possible, as never before.

We must ask what the implications of this American Revolution in Education are for special educators. Mackie (1967), formerly of the US Office of Education, addressed herself to the question: "Is the modern school changing sufficiently to provide [adequate services in general education] for large numbers of pupils who have functional mental retardation due to environmental factors [p. 5]?" In her view, hundreds—perhaps even thousands— of so called retarded pupils may make satisfactory progress in schools with diversified programs of instruction and thus will never need placement in self contained special classes. With earlier, better, and more flexible regular school programs many of the children should not need to be relegated to the type of special education we have so often provided.

In my view, the above four reasons for change are cogent ones. Much of special education for the mildly retarded is becoming obsolete. Never in our history has there been a greater urgency to take stock and to search out new roles for a large number of today's special educators.

## A Blueprint for Change

Two major suggestions which constitute my attempt at a blueprint for change are developed below. First, a fairly radical departure from conventional methods will be proposed

99

in procedures for diagnosing, placing, and teaching children with mild learning difficulties. Second, a proposal for curriculum revision will be sketched out. These are intended as proposals which should be examined, studied, and tested. What is needed are programs based on scientific evidence of worth and not more of those founded on philosophy, tradition, and expediency.

## A Thought

*There is an important difference between regular educators talking us into trying to remediate or live with the learning difficulties of pupils with which they haven't been able to deal; versus striving to evolve a special education program that is either developmental in nature, wherein we assume responsibility for the total education of more severely handicapped children from an early age, or is supportive in nature, wherein general education would continue to have central responsibility for the vast majority of the children with mild learning disabilities—with us serving as resource teachers in devising effective prescriptions and in tutoring such pupils.*

### A Clinical Approach

Existing diagnostic procedures should be replaced by expecting special educators, in large measure, to be responsible for their own diagnostic teaching and their clinical teaching. In this regard, it is suggested that we do away with many existing disability labels and the present practice of grouping children homogeneously by these labels into special classes. Instead, we should try keeping slow learning children more in the mainstream of education, with special educators serving as diagnostic, clinical, remedial, resource room, itinerant and/or team teachers, consultants, and developers of instructional materials and prescriptions for effective teaching.

The accomplishment of the above *modus operandi* will require a revolution in much of special education. A moratorium needs to be placed on the proliferation (if not continuance) of self contained special classes which enroll primarily the ethnically and/or economically disadvantaged children we have been labeling educable mentally retarded. Such pupils should be left in (or returned to) the regular elementary grades until we are "tooled up" to do something better for them.

*Prescriptive teaching.* In diagnosis one needs to know how much a child can learn, under what circumstances, and with what materials. To accomplish this, there are three administrative procedures possible. One would be for each large school system—or two or more small districts—to establish a "Special Education Diagnostic and Prescription Generating Center." Pupils with school learning problems would be enrolled in this center on a day and/or boarding school basis for a period of time—probably up to a month and hopefully until a successful prescription for effective teaching had been evolved. The core of the staff would be a variety of master teachers with different specialties—such as in motor development, perceptual training, language development, social and personality development, remedial education, and so forth. Noneducators such as physicians, psychologists, and social workers would be retained in a consultative role, or pupils would be referred out to such paraeducational professionals, as needed. A second procedure, in lieu of such centers with their cadres of educational specialists, would be for one generalist in diagnostic teaching to perform the diagnostic and prescription devising functions on her own. A third and even less desirable procedure would be for one person to combine the roles of prescriptive and clinical teacher which will be presented next. It is suggested that 15 to 20 percent of the most insightful special educators be prepared for and/or assigned to prescriptive teaching. One clear virtue of the center is that a skilled director could coordinate an inservice training program and the staff could learn through, and be stimulated by, one another. In fact, many special educators could rotate through this program.

Under any of these procedures, educators would be responsible for the administration and interpretation of individual and group psychoeducational tests on cognitive development (such as the WISC and Binet), on language development (such as the ITPA), and on social maturity (such as the Vineland Social Maturity Scale). However, these instruments—with the exception of the ITPA which yields a profile of abilities and disabilities—will be of little use except in providing baseline data on the level at which a child is functioning. In place of these psychometric tests which usually yield only global scores, diagnostic educators would need to rely heavily on a combination of the various tools of behavior shapers and clinical teachers. The first step would be to make a study of the child to find what behaviors he has acquired along the dimension being considered. Next, samples of a sequential program would be designed to move him forward from that point. In presenting the program, the utility of different reinforcers, administered under various conditions, would be investigated. Also, the method by which he can best be taught the material should be determined. Different modalities for reaching the child would also be tried. Thus, since the instructional program itself becomes the diagnostic device, this procedure can be called diagnostic teaching. Failures are program and instructor failures, not pupil failures. In large measure, we would be guided by Bruner's dictum (1967) that almost any child can be taught almost anything if it is programed correctly.*

This diagnostic procedure is viewed as the best available since it enables us to assess continuously the problem points of the instructional program against the assets of the child. After a successful and appropriate prescription has been devised, it would be communicated to the teachers in the pupil's home school and they would continue the procedure as long as it is necessary and brings results. From time to time, the child may need to return to the center for reappraisal and redirection.

Clearly the above approach to special education diagnosis and treatment is highly clinical and intuitive. In fact, it is analogous to the rural doctor of the past who depended on his insights and a few diagnostic and treatment devices carried in his small, black bag. It may remain with us for some time to come. However, it will be improved upon by more standardized procedures. Perhaps the two most outstanding, pioneering efforts in this regard are now being made by Feuerstein (1968) in Israel, and by Kirk (1966) in the United States. Feuerstein has devised a *Learning Potential Assessment Device* for determining the degree of modifiability of the behavior of an individual pupil, the level at which he is functioning, the strategies by which he can best learn, and the areas in which he needs to be taught. Also, he is developing a variety of exercises for teaching children with specific learning difficulties. Kirk and his associates have not only given us the ITPA which yields a profile of abilities and disabilities in the psycholinguistic area, but they have also devised exercises for remediating specific psycholinguistic disabilities reflected by particular types of profiles (Kirk, 1966). Both of these scientists are structuring the assessment and remediation procedures to reduce clinical judgment, although it would be undesirable to formalize to too great a degree. Like the country doctor versus modern medicine, special education in the next fifty years will move from clinical intuition to a more precise

---

* By ignoring genetic influences on the behavioral characteristics of children with learning diffiiculties, we place responsibility on an inadequate society, inadequate parents, unmotivated pupils, and/or in this case inadequate teachers. Taking this extreme environmental approach could result in placing too much blame for failure on the teacher and too much pressure on the child. While we could set our level of aspiration too high, this has hardly been the direction of our error to date in special education of the handicapped. Perhaps the sustained push proposed in this paper may not succeed, but we will not know until we try it. Insightful teachers should be able to determine when the pressures on the pupil and system are too great.

science of clinical instruction based on diagnostic instruments which yield a profile of abilities and disabilities about a specific facet of behavior and which have incorporated within them measures of a child's ability to learn samples or units of materials at each of the points on the profile. If psychoeducational tests had these two characteristics, they would accomplish essentially the same thing as does the diagnostic approach described above—only under more standardized conditions.

*Itinerant and resource room teaching.* It is proposed that a second echelon of special educators be itinerant or resource teachers. One or more resource teachers might be available to each sizable school, while an itinerant teacher would serve two or more smaller schools. General educators would refer their children with learning difficulties to these teachers. If possible, the clinical teacher would evolve an effective prescription for remediating the problem. If this is not possible, she would refer the child to the Special Education Diagnostic and Prescription Generating Center or to the more specialized prescriptive teacher who would study the child and work out an appropriate regimen of instruction for him. In either event, the key role of the resource room and itinerant clinical educators would be to develop instructional materials and lessons for implementing the prescription found effective for the child, and to consult and work with the other educators who serve the child. Thus, the job of special educators would be to work as members of the schools' instructional teams and to focus on children with mild to moderate school learning problems. Special educators would be available to all children in trouble (except the severely handicapped) regardless of whether they had, in the past, been labeled educable mentally retarded, minimally brain injured, educationally handicapped, or emotionally disturbed. Children would be regrouped continually throughout the school day. For specific help these children who had a learning problem might need to work with the itinerant or resource room special educator. But, for the remainder of the day, the special educator would probably be more effective in developing specific exercises which could be taught by others in consultation with her. Thus, the special educator would begin to function as a part of, and not apart from, general education. Clearly this proposed approach recognizes that all children have assets and deficits, not all of which are permanent. When a child was having trouble in one or more areas of learning, special educators would be available to devise a successful teaching approach for him and to tutor him when necessary. Perhaps as many as 20 to 35 percent of our present special educators are or could be prepared for this vital role.

103

*Two other observations.* First, it is recognized that some of today's special educators—especially of the educable mentally retarded—are not prepared to serve the functions discussed. These teachers would need to either withdraw from special education or develop the needed competencies. Assuming an open door policy and playing the role of the expert educational diagnostician and the prescriptive and clinical educator would place us in the limelight. Only the best will succeed. But surely this is a responsibility we will not shirk. Our avowed *raison d'etre* has been to provide special education for children unable to make adequate progress in the regular grades. More would be lost than gained by assigning less than master teachers from self contained classes to the diagnostic and clinical educator roles. Ainsworth (1959) has already compared the relative effectiveness of the special class versus itinerant special educators of the retarded and found that neither group accomplished much in pupil progress. A virtue of these new roles for special education is that they are high status positions which should appeal to the best and therefore enhance the recruitment of master regular teachers who should be outstanding in these positions after having obtained specialized graduate training in behavior shaping, psychoeducational diagnostics, remedial education, and so forth.

Second, if one accepts these procedures for special education, the need for disability labels is reduced. In their stead we may need to substitute labels which describe the educational intervention needed. We would thus talk of pupils who need special instruction in language or cognitive development, in sensory training, in personality development, in vocational training, and other areas. However, some labels may be needed for administrative reasons. If so, we need to find broad generic terms such as "school learning disorders."

### New Curricular Approaches

Master teachers are at the heart of an effective school program for children with mild to moderate learning difficulties —master teachers skilled at educational diagnosis and creative in designing and carrying out interventions to remediate the problems that exist. But what should they teach? In my view, there has been too great an emphasis in special classes on practical arts and practical academics, to the exclusion of other ingredients. Let us be honest with ourselves. Our courses of study have tended to be watered down regular curriculum. If we are to move from the clinical stage to a science of instruction, we will need a rich array of validated prescriptive programs of instruction at our disposal. To assemble these programs will take time, talent, and money; teams of specialists including creative teachers, curriculum specialists, programers, and theoreticians will be needed to do the job.

What is proposed is a chain of Special Education Curriculum Development Centers across the nation. Perhaps these could best be affiliated with colleges and universities, but could also be attached to state and local school systems. For these centers to be successful, creative educators must be found. Only a few teachers are remarkably able to develop new materials. An analogy is that some people can play music adequately, **if not brilliantly, but only a few people can compose it. Therefore, to move special education forward, some 15 to 20 percent of our most creative special educators need to be identified, freed from routine classroom instruction, and placed in a stimulating setting where they can be maximally productive in curriculum development.** These creative teachers and their associates would concentrate on developing, field testing, and modifying programs of systematic sequences of exercises for developing specific facets of human endeavor. As never before, funds are now available from the US Office of Education under Titles III and VI of PL 89-10 to embark upon at least one such venture in each state. In fact, Title III was designed to support innovations in education and 15 percent of the funds were earmarked for special education. Furthermore, most of the money is now to be administered through state departments of education which could build these curriculum centers into their state plans.

The first step in establishing specialized programs of study would be to evolve conceptual models upon which to build our treatments. In this regard the creative teachers would need to join with the theoreticians, curriculum specialists, and other behavioral scientists. Even the identification of the broad areas will take time, effort, and thought. Each would require many subdivisions and extensive internal model building. A beginning taxonomy might include the following eight broad areas: (a) environmental modifications, (b) motor development, (c) sensory and perceptual training, (d) cognitive and language development including academic instruction, (e) speech and communication training, (f) connative (or personality) development, (g) social interaction training, and (h) vocational training. (Of course, under cognitive development alone we might evolve a model of intellect with some ninety plus facets such as that of Guilford [1967], and as many training programs.)

In the area of motor development we might, for example, involve creative special and physical educators, occupational and physical therapists, and experts in recreation and physical medicine, while in the area of language development a team of speech and hearing specialists, special educators, psychologists, linguists, and others would need to come together to evolve a conceptual model, to identify the parameters, and to develop the specialized programs of exercises. No attempt is made in this article to do more than provide an overview of the problem and the approach. Conceptualizing the specific working models would be the responsibility of cadres of experts in the various specialties.

*Environmental modifications.* It would seem futile and rather unrealistic to believe we will be able to remediate the learning difficulties of children from ethnically and/or economically disadvantaged backgrounds when the schools are operating in a vacuum even though top flight special education instructional programs are used. Perhaps, if intensive around the clock and full calendar year instruction were provided beginning at the nursery school level, we might be able to counter appreciably the physiological weaknesses and inadequate home and community conditions of the child. However, the field of education would be enhanced in its chances of success if it became a part of a total ecological approach to improve the environments of these children. Thus special educators need to collaborate with others—social workers, public health officials, and other community specialists. Interventions in this category might include (a) foster home placement, (b) improved community conditions and out of school activities, (c) parent education, (d) public education, and (e) improved cultural exposures. For optimal pupil development, we should see that children are placed in a setting that is both supportive and stimulating. Therefore, we must participate in environmental manipulations and test their efficacy. We have made a slight beginning in measuring the effects of foster home placement and there is evidence that working with parents of the disadvantaged has paid off. The model cities programs would also seem to have promise. But much more human and financial effort must be invested in this area.

*Motor development.* Initial work has been done with psychomotor training programs by a number of persons including Delacato (1966), Oliver (1958), Cratty (1967), Lillie (1967), and others. But we still need sets of sequential daily activities built around an inclusive model. Under this category, we need to move from the early stages of psychomotor development to the development of fine and large movements required as vocational skills. Programs to develop improved motor skills are important for a variety of children with learning problems. In fact, one could argue that adequate psychomotor skills constitute the first link in the chain of learning.

*Sensory and perceptual training.* Much of our early efforts in special education consisted of sensory and perceptual training applied to severe handicapping conditions such as blindness, deafness, and mental deficiency. Consequently, we have made a good beginning in outlining programs of instruction in the areas of auditory, visual, and tactual training. Now we must apply our emerging technology to work out the step by step sequence of activities needed for children with mild to moderate learning difficulties. In this regard, visual perceptual training has received growing emphasis, pioneered by Frostig (1964), but auditory perceptual training has been neglected. The latter is more important for school instruction than the visual channel. Much attention needs to be given to this second link in the chain of learning. Children with learning problems need to be systematically taught the perceptual processes: they need to be able to organize and convert bits of input from the various sense modalities into units of awareness which have meaning.

*Cognitive and language development including academic instruction.* This is the heart of special education for slow learning children. Our business is to facilitate their thinking processes. We should help them not only to acquire and store knowledge, but also to generate and evaluate it. Language development could largely be included under this caption— especially the integrative components—since there is much overlap between the development of oral language and verbal intelligence. However, much of receptive language training might be considered under sensory and perceptual training, while expressive language will be considered in the next topic.

A major fault of our present courses of study is failure to focus on the third link in the chain of learning—that of teaching our children systematically in the areas of cognitive development and concept formation. A major goal of our school program should be to increase the intellectual functioning of children we are now classifying as socioculturally retarded. For such children, perhaps as much as 25 percent of the school day in the early years should be devoted to this topic. Yet the author has not seen one curriculum guide for these children with a major emphasis on cognitive development—which is a sad state of affairs indeed!

Basic psychological research by Guilford (1959) has provided us with a useful model of intellect. However, little is yet known about the trainability of the various cognitive processes. Actually, Thurstone (1948) has contributed the one established set of materials for training primary mental abilities. Thus, much work lies ahead in developing programs of instruction for the training of intellect.

We are seeing more and more sets of programed materials

in the academic areas, most of which have been designed for average children. The most exciting examples today are in the computer assisted instruction studies. Our major problem is to determine how these programed exercises need to be modified to be maximally effective for children with specific learning problems. Work will be especially needed in the classical areas of instruction including written language and mathematics. Hopefully, however, regular teachers will handle much of the instruction in science and social studies, while specialists would instruct in such areas as music and the fine arts. This will free special educators to focus on better ways of teaching the basic 3 R's, especially written language.

*Speech and communication training.* This area has received much attention, particularly from speech correctionists and teachers of the deaf. Corrective techniques for specific speech problems are probably more advanced than for any other area, yet essentially no carefully controlled research has been done on the efficacy of these programs. Speech correctionists have tended to be clinicians, not applied behavioral scientists. They often create the details of their corrective exercises while working with their clients in a one to one relationship. Thus, the programs have often been intuitive. Furthermore, public school speech therapists have been spread very thin, usually working with 75 to 100 children. Many have been convinced that only *they* could be effective in this work. But remarkable changes have recently occurred in the thinking of speech therapists; they are recognizing that total programs of oral language development go far beyond correcting articulation defects. Furthermore, some speech therapists believe they could be more productive in working with only the more severe speech handicaps and devoting much attention to the development and field testing of systematic exercises to stimulate overall language and to improve articulation, pitch, loudness, quality, duration, and other speech disorders of a mild to moderate nature. These exercises need to be programed to the point at which teachers, technicians, and perhaps teacher aides can use them. Goldman (1968) is now developing such a program of exercises to correct articulation defects. This seems to be a pioneering and heartening first step.

*Connative (or personality) development.* This emerging area requires careful attention. We must accept the position that much of a person's behavior is shaped by his environment. This applies to all aspects of human thought, including attitudes, beliefs, and mores. Research oriented clinical psychologists are providing useful information on motivation and personality development and before long we will see re-

108

ports of research in shaping insights into self, the effects of others on self, and one's effects on others. It is not too early for teams of clinical psychologists, psychiatric social workers, creative special educators (especially for the so called emotionally disturbed), and others to begin developing programs of instruction in this complex field.

*Social interaction training.* Again we have an emerging area which overlaps considerably with some of those already presented, particularly connative development. Special educators have long recognized that the ability of a handicapped individual to succeed in society depends, in large measure, on his skill to get along with his fellow man. Yet we have done little to develop his social living skills, a complex area of paramount importance. Training programs should be developed to facilitate development in this area of human behavior.

*Vocational training.* Closely tied to social interaction training is vocational training. Success on the job for persons that we have labeled educable mentally retarded has depended on good independent work habits, reliability, and social skills, rather than on academic skills. Consequently, early and continuing emphasis on developing these traits is necessary. In fact, it is likely to be even more important in the years ahead with fewer job opportunities and increasing family disintegration providing less shelter and support for the so called retarded. Therefore sophisticated programs of instruction are especially needed in this area. Even with our best efforts in this regard, it is likely that our pupils, upon reaching adolescence, will continue to need a variety of vocational services, including trade and technical schools, work study programs, and vocational training.

*Another observation.* It seems to me to be a red herring to predict that special educators will use these hundreds of specialized instructional programs indiscriminately as cookbooks. Perhaps a few of the poor teachers will. But, the clinical teachers proposed in this article would be too sophisticated and competent to do this. They would use them as points of departure, modifying the lessons so that each child would make optimal progress. Therefore, it seems to me that this library of curriculum materials is necessary to move us from a clinical and intuitive approach to a more scientific basis for special education.

## An Epilogue

The conscience of special educators needs to rub up against morality. In large measure we have been at the mercy of the general education establishment in that we accept problem pupils who have been referred out of the regular grades. In this way, we contribute to the delinquency of the general educations since we remove the pupils that are problems for them and thus reduce their need to deal with individual differences. The *entente* of mutual delusion between general and special education that special class placement will be advantageous to slow learning children of poor parents can no longer be tolerated. We must face the reality—we are asked to take children others cannot teach, and a large percentage of these are from ethnically and/or economically disadvantaged backgrounds. Thus much of special education will continue to be a sham of dreams unless we immerse ourselves into the total environment of our children from inadequate homes and backgrounds and insist on a comprehensive ecological push—with a quality educational program as part of it. This is hardly compatible with our prevalent practice of expediency in which we employ many untrained and less than master teachers to increase the number of special day classes in response to the pressures of waiting lists. Because of these pressures from the school system, we have been guilty of fostering quantity with little regard for quality of special education instruction. Our first responsibility is to have an abiding commitment to the less fortunate children we aim to serve. Our honor, integrity, and honesty should no longer be subverted and rationalized by what we hope and may believe we are doing for these children—hopes and beliefs which have little basis in reality.

Embarking on an American Revolution in Special Education will require strength of purpose. It is recognized that the structure of most, if not all, school programs becomes self perpetuating. Teachers and state and local directors and supervisors of special education have much at stake in terms of their jobs, their security, and their programs which they have built up over the years. But can we keep our self respect and continue to increase the numbers of these self contained special classes for the educable mentally retarded which are of questionable value for many of the children they are intended to serve? As Ray Graham said in his last article in 1960: [p. 4.]

We can look at our accomplishments and be proud of the progress we have made; but satisfaction with the past does not assure progress in the future. New developments, ideas, and facts may show us that our past practices have become out-moded. A growing child cannot remain static—he either grows or dies. We cannot become satisfied with a job one-third done. We have a long way to go before we can rest assured that the desires of the parents and the educational needs of handicapped children are being fulfilled [p. 4].

# References

Ainsworth, S. H. *An exploratory study of educational, social and emotional factors in the education of mentally retarded children in Georgia public schools.* US Office of Education Cooperative Research Project Report No. 171(6470). Athens, Ga.: University of Georgia, 1959.

Bereiter, C., & Engelmann, S. *Teaching disadvantaged children in the preschool.* Englewood Cliffs, N.J.: Prentice-Hall, 1966.

Bruner, J. S., Olver, R. R., & Greenfield, P. M. *Studies in cognitive growth.* New York: Wiley, 1967.

Coleman, J. S., et al. *Equality of educational opportunity.* Washington, D.C.: USGPO, 1966.

Cratty, P. J. *Developmental sequences of perceptual motor tasks.* Freeport, Long Island, N.Y.: Educational Activities, 1967.

Delacato, C. H. (Ed.) *Neurological organization and reading problems.* Springfield, Ill.: Charles C Thomas, 1966.

Feuerstein, R. *The Learning Potential Assessment Device* Jerusalem, Israel: Haddassa Wizo Canada Child Guidance Clinic and Research Unit, 1968.

Frostig, M., & Horne, D. *The Frostig program for the development of visual perception.* Chicago: Follett, 1964.

Graham, R. Special education for the sixties. *Illinois Educational Association Study Unit,* 1960, 23, 1-4.

Goffman, E. *Asylums: Essays on the social situation of mental patients and other inmates.* Garden City, N.Y.: Anchor, 1961.

Goldman, R. *The phonemic-visual-oral association technique for modifying articulation disorders in young children.* Nashville, Tenn.: Bill Wilkerson Hearing and Speech Center, 1968.

Guilford, J. P. *The nature of human intelligence.* New York: McGraw-Hill, 1967.

Hoelke, G. M. *Effectiveness of special class placement for educable mentally retarded children.* Lincoln, Neb.: University of Nebraska, 1966.

Hollingworth, L. S. *The psychology of subnormal children.* New York: MacMillan, 1923.

Johnson, G. O. Special education for mentally handicapped—a paradox. *Exceptional Children,* 1962, 19, 62-69.

Kirk, S. A. Research in education. In H. A. Stevens & R. Heber (Eds.), *Mental retardation.* Chicago, Ill.: University of Chicago Press, 1964.

Kirk, S. A. *The diagnosis and remediation of psycholinguistic disabilities.* Urbana, Ill.: University of Illinois Press, 1966.

Lillie, D. L. The development of motor proficiency of educable mentally retarded children. *Education and Training of the Mentally Retarded,* 1967, 2, 29-32.

Mackie, R. P. *Functional handicaps among school children due to cultural or economic deprivation.* Paper presented at the First Congress of the International Association for the Scientific Study of Mental Deficiency, Montpellier, France, September, 1967.

Meyerowitz, J. H. Family background of educable mentally retarded children. In H. Goldstein, J. W. Moss & L. J. Jordan. *The efficacy of special education training on the development of mentally retarded children.* Urbana, Ill.: University of Illinois Institute for Research on Exceptional Children, 1965. Pp. 152-182.

Meyerowitz, J. H. Peer groups and special classes. *Mental Retardation,* 1967, 5, 23-26.

Oliver, J. N. The effects of physical conditioning exercises and activities on the mental characteristics of educationally sub-normal boys. *British Journal of Educational Psychology,* 1958, **28,** 155-165.

Passow, A. H. *A summary of findings and recommendations of a study of the Washington, D.C. schools.* New York: Teachers College, Columbia University, 1967.

Rosenthal, R., & Jacobson, L. Teachers' expectancies: Determinants of pupils' IQ gains. *Psychological Reports,* 1966, **19,** 115-118.

Rubin, E. Z., Senison, C. B., & Betwee, M. C. *Emotionally handicapped children in the elementary school.* Detroit: Wayne State University Press, 1966.

Smith, H. W., & Kennedy, W. A. Effects of three educational programs on mentally retarded children. *Perceptual and Motor Skills,* 1967, **24,** 174.

Thurstone, T. G. *Learning to think series.* Chicago, Ill.: Science Research Associates, 1948.

Wright, Judge J. S. *Hobson vs Hansen: U. S. Court of Appeals decision on the District of Columbia's track system. Civil Action No. 82-66.* Washington, D. C.: US Court of Appeals, 1967.

# Long Term Effects
# of Special Class Intervention
# for Emotionally Disturbed Children

NICHOLAS A. VACC

The school, as an instrument of society, attempts to provide the opportunity for all children to be educated to their fullest extent. One approach in this attempt is the education of emotionally disturbed children through special class programs. Recently, there has been a flourish of public school programs in which emotionally disturbed children are segregated for educational rehabilitation. Since 1962, three times the number of states and United States associated territories have reported teacher education programs for disturbed children (Scheuer, 1966). Federal support and the recent interest of states have served to energize special education classes for emotionally disturbed children.

This study questions the basic assumption underlying special classes—that emotionally disturbed children placed in a special program show greater benefit than emotionally disturbed children remaining in their respective regular classes. This policy of segregating emotionally disturbed children, however, has not been evaluated adequately. The final test of any special class program is the degree to which a child's improvement, resulting from the special class procedure, is maintained after his return to a regular class. If a long range study of educational facilities for emotionally disturbed children were to provide (a) assessment of change in achievement, (b) a measure of overt

EXCEPTIONAL CHILDREN, September 1972, pp. 15-22.

behavior change, and (c) a consideration of peer acceptance, the findings would be useful in providing information about educational programs for emotionally disturbed children.

Because the experimental literature on overt behavior change, achievement, and social relations of school children is not easily applicable to treatment, comparatively little research has been published regarding emotionally disturbed children in school settings. Glavin and Quay (1969) reported that most articles concerning emotionally disturbed children have been descriptions of projects, clinical case studies, or suggested methodologies for programs. These findings have been supported by numerous other writers (Morse & Dyer, 1963; Balow, 1966; Goldman & May, 1967).

Studies with results indicating successful educational intervention include Vacc (1968), Cruickshank, Bentzen, Ratzeburg, and Tannhauser (1961), Haring and Phillips (1962), and Radin, Cary, Chorost, Kaplan, and Garcea (1966). Not all programs reported for educating emotionally disturbed children in schools have indicated that special classes have produced results different from regular classes. Rubin, Simson, and Betwee (1966) noted that special classes did not result in increased academic achievement. Knoblock (1966) has suggested that much programing for emotionally disturbed children can be accomplished within the regular classroom.

Considering this controversy concerning special classes and the increasing pressure to establish more of them, little has been done to measure the long range consequences of their existence. Many children demonstrate problem behavior in the course of development. But the question arises, does a child grow out of his problem behavior with increasing age without intervention or does he become a disturbed adult? Findings related to this question have been conflicting.

The work of Renaud and Estess (1961), Schofield and Balian (1959), Morris, Soroker, and Burruss (1954) provided indications that problem behavior of children does not necessar-

114

ily produce disturbed adults. Clarizio (1968) stated that "normal problem behavior that occurs as developmental phenomena seems to have a very high probability of being resolved with increasing age. Clinical problems, though having a lower probability of improvement than those of a developmental nature, also seem to have a reasonably high probability of spontaneous remission [p. 291]."

This study was designed to investigate long term changes in achievement and overt behavior of children identified as emotionally handicapped. Changes were measured for two groups of emotionally disturbed children: those who had experienced special class placement and had returned to regular classes for at least 2 years and those who had not experienced the special class procedure. A secondary objective of the study was to compare the social positions of the following groups: (a) emotionally disturbed children receiving special class intervention, (b) emotionally disturbed children who remained in the regular class, and (c) normal children.

In regard to the main objectives of this study, the following questions were developed to permit an examination of the success of emotionally disturbed children who received special class intervention.

1. What is the change in achievement of emotionally disturbed children who received special class intervention as compared to that of emotionally disturbed children remaining in a regular class, as measured by the *Wide Range Achievement Test*?

2. What is the change in overt behavior of emotionally disturbed children who received special class intervention as compared to that of emotionally disturbed children remaining in a regular class, as measured by the Behavior Rating Scale (Haring & Phillips, 1962)?

3. What is the degree to which emotionally disturbed children who received special class intervention are receiving social

choice selection and rejections as compared to emotionally disturbed children who remained in a regular class, as measured by A Class Play (Bower, 1958)?

4. What is the degree to which each group of emotionally disturbed children is receiving social choice selections and rejections as compared to the normal children as measured by A Class Play?

In addition, attention was directed to determining the percentage of stars, isolates, and rejectees formed within each group of emotionally disturbed children and the normal children.

### Definition of Terms

The following terms used throughout this study could be interpreted in various ways. Therefore, definitions are stipulated in order to limit the possible connotations given to these terms.

*Emotionally disturbed.* The term, emotionally disturbed, refers to children identified by a school psychologist and a psychiatrist as being emotionally handicapped, requiring placement in a special class as indicated by New York state law.

*Isolate.* An isolate is a person in a classroom sociometric situation who has been chosen for positive roles so seldom in comparison with chance expectancy as to confirm the existence of social forces of neglect or rejection.

*Normal.* Any child not classified as being emotionally disturbed is classified as being normal.

*Rejectee.* A rejectee is a person in a classroom sociometric situation who is chosen for negative roles so much in excess of chance expectancy as to confirm the existence of social forces of rejection.

*Sociometric.* The definition of sociometric employed throughout this study was given by Bronfenbrenner (1943): " . . . a method for discovering, describing, and evaluating social status, structure, and development through measuring the extent of acceptance or

116

rejection between individuals in a group [p. 364]."

*Star.* A star is a person in a classroom sociometric situation who is chosen for positive roles so much in excess of chance expectancy as to confirm the existence of social forces of acceptance.

## Method

### Population Studied

The population studied consisted of children attending public schools in the centralized districts of Chautauqua County, New York. The process of identification and selection of emotionally disturbed children was as follows. Children were referred to school psychologists for various reasons by school personnel. After a thorough evaluation was made by the psychologist and the child was screened as a candidate for a special class, a parent conference was held and the child was referred to either the child guidance clinic or a private practitioner. Attendance in the special class group was dependent on the completion of a child's identification procedure as well as the district's participation in the program.

At the beginning of the study (entry), each child in the special class was equated with a child in the regular class on several variables. A group of 16 emotionally disturbed children was selected from the regular grades by matching each with a member of two special classes, each of which contained 8 emotionally disturbed children. Matching of the groups included the following variables: (a) intelligence, (b) chronological age, (c) grade placement, (d) achievement level, (e) comparison of social class position, and (f) the opinion of the supervising psychologist.

The groups were tested at entry and at the end of 1 year and the results were reported by Vacc (1968). Results indicated greater gains by those children in the special classes on all areas tested. The present study, a followup made 5 years and 8 months from the date of entry of the group of emotionally disturbed children, will examine if these gains are lasting. The followup groups were smaller because of the

117

**TABLE 1**

**Comparison at Entry of the Groups
of Emotionally Disturbed Children**

| Variable | Special classes (Intervention) | | Regular classes (No intervention) | |
|---|---|---|---|---|
| | 1 year study (N = 16) Mean | Followup (N = 11) Mean | 1 year study (N = 16) Mean | Followup (N = 10) Mean |
| Social class | 5.12 | 4.91 | 5.43 | 5.00 |
| Grade level | 3.56 | 3.09 | 3.62 | 3.40 |
| Intelligence | 95 | 96.55 | 93 | 92.20 |
| Age in months | 124 | 121 | 121 | 116 |
| Achievement level | 2.71 | 2.82 | 3.00 | 3.05 |

NOTE: For all variables tested, no significant differences existed between either the original entry group or the remaining followup group.

following factors: (a) five students had dropped out of school, (b) no records of location were available to the researcher for five other students, and (c) one student had been placed in a special class for educable mentally retarded children.

Table 1 presents a comparison of the groups used for the 1 year study as well as the groups used for the followup study. The comparisons are based on data at entry. For the variables tested, the findings indicate no significant differences between the groups used for the 1 year study and the followup groups after attrition. The computed $F$ ratio suggests homogeneity of variance between the groups. On the basis of these statistical tests, it would seem that the emotionally disturbed children in both the regular and special classes of both studies, the 1 year and the followup, came from the same population.

### Instruments Used

*Wide Range Achievement Test.* This test was devised by Jastak (1946) for determining achievement level in the basic school subjects of reading, spelling, and arithmetic. The range of the instrument extends from kindergarten to college. The reliability coefficients determined by repeated testing of 280 cases ranged from .88 to .95. Jastak (1946) reported that the test provided a suitable achievement measure for clinical work.

The same procedure that was used at entry and at the end of 1 year was used during the current research with the test administered to each subject by a school psychologist.

*Behavior Rating Scale.* The Behavior Rating Scale was developed by Haring and Phillips (1962) for use in measuring change in overt behavior of emotionally disturbed children. The Behavior Rating Scale is a 7 point Likert-type scale consisting of 26 items. The judge rates a child from 1 to 7 on an item of descriptive behavior. As was done at entry and at the end of 1 year, two Behavior Rating Scales were completed for each child during the followup

119

study—one by a teacher and one by a school psychologist—with an observation period consisting of a minimum of 35 minutes for each child required before completing the rating scale. The values of the items and raters are averaged to yield a single score. As reported by Vacc (1968), the test reliability of 36 means of two raters was .95. Internal consistency of each item to the single score provided data that 23 of the 26 items were consistent at the .01 level. Additional analysis of the Behavior Rating Scale has been reported concerning rater agreement which illustrated agreement in scoring (Vacc, 1968).

*Sociometric questionnaire.* Since the subjects were in regular classes, the sociometric questionnaire was administered to every child in a regular class that contained one of the emotionally disturbed children being studied in the present research. The sociometric questionnaire used was A Class Play devised by Bower (1958) for use as a sociometric device with elementary children. Certain parts in A Class Play are representative of negative roles, and others positive. These roles are based on commonly accepted cultural perceptions. The student is asked to indicate a child in his class who best fits the role as described by his teacher. A child received an acceptance score of 1 each time his name was given by any classmate in response to a positive question. Since there is no method of determining the extent of acceptance or rejection, there was no adequate basis on which to assign weights to the scores. For data analysis, it was assumed that each child named was accepted or rejected equally on each question.

In its original form, A Class Play contained 12 roles, but for purposes of this study the 6 roles with the highest discrimination value based on factor analysis (numbers 1, 2, 3, 4, 10, and 11) were employed (Bower, 1958).

Test-retest reliability for 108 children was reported to be .92 for this instrument (Bowers, 1960).

### Results

The data were analyzed to determine what

## TABLE 2
### Comparison of Emotionally Disturbed Children Who Received Special Class Intervention and Those Who Did Not on the *Wide Range Achievement Test*

| Emotionally disturbed children | | 1 year | | | | | | | | Followup | | | | | |
|---|---|---|---|---|---|---|---|---|---|---|---|---|---|---|---|
| | | Entry[1] | | End of 1 year | | Mean gain in grade achievement | | | | Entry[1] | | End of 5 years and 8 months | | Mean gain in grade achievement | |
| | N | Mean | SD | Mean | SD | | F | t | N | Mean | SD | Mean | SD | | F | t |
| Special class | 16 | 2.71 | 1.60 | 3.26 | .98 | .56 | | | 11 | 2.81 | 1.69 | 4.96 | 2.26 | 2.15 | | |
| Regular class | 16 | 3.00 | 1.04 | 3.30 | 1.09 | .30 | 1.37 | 2.60* | 10 | 3.05 | 1.14 | 6.74 | 2.55 | 3.69 | 1.71 | 1.86 |

[1]Pretest not significantly different at .05 level
*p<.05

## TABLE 3
### Comparison of Emotionally Disturbed Children Who Received Special Class Intervention and Those Who Did Not on the Behavior Rating Scale

| Emotionally disturbed children | | One year | | | | | | | | Followup | | | | | |
|---|---|---|---|---|---|---|---|---|---|---|---|---|---|---|---|
| | | Entry[1] | | End of 1 year | | Mean gain | | | | Entry[1] | | End of 5 years and 8 months | | Mean gain | |
| | N | Mean | SD | Mean | SD | | F | t | N | Mean | SD | Mean | SD | | F | t |
| Special class | 16 | 4.19 | .52 | 3.77 | .76 | .42 | | | 1 | 4.15 | .78 | 3.60 | .75 | .55 | | |
| Regular class | 16 | 4.02 | .96 | 4.26 | .85 | -.24 | 1.19 | 4.33* | 10 | 3.86 | .82 | 3.90 | .74 | -.04 | 1.55 | 1.37 |

[1]Pretest not significantly different at .05 level
*p<.05

changes took place from entry to followup. Change was measured for those children who experienced special class placement and had returned to regular classes for at least 2 years and those who did not experience the special class procedure. Tables 2, 3, 4, and 5 contain this data regarding changes measured. Tables 2 and 3 also present the results of a previous investigation which measured change in achievement and overt behavior from entry to 1 year (Vacc, 1968).

### Wide Range Achievement Test

Table 2 presents the mean gain scores of the emotionally disturbed children who experienced special class intervention and those who did not as measured by the *Wide Range Achievement Test*. The *t* value between the two groups at followup was not significant at the .05 level. This suggests that during the 5 years and 8 months from entry, the achievement gains made by the emotionally disturbed children who experienced special class placement were not different from the emotionally disturbed children who remained in regular classes. The trend in improvement, while not significant, was achieved by the emotionally disturbed children who did not experience special class intervention.

### Behavior Rating Scale

The data in Table 3 contain the mean gain scores of the emotionally disturbed children who experienced special class intervention and those who did not, as measured by the Behavior Rating Scale. The *t* value between the two groups was not significant at the .05 level. The results indicated that the mean gain scores of emotionally disturbed children receiving special class intervention did not exceed those made by the emotionally disturbed children who remained in the regular classes.

### Sociometric Questionnaire

The sociometric questionnaire was administered at followup in order to determine if any difference existed between the social positions

122

## TABLE 4
### Comparison of Positive and Negative Selection Scores of Emotionally Disturbed Children Who Received Special Class Intervention (EDC-I) and Those Who Did Not (EDC-NI)

| | N | | Mean | | SD | | D | t |
|---|---|---|---|---|---|---|---|---|
| Scores | EDC-I | EDC-NI | EDC-I | EDC-NI | EDC-I | EDC-NI | | |
| Positive selection score | 11 | 10 | .73 | .90 | 1.05 | 1.33 | .17 | .26 |
| Negative selection score | 11 | 10 | 5.09 | 6.70 | 4.37 | 8.57 | 1.61 | .54 |

## TABLE 5
### Comparison of Positive and Negative Selection Scores of Normal Children with Each Group of Emotionally Disturbed Children

| | Normal | | EDC-NI | | EDC-I | | D | | t | |
|---|---|---|---|---|---|---|---|---|---|---|
| Scores | N | Mean | N | Mean | N | Mean | Normal and EDC-I | Normal and EDC-NI | Normal and EDC-I | Normal and EDC-NI |
| Positive selection score | 421 | 3.07 | 10 | .90 | 11 | .73 | 2.34 | 2.17 | 3.08* | 2.68* |
| Negative selection score | 421 | 3.05 | 10 | 6.70 | 11 | 5.09 | 2.04 | 3.65 | 1.40 | .89 |

*$p < .05$

123

of emotionally disturbed children who received special class intervention as compared to those who remained in the regular classes. In addition, a comparison was made between the groups of emotionally disturbed children and the normal children.

The results of the positive and negative selection scores for the emotionally disturbed children are presented in Table 4. The data present the comparison of the mean positive and negative selection scores of the emotionally disturbed children receiving special class intervention and those who did not. The results indicated that emotionally disturbed children receiving special class intervention received no more positive or negative selection scores than the emotionally disturbed children who remained in the regular classes. The difference between the means of the positive and negative selection scores of the two groups was not statistically significant at the .05 level.

The data presented in Table 5 contain the $t$ values derived from the comparison of the positive and negative selection scores of the normal children with each group of emotionally disturbed children. An analysis of the results of the negative selections indicated that no significant difference existed between any of the groups tested. The results of the positive selections indicated that both groups of emotionally disturbed children were not as accepted within their classes as were the normal children. The difference between mean positive selection scores of the groups was statistically significant at the .05 level.

Figure 1 presents a graphic illustration of the stars, isolates, and rejectees of the normal and emotionally disturbed groups. The emotionally disturbed children are presented in two groups—those children who received special class intervention and those who did not. The method of determining stars, isolates, and rejectees follows that of Bronfenbrenner (1943). A chance expectancy index is calculated for each class. With these values it was possible to determine the equivalent $t$ for each cumulative frequency. For example, a significantly low acceptance score indicated an iso-

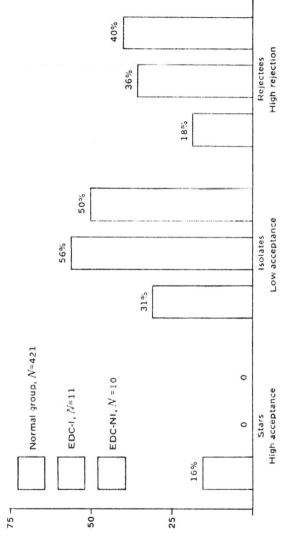

FIGURE 1. Comparison of stars, isolates, and rejectees.

late, a significantly high acceptance score indicated a star, and a significantly high rejection score indicated a rejectee. It was possible that a child could be classified into one or more categories providing significance was achieved in each category; " . . . it permits identification of statistically significant results . . . the concept provides a constant frame of reference against which data from diverse sociometric situations may be projected without distortion [pp. 371-372]."

An examination of Figure 1 presents the following information: (a) No emotionally disturbed child in either the group that received intervention or the group that remained in the regular classes was classified as a star, while 16 percent of the normal group were stars. (b) The percentage of isolates was greater in both groups of emotionally disturbed children than in the normal group. The two groups of emotionally disturbed children did not differ to any appreciable degree as to the percentage of isolates. (c) Each group of emotionally disturbed children contained a similar percentage of rejectees whereas the normal group contained approximately one-half that percentage.

### Conclusions

The findings from the present study suggest that special classes do not result in long term changes for emotionally disturbed children as compared to emotionally disturbed children placed in regular classes. This followup study, while limited in subjects, indicates that if special classes have any advantages over regular classes for emotionally disturbed children, it exists only as long as the children remain in the special program.

The following salient points reflected by the analyzed data appear justified:

1.  The achievement gains made by emotionally disturbed children receiving special class intervention did not exceed those made by the emotionally disturbed children who remained in the regular classes. While not significantly different, the results of the mean gain scores indicated a

126

greater degree of achievement growth by emotionally disturbed children who remained in the regular classes than that reflected by the emotionally disturbed children receiving special class intervention.

2.  When the emotionally disturbed children receiving special class intervention were compared at followup on overt behavior with the emotionally disturbed children remaining in regular classes, there were no significant differences between the two groups.

3.  The emotionally disturbed children who experienced special class intervention did not receive more positive or negative selection choices than the emotionally disturbed children who did not experience special class intervention.

4.  No significant differences were found for the positive selection scores when each group of emotionally disturbed children were compared to normal children. However, both groups of emotionally disturbed children were less accepted than the normal children in the regular classes.

5.  The analysis of the sociometric data for stars, isolates, and rejectees revealed that: (a) the percentages of stars in the two groups of emotionally disturbed children were consistent with each other, with the emotionally disturbed children not being chosen positively to any appreciable degree; (b) the percentage of isolates, which was similar between the two groups of emotionally disturbed children, was greater among the groups of emotionally disturbed children than the normal group; and (c) the largest percentage of rejectees was found in both groups of emotionally disturbed children.

In summary, it can be concluded that the data from this study support the notion that emotionally disturbed children who did not receive special class intervention are accomplishing the objectives of academic achievement, overt behavior, and social position at the same level as children who did have the advantage of a special class. Thus, the conception of placing emotionally disturbed children in special classes for rehabilitation is called into question.

## References

Balow, B. The emotionally and socially handicapped. *Review of Educational Research*, 1966, 36, 120-133.

Bower, E.M. A process for early identification of emotionally disturbed children. *California State Department of Education Bulletin*, 1958, 27, 1-8.

Bower, E.M. *Early identification of emotionally handicapped children in school.* Springfield, Ill.: Charles C Thomas, 1960.

Bronfenbrenner, U. A constant frame of reference for sociometric research: Part 1. *Sociometry*, 1943, 6, 363-397.

Clarizio, H. Stability of deviant behavior through time. *Mental Hygiene*, 1968, 52, 288-293.

Cruickshank, W.M., Bentzen, F.A., Ratzeburg, F.H., & Tannhauser, M.T. *Teaching methodology for brain injured and hyperactive children.* Syracuse: Syracuse University Press, 1961.

Glavin, J.P., & Quay, H.C. Behavior disorders. *Review of Educational Research*, 1969, 39 (1), 83-102.

Goldman, W.J., & May, A. Dynamics of classroom structure for emotionally disturbed children. *The Journal of School Health*, 1967, 37, 200-202.

Haring, N.G., & Phillips, E.L. *Educating emotionally disturbed children.* New York: McGraw-Hill, 1962.

Jastak, J. *Wide Range Achievement Test.* Wilmington, Del.: C.L. Story, 1946.

Knoblock, P. *Intervention approaches in educating emotionally disturbed children.* Syracuse: Syracuse University Press, 1966.

Morris, D.P., Soroker, E., & Burruss, G. Follow-up studies of shy, withdrawn children—I. Evaluation of later adjustment. *American Journal of Orthopsychiatry*, 1954, 24, 743-754.

Morse, W.C., & Dyer, C.O. The emotionally and socially handicapped. *Review of Educational Research*, 1963, 33 (1), 109-125.

Radin, S.S., Cary, G.L., Chorost, S.B., Kaplan, S.G., &

Garcea, R.A. Orthopsychiatry and special services for emotionally disturbed children in the public school setting: Syracuse Scholastic Rehabilitation Program. *Journal of School Health*, 1966, 36, 245-248.

Renaud, H., & Estess, F. Life history interviews with one hundred normal American males: "Pathogenicity" of childhood. *American Journal of Abnormal and Social Psychology*, 1961, 31, 786-802.

Rubin, E.Z., Simson, C.B., & Betwee, M.C. *Emotionally handicapped children and the elementary school.* Detroit, Mich.: Wayne State University Press, 1966.

Scheuer, A.L. Certification, teacher preparation, and special classes for the emotionally disturbed and socially maladjusted: Report by states. *Exceptional Children*, 1966, 33, 120-121.

Schofield, W., & Balian, L. A comparative study of the personal histories of schizophrenic and nonpsychiatric patients. *Journal of Abnormal and Social Psychology*, 1959, 59, 216-225.

Vacc, N. A. A study of emotionally disturbed children in regular and special classes. *Exceptional Children*, 1968, 35, 197-204.

# THE REINFORCEMENT OF BEHAVIOR
# IN INSTITUTIONAL SETTINGS*

R. E. BUEHLER

G. R. PATTERSON

and

J. M. FURNISS

Summary—Three studies are reported which identified and measured social reinforcers occurring among inmates and staff in institutions for delinquent children. Observation and coding procedures were derived from interpersonal communication and operant conditioning research. Results indicate that the social living system of a correctional institution tends to reinforce delinquent responses and to punish socially conforming responses and, the delinquency reinforcing responses tend to occur on non-verbal levels of communication. Implications for re-scheduling reinforcers within the social system are discussed.

## INTRODUCTION

THE IMPORTANCE of the peer group in shaping and controlling behavior has been stressed by both socio-cultural and psychological theorists. The present report summarizes a series of pilot studies which identify some of the behavioral processes associated with shaping and controlling behavior within a peer group of delinquent adolescents.

The assumptions implicit in these studies are derived from recent literature on social learning and interpersonal communications behavior. Specifically, it is assumed that the interpersonal communication transactions within a peer group function as reinforcers. When put in terms of a reinforcement paradigm this means that in the peer group situation behavior operates upon the social environment. The nature of the environmental response(s) (which often is not a single act but multifarious movements on the part of several persons) influences the future probabilities of the recurrence of the behavior. If the environmental response is rewarding to the actor, the act will tend to be repeated. If the response is aversive the act tends not to recur. Within this general framework, outlined initially by Skinner (1953), we are suggesting that the delinquent peer group provides massive schedules of positive reinforcement for deviant behavior and negative reinforcement or punishment for socially conforming behavior. If these hypotheses are correct, it would appear that settings which provide prolonged interpersonal transactions among delinquent adolescents might be expected to provide an excellent opportunity for maintaining existing deviant

* These studies were supported in part by research grants from the Office of the Institution Research Coordinator, Board of Control, State of Oregon, Salem, Oregon.

BEHAVIOR RESEARCH AND THERAPY, 1966, Vol. 4, pp. 157-167.

behavior and, for the "novice", an opportunity to acquire new sets of deviant behavior. We would hypothesize too that within the institutional setting, the majority of social reinforcers are provided by the peer group rather than by the staff. The institutional setting thus would be seen as a "teaching machine" programmed for the maintenance and acquisition of deviant behavior rather than for retraining the child to more socially adaptive behavior.

## STUDY NUMBER ONE

A pilot study by Patterson (1963) provided a preliminary test for these hypotheses. Fifteen 2-hr observations were made in a detention home for delinquent children. The observer sampled most of her observations from a small group of delinquent girls. After observing for a period of time, the observer would withdraw and write a descriptive account of each episode in which either a delinquent response or a response which was obviously conforming to social norms occurred. Each behavioral description also outlined the consequences of these responses; e.g. Roberta: "She is sickening (referring to the housemother); Steve: "Not very smart either". Karen laughs. This direct criticism of an adult authority figure is reinforced immediately by two different members of the peer group. The various delinquent responses were classified into responses reflecting delinquent value systems; i.e. deviant sex behaviors, breaking rules, any form of rejection of adult authority, aggressive talk and expressing ideas consistent with delinquent behavior. The other major category of responses consisted of behavior corresponding to societal norms; i.e. talking of going to college, admission of feelings of guilt and regret for having indulged in delinquent acts, expressions of expectations regarding avoidance of delinquent behavior, saying they liked someone on the staff, and expressions of cooperation with the treatment program etc.

The consequences of this behavior were classified in two general categories: "positive reinforcement" and "punishment". Under the heading of positive reinforcement were included such peer reactions as: approval, agreement, interest, attention, laughing, smiling, imitating the speaker, etc. Under the heading of punishment were categorized such behaviors as: disagreeing, threatening, frowning, ignoring, sneering, etc.

The data were clear in showing overwhelming positive reinforcement (70 per cent) for such behavior as rule breaking, criticims of adults and adult rules, agressive behavior, and "kicks". In keeping with the hypotheses the peer group was most likely to disapprove when the behavior in question deviated from the delinquent norms. These data, of course, represented a limited sample obtained by one observer from one group in a single institutional setting. Although the results obtained were in keeping with the general predictions made, it was necessary to carry out an extensive replication before placing any confidence in the conclusions. Such a replication was carried out in Study Number Two which is reported in more detail below.

## STUDY NUMBER TWO

The methodology in a study conducted by Furniss (1964) was derived from the social reinforcement model utilized by Patterson and an interpersonal communications behavior analysis method developed by Buehler and Richmond (1963). These two methodologies were combined because it appeared to the writers that each set of procedures would contribute something unique to our understanding of delinquent behavior. Social learning research has tended to simply classify communication behavior as verbal or non-verbal, without identifying the specific communication behavior which is utilized by members of particular sub-groups of the population. Since socio-cultural studies have long indicated that there are wide variations among people in the use of interpersonal communication behavior, it follows that there are no standard reinforcement contingencies which cross all age, sex, and cultural sub-groups. As a means for obtaining more precise measures of peer group social reinforcement behavior in an institutional setting Furniss combined the inter-interpersonal communication behavior analysis method and the social reinforcement method utilized previously by Patterson.

The interpersonal communication analysis method is a method for observing and measuring interpersonal communication behavior in terms of four postulated levels of communication (Richmond and Buehler, 1962; Buehler and Richmond, 1963 a and b). This method, developed within a transactional rather than a self-action or interactional frame of reference (as defined by Dewey and Bentley, 1949) is based upon the postulate that all interpersonal behavior is communication and that this behavior occurs on four primary levels. These levels are: (1) bio-chemical; (2) motor movement; (3) speech and (4) technology. Each of the four levels or categories has sub-categories which are defined operationally in terms of observable movement on the part of a person during interpersonal transactional episodes. The unit of measure is a time interval of 2.5 sec. All behavior which occurs in any category is scored once in each interval. Meaning, intent, effects, etc. are rigorously excluded from scoring system as these are seen as observer's subjective interpretations of the observed behavior and should be derived, if necessary, from analyses of the sequences of ongoing behavior rather then imputed to the behavior by the observer.

It was predicted that the combination of these two methods and their implicit coding systems would result in a more powerful instrument for measuring the specific reinforcement processes within a peer group. Furniss' study was done in a State institution for girls who had been committed by Juvenile Courts for a variety of socially maladaptive behavior.


## METHODS

Observations were made during students' leisure time hours on the cottages. The observer would note all interaction episodes on the part of the subject or subjects being observed at the time and write, immediately after, a detailed list of all behavior which she observed. These lists were later coded independently by two judges for: level of communication on which each observed act occurred; whether the act was in accordance with delinquent or socially appropriate norms; and the peer response(s) (reinforcements). Responses were categorized as positive reinforcements if there was an indication of attention or approval given the subject by a peer or peers, and as punishments if the peer response was disinterest or disapproval. The criteria used in classifying behavior as delinquent or non-delinquent were derived from the Girl's Handbook of the institution which listed the institution's expectations regarding inmate behavior. The congruence between the social norms expressed in the Handbook and those operant in the culture of the communities from which the girls came has never been validated empirically, but was accepted tentatively for purposes of the study.

It was hypothesized that the peer group would provide more social approval than disapproval for delinquent behavior. Second, it was hypothesized that the schedule of rewards for delinquent behavior and the amount of delinquent behavior would not vary as a function of the differences in the social living situations (cottages) within the institution. Third, it was hypothesized that the reinforcing behavior would be significantly more frequent on the non-verbal than the verbal levels of communication.*

Six subjects were randomly selected in each of two "open" (less restricted, presumably less delinquent girls) and two "closed" (more restricted, presumably more delinquent girls) cottages, or a total of twenty-four subjects. The subjects' age range was 13.5–18 yr. Length of institutionalization varied from 2 to 30 months. Prior institutionalization was not checked. On each of the four cottages the groups were heterogenous with respect to age, length of residence in the institution, and behavior which led to commitment by the Courts.

Each subject's interpersonal transactions with peers were observed for a total of 50 min, composed of two 25-min periods on two different days. The order of subject observations was random on each cottage and observations were distributed equally, over time, on all cottages.

## RESULTS

Analysis of the data yielded the following results:

1. In peer reinforcement of delinquent behavior, the non-verbal levels of communications were used in 82 per cent of the reinforcing responses, while verbal reinforcement was used in only 18 per cent of the responses, on all sample cottages.

2. In peer reinforcement of socially conforming behavior, 36 per cent of the reinforcers occurred on the level of speech and 64 per cent occurred on the non-verbal levels.

3. The frequency of delinquent responses did not differ with respect to "open" versus "closed" cottages. Consequently, "open" as compared to "closed" cottage status did not signify any significant difference in the frequency of delinquent behavior within the peer group.

4. Delinquent behavior was rewarded by the peer group on the open cottages as frequently as it was rewarded on the closed cottages.

5. On all sample cottages (four of the institution's eight) the reinforcement of delinquent responses by peers occurred significantly more often ($P<.001$) than the punishment of delinquent responses.

6. On all sample cottages the peer group punished socially conforming behavior more frequently ($P<.01$) than they rewarded such behavior.

These results are extremely suggestive as to what learning takes place within the inmate social system in an institution and what is involved in altering behavior in treatment institutions. In the main, *delinquent behavior* on the part of the peer group and its members *occurs* and is *reinforced* on the *non-verbal level of behavior*. In other words, the bulk of the teaching among the girls is non-verbal. This corresponds with well-known postulates regarding communication behavior as articulated by Mead (1934), Hall (1959) and others.

* This hypothesis was not stated in Miss Furniss' original research design but was added by Buehler and Patterson in analyzing her data.

In terms of treatment processes, it becomes obvious that the continuous peer group reinforcement of behavior by non-verbal communications must be taken into account and dealt with. It is clear that verbal behavior among peers does not alone accurately represent the teaching process which actually takes place within peer groups. Furthermore the data from the closed cottages suggest that institutional criteria for "improved behavior" may be related simply to "security" (more or less locked doors) and other maintenance variables rather than to *changed social attitudes and behavior*. In actual ratio of punishment versus reward for delinquent or nondelinquent behavior, Furniss' data agree essentially with those previously obtained (in a smaller institution) by Patterson, namely, in 132 responses to delinquent behavior, 116 (88 per cent) were rewarding and 16 (12 per cent) were punishing. Thus, regardless of institution size, the peer group communication transactions tend to maintain the very attitudes and behavior which led to institutionalization.

## STUDY NUMBER THREE

The next in this series of pilot studies consisted of efforts to test some methods for developing a specific behavioral analysis for each individual member of a delinquent peer group in an institution, to refine the methods for determining the peer group reinforcement contingencies, and to develop procedures for determining schedules of reinforcement to be administered initially by the staff and eventually by the peer group itself.

The two previous pilot studies, while focusing for empirical purposes only upon the peer group, did nevertheless lead to the definite impression that staff members in both settings tended to reward and punish indiscriminately. The focus of attention in the third study was upon the peer group behavior and the reinforcement contingencies dispensed by the immediate staff members.

The assumption in this study was borrowed directly from current social reinforcement literature. This assumption involves both the interpersonal communication and the social reinforcement paradigms discussed previously. An analysis of current literature indicates that: first, the behavior which needs to be either reinforced or extinguished must be identified specifically; second, the environmental response (reinforcing agent) must be on the same level of communication as the act which is to be reinforced. There are exceptions to this, of course, but this is assumed to be a general rule: e.g. smiling or frowning is a more spontaneous response to a smile than is a verbal statement such as "I am glad to see you smile" or "stop your smiling". In an official communication system such as presented by a school, a verbal punishment or reward may be used by the teacher in response to a non-verbal act on the part of the student, but within the peer group itself, as Furniss' data indicated, there is a high level of congruence between the level of communication utilized by the actor and the peer group respondents. We would speculate that this congruence in levels of communication through which reinforcements are continuously dispensed in ongoing peer group transactions may be one reason why the peer group is so effective in shaping and controlling behavior.

These considerations, among others, suggested to Buehler and Patterson that the field of investigation should be enlarged to include the reinforcing behavior operant in the total social system of one residential cottage in the institution for delinquent girls which was utilized in Furniss' study. This involved refining the methods for identifying the schedules of reinforcement within the peer group of girls and the reinforcing behavior of the staff members with reference to the girls' behavior.

# METHODS

Behavioral observations were made by an observer equipped with a small portable dictation machine with a microphone inserted in a rubber mask which covered the observer's mouth. As a means for obtaining a maximum amount of data on individual girls, a sample of six subjects was selected randomly for daily observations. The observer went on the cottage at 4 p.m. on five days a week and remained until the girls' bedtime at 9 p.m. The observations included two 1-hr group meetings each week which were conducted by the senior author. Two cottage supervisors (housemothers) and a staff social worker attended the group meetings along with the twenty-four resident girls.

The observer focused her attention on the interpersonal transactions on the part of the six subjects, including their transactions with staff members. The tapes were transcribed each day and separate sheets were extracted for each of the six subjects and each staff member. These individual behavioral protocols were coded in terms of communication and reinforcement categories.

# BEHAVIORAL DIAGNOSES

The behavioral protocols obtained in the manner described above were utilized along with behavioral data in the subject's case folder in developing a specific behavioral diagnosis for each subject. The following data presents in some detail a sample of a behavioral diagnosis and a reinforcement prescription for one subject:

*Personal history.* I.Q. 124. Father inconsistent in his reinforcing behavior, ranging from over-indulgence to physical cruelty. Mother indulged in frequent outbursts of anger and unreasonable accusations. The unreasonable demands made upon the subject by her parents led to a cruelty petition against the home by the Juvenile Court. Subject was committed to the institution after several unsatisfactory foster home placements. Intake information indicated that the subject defied family authority, had few friends, considerable heterosexual activity with a variety of partners, AWOL from foster homes. She alternated between affectionate and hostile behavior with reference to adults. When she felt rejected, she became immature and demanding. Adults generally found her annoying and troublesome and rejected her. Her response to adult rejection was to act out as described above. She had one illegitimate child and refused to give it up. The child was being cared for by the subject's mother and this led to constant friction between the subject and her mother. Subject wanted to live away from her family and care for her child.

The institutional staff reported of the same ambivalent pattern toward adults. The subject appeared to the staff to be eager to please, demanded much attention, manipulated adults and peers, refused to obey rules, tended to be loud, noisy, disruptive and coercive. The staff saw her as acting in a superior manner toward her peers, attempting to boss them, and as being generally rejected by her peers.

The subject's interpersonal transactional behavior was observed at intervals over a period of 5 days. The kind of reinforcements she was being given by her peer group and by the staff and her responses are presented in Table 1.

These behavioral data indicate that the peer group punished the subject for identifying with social norms in a ratio of almost three to one, while the staff rewarded her in a ratio of nine to one. However, the frequency of the reinforcements that were dispensed by the peers greatly outnumbered those dispensed by the staff. Furthermore, when she was hostile toward her peers they rewarded her in a greater than two to one ratio and when she was hostile toward adults, the adults punished her more or less consistently. She tended to punish her peers when they made social gestures toward her, although she rewarded adults for doing the same thing. The peer group's persistent punishment when the subject

TABLE 1.

| Behavior | Reward for subject's behavior | | | | Subject's reward to others | | | |
| --- | --- | --- | --- | --- | --- | --- | --- | --- |
| | From peers | | From adults | | To peers | | To adults | |
| | No. ob- served | Re- inforce- ment | No. ob- served | Re- inforce- ment | No. ob- served | Re- inforce- ment | No. ob- served | Re- inforce- ment |
| Social | 29 | 12+ 17− | 23 | 16+ 7− | 8 | 3+ 5− | 5 | 5+ 0− |
| Hostility | 19 | 13+ 6− | 5 | 0+ 5− | 2 | 0+ 2− | 0 | |
| Coercive | 9 | 1+ 8− | 3 | 0+ 3− | 5 | 1+ 4− | 1 | 0+ 1− |
| Identification with delinquency | 1 | 0+ 1− | 1 | 1+ 0− | 0 | | 0 | |
| Identification with social norms | 37 | 10+ 27− | 20 | 18+ 2− | 2 | 1+ 1− | 0 | |

+positive reward.
−punishment.

verbalized identifications with social norms is very clear. She expressed thirty-seven such identifications and the peer group punished her twenty-seven times and rewarded her ten times. The staff, on the other hand, rewarded her eighteen out of twenty times that she identified with social norms in their presence.

These observations indicate that the reinforcement system for the subject tended to be very inconsistent. Her peers tended to reward her for being a delinquent and to punish her whenever she made moves toward socially appropriate behavior, while the staff would alternately reward her and punish her for the same acts.

In the group sessions the subject behaved as would be predicted from the reports and observations shown above. She would verbally identify herself with social norms (getting a job and taking care of her child, staying out of further trouble with Juvenile Court, etc.) and was persistently punished by her peers for these identifications. She would retaliate and some of her peers would counter-retaliate. This intra-group conflict would rise in intensity as long as the group discussion leader played a non-directive role. When the leader's role shifted to identifying the group's behavior (i.e. "S is trying to say that she wants to leave this institution, get a job, etc. and some of you girls are punishing her for wanting to do these things"), the girls who silently approved S's behavior would begin to reward her.

It was noticeable in the group meetings that the more aggressive, dominating and coercive girls tended to punish those girls who attempted to show some socially conforming attitudes, expectations, and behavior. This was particularly true of another subject who was the leader of an informal sub-group of girls on the cottage. This girl saw the group meetings as a distinct threat to her control over her domineering "gang". A previous group leader had given in to the two rival informal groups on the cottage and was meeting separately with each of them. Under the former leader's non-directive leadership the two rival gangs remained intact and in daily conflict for control of the communal life on the

136

cottage. When this gang behavior was pointed up in meetings of all the girls and the staff, the two gang leaders would aggressively punish every girl who in one way or another supported the discussion leader's efforts to elicit cooperation in seeking solutions to the intra-cottage problems. This behavior strengthened the authors' assumption that if schedules of reinforcement within the peer group are to be changed in the direction of socially appropriate behavior, something other than "non-directive" evocative therapy is required.

The behavioral analyses described above suggested that the initial treatment prescription for the subject may be as follows:

*Reward*

(1) Every socially appropriate approach to an adult;
(2) all of the subject's references to her maternal role and her maternal role responsibilities;
(3) give the subject much attention and praise when she engages in socially responsible acts toward her peers;
(4) reward the subject's peers when they reward her socially appropriate acts, and
(5) reward the subject's peers when they resist being coerced by the subject.

*Punish*

(1) Ignore the subject's loud, boisterous, coercive and bossy behavior, and
(2) confront, and in any other appropriate way, punish the subject's peers when they punish her for her efforts to conform to socially appropriate norms.

Each of the six subjects' behavior was observed and analyzed in the manner described above. The specific behavioral categories for each girl varied, however. Such categories as: isolation from peers, passive resistance, or physical aggression were also used in order to tailor-make the descriptive system for each girl. One subject in particular, a very attractive girl who was a strong leader among her peers, showed thirteen coercive acts towards her peers for which she was rewarded nine times and punished only four times. She also showed fourteen coercive acts towards adults and was rewarded seven times and punished seven times by adults. She showed hostility towards adults in the presence of her peers a total of twenty-six times and was rewarded by her peers twelve times and punished fourteen times. For the same behavior she was rewarded three times and punished twenty-three times by adults. This suggested how she was being taught by her peer group to be an aggressive, coercive leader and to continue to be hostile and defiant toward adults.

The observed transactions between the staff and the girls were not as frequent as were the transactions among the peers because the adult staff members showed a tendency to remain in their offices or to sit on the periphery of the social group. However, the observed adult behavior of six staff members who at one time or the other were on the cottage over a period of a week, is summarized in Table 2.

These data support the impression obtained in the preceding studies, namely, that staff members tended to reinforce and to punish indiscriminately. Such vacillating schedules of reinforcement would tend, we assume, to reduce severely the effectiveness of the staff in influencing inmate behavior in any direction. In the two classes of behavior with the greatest frequency, social and coercive, the staff response was approximately equal in punishment and in reward. It is interesting to note too that the girls reinforced and punished the staff in an equally inconsistent manner. The peer group's response to coping behavior on the part of the staff is particulary interesting in view of the traditions of staff

137

| Behavior | Reinforcement given to girls | | Reinforcement received from girls | |
|---|---|---|---|---|
| | No. observed | Ratio | No. observed | Ratio |
| Social | 18 | 11+<br>7− | 19 | 10+<br>9− |
| Coercive | 20 | 11+<br>9− | 14 | 11+<br>3− |
| Hostile | 1 | 1+<br>0− | 16 | 8+<br>8− |
| Information giving | 3 | 1+<br>2− | 4 | 3+<br>1− |
| Information asked | 5 | 3+<br>2− | | |
| Usurping role of student | 5 | 3+<br>2− | | |
| Coping with problems | | | 4 | 1+<br>3− |
| Not coping | | | 12 | 3+<br>9− |
| Decision making:<br>    Self | | | 15 | 10+<br>5− |
|     Refer decision to girl | | | 7 | 4+<br>3− |
|     Refer decision to group | | | 7 | 1+<br>6− |
|     Refer decision to administrator | | | 11 | 3+<br>8− |

authority and responsibility in penal institutions. When the staff failed to cope with problems they were punished in a three to one ratio. When staff referred problems back to the group for group action and/or decision the staff was punished by the peer group in a ratio of six to one. Also, when staff referred problems to the administration the peer group punished them consistently (8 : 3). The implications of these data for further research and theory construction with reference to therapeutic and/or educational social systems are challenging indeed.

# DISCUSSION

The persistence of delinquent behavior in institutions where the official aim is to "correct" such behavior has been documented repeatedly in long and melancholy "recidivism" lists. Of equal note is the fact, frequently mentioned in the literature, that during the process of institutionalization many cases of adolescent deviation (e.g. truancy, running away from home, etc.) are converted into severe criminal offenders. The "peer group culture" has been blamed for these reversals of official intentions, but *how* the peer group achieves these effects has not been identified or described in *behavioral* terms. Nor has the staff behavior which contributes to these effects been documented. The data in the three studies reviewed above identify two separate behavioral systems within a single peer group and the other is operated by the staff. While no data were obtained in these pilot studies on the relative effects of the two behavioral systems, other data on peer group phenomena (Patterson, 1963; Schrag, 1961; and others) permit us to hypothesize that it is the peer group behavioral system which has the predominating effects. In fact, it is reasonable to hypothesize that the inmate behavioral system not only shapes and controls its own members but also it shapes and controls the behavior of the staff.

The problem as we see it is to identify and to establish controls over the behavior occurring in peer groups which keeps the group resistant to institutional treatment objectives. We emphasize the term "treatment objective" because these data suggest that while the objective of the institutions in which the data were obtained was to "correct" the delinquency, the behavioral operations of the staff tended to reward or punish delinquent behavior indiscriminately. There is ample evidence in social reinforcement research that when reinforcements are inconsistent the reinforcing agent has no effect.

These data suggest that a social reinforcement approach to behavioral diagnosis and treatment planning and operations is feasible. The impressive data on behavior modification which has been summarized in part by Krasner and Ullmann (1965) and by Bandura and Walters (1963), as well as in a wide range of scientific journals, suggest that this may be a promising approach to treatment operations in a "correctional" setting.

As an initial step to modifying delinquent schedules of reinforcement within a peer group, we assume that a rigorous behavioral approach needs to be adopted by the staff. It was noted by the authors in informal conversations with staff members that they had a marked tendency to attach moral labels to the inmates and would respond to the label rather than to specific behavior of the labeled girl; e.g. Mary is "good" therefore she will be rewarded persistently regardless of her behavior, Susie is "bad" therefore she will be punished persistently regardless of whatever moves she makes toward socially conforming behavior. Once a behavioral frame of reference is adopted, the next step in this paradigm would be to adopt a rigorous observational system for identifying the specific behaviors and reinforcing contingencies within the inmate peer groups. The method of observing the behavior as described above is simple, requires no instruments and can be adopted easily by relatively untrained persons (the Research Assistant in Study No. 3 was a college sophomore). The final steps would be to tailor-make a schedule of reinforcement to fit each separate inmate and the group as a whole, and to teach the staff how to use their own interpersonal communication behavior as a source of reinforcement.

139

# REFERENCES

BANDURA A. and WALTERS R. H. (1963) *Social Learning and Personality Development.* Holt, Rinehart and Winston, New York.

BUEHLER R. E. and RICHMOND J. F. (1963a) Interpersonal communication behavior analysis: a research method. *J. Commun.* **XIII**, No. 3.

BUEHLER R. E. and RICHMOND J. F. (1963b) Pilot study on interpersonal communication behavior analysis method. *Research Report*, Board of Control, Salem, Oregon.

DEWEY J. and BENTLEY A. F. (1949) *Knowing and the Known.* Beacon Press, Boston.

FURNISS JEAN (1964) *Peer Reinforcement of Behavior in an Institution for Delinquent Girls.* Unpublished Master's Thesis, Oregon State University.

HALL E. T. (1959) *The Silent Language.* Doubleday, New York.

KRASNER L. and ULLMANN L. P. (1965) *Case Studies in Behavior Modification.* Holt, Rinehart and Winston New York.

MEAD G. H. (1934) *Mind, Self and Society.* University of Chicago Press, Chicago.

PATTERSON G. R. (1963) *The Peer Group as Delinquency Reinforcement Agent.* Unpublished Research Report, Child Research Laboratory, University of Oregon, Eugene, Oregon.

PATTERSON G. R. and ANDERSON D. (1964) Peers as reinforcers. *Child Dev.* **35**, 951–960.

RICHMOND J. F. and BUEHLER R. E. (1962) Interpersonal communication: a theoretical formation. *J. Commun.* **XII**, No. 1.

SCHRAG C. (1961) Some foundations for a theory of corrections. *Cressey, The Prison.* Holt, Rinehart and Winston, New York.

SKINNER B. F. (1953) *Science and Human Behavior.* Macmillan, New York.

# PART III

# RULES, PRAISE, AND IGNORING: ELEMENTS OF ELEMENTARY CLASSROOM CONTROL[1]

## Charles H. Madsen, Jr., Wesley C. Becker, and Don R. Thomas

An attempt was made to vary systematically the behavior of two elementary school teachers to determine the effects on classroom behavior of Rules, Ignoring Inappropriate Behaviors, and showing Approval for Appropriate Behavior. Behaviors of two children in one class and one child in the other class were recorded by observers, as were samples of the teachers' behavior. Following baseline recordings, Rules, Ignoring, and Approval conditions were introduced one at a time. In one class a reversal of conditions was carried out. The main conclusions were that: (a) Rules alone exerted little effect on classroom behavior, (b) Ignoring Inappropriate Behavior and showing Approval for Appropriate Behavior (in combination) were very effective in achieving better classroom behavior, and (c) showing Approval for Appropriate Behaviors is probably the key to effective classroom management.

Modern learning theory is slowly but surely increasing its potential for impact upon social problems. As problems in social development and interaction are more closely examined through the methods of experimental analysis, the importance of learning principles in everyday life becomes clearer. The potential contribution of these developments to childrearing and education appears to be especially significant. This report is a part of a series of studies aimed at demonstrating what the teacher can do to achieve a "happier", more effective classroom through the systematic use of learning principles. The study grows out of a body of laboratory and field research demonstrating the importance of social reinforcers (smiles, praise, contact, nearness, attention) in establishing and maintaining effective behaviors in children. Extensive field studies in experimental nursery schools by Wolf, Bijou, Baer, and their students (e.g., Hart, Reynolds, Baer, Brawley, and Harris, 1968; Allen, Hart, Buell, Harris, and Wolf, 1965; Bijou and Baer, 1963) provided a background for the extension of their work by the present authors to special and typical elementary classrooms. In general, we have found to date that teachers with various "personalities" and backgrounds can be trained systematically to control their own behavior in ways which will improve the behavior of the children they are teaching. (Becker, Madsen, Arnold, and Thomas, 1967). We have also found that teachers can "create" problem behaviors in the classroom by controlling the ways in which they respond to their pupils (Thomas, Becker, and Armstrong, 1968; Madsen, Becker, Thomas, Koser, and Plager, 1968). It is hoped that field studies of this sort will contribute to more effective teacher training.

The present study is a refinement of an earlier study of Becker et al. (1967), in which the behavior of two children in each of five classrooms was recorded and related to experimentally controlled changes in teacher behaviors. The teachers were instructed and guided to follow a program which involved making classroom rules explicit, ignoring disruptive behaviors unless someone was getting hurt, and praising appropriate classroom behaviors. Under this program, most of the severe problem children under study showed remarkable improvements in classroom behavior. However, that study lacked certain controls which the present study sought to correct. First, the teachers in the earlier study were in a seminar

[1] We wish to express our appreciation to the teachers involved, Mrs. Barbara L. Weed and Mrs. Margaret Larson, for their cooperation in a study which involved using and applying procedures which at times made their teaching duties very difficult. Gratitude is expressed to the Director of Elementary Education, Unit District #116, Urbana, Illinois, Dr. Lowell M. Johnson, and to the principals of Thomas Paine and Prairie Schools, Richard Sturgeon and Donald Holste. This study was supported by Grant HD-00881-05 from the National Institutes of Health.

142

on behavior theory and practice during baseline conditions. Some target children improved during baseline, apparently because some teachers were beginning to apply what they were learning even though they had been requested not to do so. Second, public relations and time considerations did not make it possible to introduce the components of the experimental program one at a time (rules, ignoring, and praise) to better study their individual contributions. Third, a reversal of teacher behavior was not attempted. Such a reversal would more conclusively show the importance of teacher's behavior in producing the obtained changes. Fourth, extensive recordings of teacher behavior under all experimental conditions were not undertaken in the earlier study. The present study attempted to deal with each of these problems.

## METHOD

*Procedures*

Teachers in a public elementary school volunteered to participate in the study. After consultation with teachers and observation of the children in the classroom, two children with a high frequency of problem behavior were selected for study in each class. Previously developed behavioral categories (Becker *et al.*, 1967) were modified for use with these particular children and baseline recordings were made to determine the frequency of problem behaviors. At the end of the baseline period the teachers entered a workshop on applications of behavioral principles in the classroom which provided them with the rationale and principles behind the procedures being introduced in their classes. Various experimental procedures were then introduced, one at a time, and the effects on the target children's behaviors observed. The experiments were begun in late November and continued to the end of the school year.

*Subjects*

*Classroom A.* There were 29 children in Mrs. A's middle-primary (second grade) room who ranged in school progress from mid-first-grade level to early-third-grade level. Cliff and Frank were chosen as the target children.

Cliff was chosen because he displayed no interest in school. In Mrs. A's words, "he would sit throughout entire work periods fiddling

with objects in his desk, talking, doing nothing, or misbehaving by bothering others and walking around the room. Lately he has started hitting others for no apparent reason. When Cliff was required to stay in at recess to do his work, he would complete the work in a short time and it was usually completely accurate. I was unable to motivate him into working on any task during the regular work periods." Cliff is the son of a university professor who was born in Europe and immigrated when Cliff was 5-yr old. Cliff scored 91 on an early (CA 5-3) intelligence test. This score was discounted by the examiner because of language problems. His group IQ scores rose steadily (CA 5-9, IQ 103; CA 6-2, IQ 119; CA 7-1, IQ 123). His achievement scores indicated a low second-grade level at the beginning of the present study. Cliff was seen by the school social worker throughout the entire first grade and throughout this entire study.

Cliff was observed early in the year and it was noted that he did not respond once to teacher's questions. He played with his fingers, scratched himself repeatedly, played in his desk, paid no attention to the assignment and had to stay in at recess to finish his work. Almost continually he made blowing sounds and talked to himself. On occasions he was out of his seat making noises and talking. He would leave the room without permission. Before the study began the observers made the following notes: "What a silly kid, writing on the bottom of his shoes, writing on his arms, blowing kisses at the girls. He was vying for the attention of the girl behind him, but she ignored him. . . . Poor Cliff! he acts so silly for his age. He tried to talk to the other kids, but none of them would pay attention to him. . . . Cliff seems concerned with the little girl beside him (girl behind him last week). He has a sign on his desk which reads, 'Do you love me?'. . . ."

Frank was described by his teacher as a likable child. He had a record of misbehavior in the classroom and intense fighting on the playground. He was often out of his seat talking to other children and did not respond to "discipline". If someone was reprimanded for doing something, Frank would often do the same thing. Test scores indicated an IQ of 106 (Stanford-Binet) and achievement level just under beginning second grade at the start of school (average California Achievement Test scores 1.6 grades). The school psychologist noted that Frank's mother was a person "who willingly permitted others to make decisions for her and did not seem able to discipline Frank." Father was absent from the home during the entire year in the Air Force.

*Classroom B.* Twenty children were assigned to Mrs. B's kindergarten room. Two children were observed initially; one moved from the community shortly after baseline was taken, leaving only Stan for the study.

Stan was described as coming from a truly pathetic home environment. The mother was not married and the family of four children subsisted on state aid. One older brother was enrolled in a special class for the educable retarded. At the beginning of the year, Stan's behavior was characterized by the teacher as "wild". She reported that, "Stan would push and hit and grab at objects and at children. He had no respect for authority and apparently didn't even hear directions. He knew how to swear profusely, and I would have to check his pockets so I would know he wasn't taking home school equipment. He would wander around the room and it was difficult to get him to engage in constructive work. He would frequently destroy any work he did rather than take it home."

The difficult home situation was made manifest during the month of March. Stan had been absent for two weeks and it was reported that his mother was taking her children out of public school and placing them in a local parochial school. Investigation by school personnel indicated that Stan's mother had moved the children into a relative's home and had gone to the hospital to have another illegitimate baby. A truancy notice was filed for all four children including Stan. Following legal notice the children were returned to school.

### Rating of Child Behavior

The same rating schedule was used in both classrooms except that Isolate Play was added to the list of Inappropriate Behaviors for the kindergarten. Since the children were expected to be involved in structured group activities during observation periods, going off by oneself to play with the many toys or materials in the room was considered inappropriate by the kindergarten teacher. Inappropriate Behavior was defined as the occurrence of one or more of the behaviors listed under Inappropriate Behavior in Table 1 during any observation interval.

Observers were trained in the reliable use of the rating schedule before baseline recordings began. Training consisted of practice in use of the rating schedule in the classroom. Two observers would each rate the same child for 20 min and then return to the research office to compare their ratings and discuss their differences with their supervisor. Training was continued until reliability was above 80% on each behavior code. Training lasted approximately two weeks. Reliability was determined periodically throughout the study by dividing the number of agreements by the number of agreements plus disagreements. An agreement was defined as a rating of the same behavior class in the same observation interval. Average reliability over children, behavior classes, and days for the 69 occasions (out of 238) on which it was checked was 81%. Single day reliabilities ranged from 68% to 96%. Reliabilities were checked in each phase of the study.

Instructions to observers followed those used by Becker *et al.* (1967). In essence, the observers were not to respond to the children, but to fade into the background as much as possible. Teachers, as well as children, quickly learned not to respond to the observers, although early in the study one observer was attacked by a kindergarten child. The observer did not respond to the behavior and it quickly disappeared. Experimental changes were initiated without informing observers in an attempt to control any observer bias. However, the changes were often dramatic enough that observer comments clearly reflected programmed changes in teacher's behavior.

The target children were observed for 20 min per day, three days a week. In the middle-primary class, observations were taken when the children were engaged in seat work or group instruction. In the kindergarten class, observations were made when structured activities, rather than free play, were expected. Each observer had a clipboard, stopwatch, and rating sheet. The observer would watch for 10 sec and use symbols to record the occurrence of behaviors. In each minute, ratings would be made in five consecutive 10-sec intervals and the final 10 sec would be used for recording comments. Each behavior category could be rated only once in a 10-sec interval.

## Table 1

### Behavioral Coding Categories for Children

I. Inappropriate Behaviors

A. *Gross Motor.* Getting out of seat, standing up, running, hopping, skipping, jumping, walking around, moving chair, *etc.*

B. *Object Noise.* Tapping pencil or other objects, clapping, tapping feet, rattling or tearing paper, throwing book on desk, slamming desk. Be conservative, only rate if you can hear the noise when eyes are closed. Do *not* include accidental dropping of objects.

C. *Disturbance of Other's Property.* Grabbing objects or work, knocking neighbor's books off desk, destroying another's property, pushing with desk (only rate if someone is there). Throwing objects at another person without hitting them.

D. *Contact (high and low intensity).* Hitting, kicking, shoving, pinching, slapping, striking with object, throwing object which hits another person, poking with object, biting, pulling hair, touching, patting, *etc.* Any physical contact is rated.

E. *Verbalization.* Carrying on conversations with other children when it is not permitted. Answers teacher without raising hand or without being called on; making comments or calling out remarks when no questions have been asked; calling teacher's name to get her attention; crying, screaming, singing, whistling, laughing, coughing, or blowing loudly. These responses may be directed to teacher or children.

F. *Turning Around.* Turning head or head and body to look at another person, showing objects to another child, attending to another child. Must be of 4-sec duration, or more than 90 degrees using desk as a reference. Not rated unless seated. If this response overlaps two time intervals and cannot be rated in the first because it is less than 4-sec duration, then rate in the interval in which the end of the response occurs.

G. *Other Inappropriate Behavior.* Ignores teacher's question or command. Does something different from that directed to do, including minor motor behavior such as playing with pencil or eraser when supposed to be writing, coloring while the record is on, doing spelling during the arithmetic lesson, playing with objects. *The child involves himself in a task that is not appropriate.* Not rated when other Inappropriate Behaviors are rated. Must be time off task

H. *Mouthing Objects.* Bringing thumb, fingers, pencils, or any object in contact with the mouth.

I. *Isolate Play. Limited to kindergarten* free-play period. Child must be farther than 3 ft from any person, neither initiates or responds to verbalizations with other people, engages in no interaction of a non-verbal nature with other children for the entire 10-sec period.

II. Appropriate Behavior

Time on task; *e.g.,* answers question, listens, raises hand, works on assignment. Must include whole 10-sec interval except for Turning Around responses of less than 4-sec duration.

---

The primary dependent variable was percentage of intervals in which an Inappropriate Behavior occurred. Since the varieties of Inappropriate Behavior permitted a more detailed analysis with the schedule used, the presentation of results is focussed on them, even though functionally their converse (Appropriate Behavior) was the main behavior being manipulated.

### Ratings of Teacher Behavior

Ratings of teacher behavior were obtained to clarify relationships between changes in teacher behavior and changes in child behavior. Recordings of teacher behavior were also used by the experimenters to help the teachers learn the contingent use of Approval and Disapproval Behaviors. The teacher rating schedule is presented in Table 2. Teacher behaviors were recorded by subclasses in relation to child behaviors. That is, the record would show whether a teacher response followed Appropriate child classroom behavior or whether it

followed one of the categories of Inappropriate Behavior. Responses to all children were rated. Teacher behavior was scored as the frequency of occurrence of a specified class of behavior during a 20-min interval. Teacher ratings were either recorded during one of the periods when a target child was being rated by another observer, or immediately thereafter when only one observer made both ratings. Teacher behavior was rated on the average of once a week, except during experimental transitions, when more frequent ratings were made. The number of days teacher behavior was rated under each condition is given in Table 3. Most recorded teacher behavior (about 85%) fell in the *Verbal* Approval or Disapproval categories. For this reason we have used the term *Praise* interchangeably with Approval Behaviors and *Criticism* interchangeably with Disapproval Behaviors.

Reliability of measures of teacher behavior were checked approximately every other rating day (21 of 42 occasions for the two teachers)

Table 2

Coding Definitions for Teacher Behaviors

Appropriate child behavior is defined by the child rating categories. The teacher's rules for classroom behavior must be considered when judging whether the child's behavior is Appropriate or Inappropriate.

I. Teacher Approval following Appropriate Child Behavior
   A. *Contact.* Positive physical contact such as embracing, kissing, patting, holding arm or hand, sitting on lap.
   B. *Praise.* Verbal comments indicating approval, commendation or achievement. Examples: that's good, you are doing right, you are studying well, I like you, thank you, you make me happy.
   C. *Facial attention.* Smiling at child.

II. Teacher Approval following Inappropriate Child Behavior
   Same codes as under I

III. Teacher Disapproval following Appropriate Child Behavior
   A. *Holding the child.* Forcibly holding the child, putting child out in the hall, grabbing, hitting, spanking, slapping, shaking the child.
   B. *Criticism.* Critical comments of high or low intensity, yelling, scolding, raising voice. Ex-

amples: that's wrong, don't do that, stop talking, did I call on you, you are wasting your time, don't laugh, you know what you are supposed to do.
   C. *Threats.* Consequences mentioned by the teacher to be used at a later time. If _____ then _____ comments.
   D. *Facial attention.* Frowning or grimacing at a child.

IV. Teacher Disapproval following Inappropriate Child Behavior
   Same codes as under III.

V. "Timeout" Procedures[a]
   A. The teacher turns out the lights and says nothing.
   B. The teacher turns her back and waits for silence.
   C. The teacher stops talking and waits for quiet.
   D. Keeping in for recess.
   E. Sending child to office.
   F. Depriving child in the classroom of some privilege.

VI. Academic Recognition
   Calling on a child for an answer. Giving "feedback" for academic correctness.

[a]These are procedural definitions of teacher behaviors possibly involving the withdrawal of reinforcers as a consequence of disruptive behaviors which teacher could not ignore.

by dividing the agreements as to time interval and behavior codes by the agreements plus disagreements. Average reliability over behavior classes, teachers, and days was 84% with a range from 70% to 96% for individual day measures.

*Experimental Conditions*

In the middle-primary class (Class A) the experimental conditions may be summarized as consisting of *Baseline;* introduction of *Rules; Rules* plus *Ignoring* deviant behavior; *Rules* plus *Ignoring* plus *Praise* for appropriate behavior; return to Baseline; and finally reinstatement of *Rules, Ignoring,* and *Praise.* In the kindergarten class (Class B) the experimental conditions consisted of *Baseline;* introduction of *Rules; Ignoring* Inappropriate Behavior (without continuing to emphasize rules); and the combination of *Rules, Ignoring,* and *Praise.*

The various experimental procedures were to be used by the teachers for the classroom as a whole throughout the day, not just for the children whose behavior was being recorded, and not just when observers were present.

*Baseline.* During the Baseline period the teachers conducted their classes in their typical way. No attempt was made to influence their behavior.

*Rules.* Many people would argue that just telling children what is expected should have considerable effect on their behavior. We wished to explore this question empirically. Teachers were instructed individually and given written instructions as follows:

"The first phase of your participation in the use of behavioral principles to modify classroom behaviors is to specify explicit rules of classroom conduct. When this is done, there is no doubt as to what is expected of the children in your classroom. However, do not expect a dramatic shift in classroom control, as we all know that knowing the prohibitions does not always keep people from "sin". This is the first phase in the program and inappropriate behavior should be reduced, but perhaps not eliminated. The rules should be formulated with the class and posted in a conspicuous location (a chart in front of the room or a special place on the chalkboard where they will not be erased). Go over the rules three or four times asking the class to repeat them back to you when they are initially formulated and use the following guidelines:

"(a) Make the rules short and to the point so they can be easily memorized.

"(b) Five or six rules are adequate. Special instructions for specific occasions are best given when the occasion arises. Children will not remember long lists of rules.

"(c) Where possible phrase the rules in a positive not a negative manner (for example, "Sit quietly while working," rather than, "Don't talk to your neighbors"). We want to emphasize positive actions.

"(d) Keep a sheet on your desk and record the number of times you review the rules with the class (strive for at least four to six repetitions per day). Remember that young children do not have the retention span of an adult and frequent reminders are necessary. Let the children recite the rules as you ask them, rather than always enumerating them yourself.

"(e) Remind the class of the rules at times other than when someone has misbehaved.

"(f) Try to change no other aspects of your classroom conduct except for the presentation of the rules at appropriate times."

Teacher tally sheets indicated that these instructions were followed quite explicitly. The average number of presentations of rules was 5.2 per day.

*Ignoring Inappropriate Behavior.* The second experimental phase involved Ignoring Inappropriate Behavior. In Class A, repetition of rules was also continued. Individual conferences to explain written instructions were given both teachers. Both teachers were given the following instructions:

"The first aspect of the study was to make expectations explicit. This you have been doing over the past few weeks. During the next phase of the study you should learn to *ignore* (do not attend to) behaviors which interfere with learning or teaching, unless of course, a child is being hurt by another, in which case use a punishment which seems appropriate,

preferably withdrawal of some positive reinforcement. Learning to ignore is rather difficult. Most of us pay attention to the violations. For example, instead of ignoring we often say such things as the following: "Johnny, you know you are supposed to be working"; "Sue, will you stop bothering your neighbors"; "Henrieta, you have been at that window for a long time;" "Jack, can you keep your hands off Bill"; "Susie, will you please sit down"; "Alex, stop running around and do your work"; "Jane, will you please stop rocking on your chair."

"Behaviors which are to be ignored include motor behaviors such as getting out of seat, standing up, running, walking around the room, moving chairs, or sitting in a contorted manner. Any verbal comment or noise not connected with the assignments should also be ignored, such as: carrying on conversations with other children when it is not permitted, answering questions without raising hands or being called on, making remarks when no questions have been asked, calling your name to get attention, and extraneous noises such as crying, whistling, laughing loudly, blowing noise, or coughing. An additional important group of behaviors to be ignored are those which the student engages in when he is supposed to be doing other things, e.g., when the child ignores your instructions you are to ignore him. Any noises made with objects, playing with pencils or other materials should be ignored, as well as, taking things from or disturbing another student by turning around and touching or grabbing him.

"The reason for this phase of the experiment is to test the possibility that attention to Inappropriate Behavior may serve to strengthen the very behavior that the attention is intended to diminish. Inappropriate Behavior may be strengthened by paying attention to it even though you may think that you are punishing the behavior."

*Praise for Appropriate Behavior.* The third phase of the experiment included individual contacts with teachers to encourage and train Praising of Appropriate Behavior. The Praise instructions to the teachers were as follows:

"The first phase included specifying explicit rules, writing them on the board and reviewing them 4-6 times per day. The second phase was designed to reduce the amount of attention paid to behaviors which were unwanted by ignoring them. This third phase is primarily directed toward *increasing* Appropriate Behaviors through praise and other forms of approval. Teachers are inclined to take good behavior for granted and pay attention only when a child acts up or misbehaves. We are now asking you to try something different. This procedure is characterized as "catching the child being good" and making a comment designed to reward the child for good behavior. Give praise, attention, or smile when the child is doing what is expected during the particular class period in question. Inappropriate Behavior would not be a problem if all children were engaging in a great deal of study and school behavior, therefore, it is necessary to apply what you have learned in the workshop. Shape by successive approximations the behavior desired by using praise and attention. Start "small" by giving praise and attention at the first signs of Appropriate Behavior and work toward greater goals. Pay close attention to those children who normally engage in a great deal of misbehavior. Watch carefully and when the child begins to behave appropriately, make a comment such as, "You're going a fine job, (name) ." It is very important during the first few days to catch as many good behaviors as possible. Even though a child has just thrown an eraser at the teacher (one minute ago) and is now studying, you should praise the study behavior. (It might also decrease the rate of eraser throwing.) We are assuming that your commendation and praise are important to the child. This is generally the case, but sometimes it takes a while for praise to become effective. Persistence in catching children being good and delivering praise and attention should eventually pay off in a better behaved classroom.

"Some examples of praise comments are as follows:

I like the way you're doing your work quietly (name) .

That's the way I like to see you work _____.

That's a very good job _____.
You're doing fine _____.
You got two right _____, that's very good (if he generally gets no answers right).

"In general, give praise for achievement, prosocial behavior, and following the group rules. Specifically, you can praise for concentrating on individual work, raising hand when appropriate, responding to questions, paying attention to directions and following through, sitting in desk and studying, sitting quietly if noise has been a problem. Try to use variety and expression in your comments. Stay away from sarcasm. Attempt to become spontaneous in your praise and smile when delivering praise. At first you will probably get the feeling that you are praising a great deal and it sounds a little phony to your ears. This is a typical reaction and it becomes more natural with the passage of time. Spread your praise and attention around. If comments sometimes might interfere with the ongoing class activities then use facial attention and smiles. Walk around the room during study time and pat or place your hand on the back of a child who is doing a good job. Praise quietly spoken to the children has been found effective in combination with some physical sign of approval.

"General Rule: Give *praise* and *attention* to behaviors which facilitate learning. Tell the child what he is being praised for. Try to reinforce behaviors incompatible with those you wish to decrease."

The teachers were also instructed to continue to ignore deviant behavior and to repeat the rules several times a day.

Additional training given teachers consisted of: (a) discussion of problems with suggested solutions during weekly seminars on behavior analysis, and (b) specific suggestions from the experimenter on possible alternative responses in specific situations based on the experimenter's observations of the teachers during experimental transitions, or based on observer data and notes at other times when the data showed that the teachers were not on program.

Additional cues were provided to implement the program. Cards were placed on the teachers' desks containing the instructions for the experimental phase in which they were engaged.

*Reversal.* In Class A the final experimental conditions involved an attempt to return to Baseline, followed by a reinstatement of the *Rules, Praise,* and *Ignore* condition. On the basis of the earlier observations of Teacher A, we were able to specify to her how frequently she made disapproving and approving comments. The success of this procedure can be judged from the data.

## RESULTS

Percentage of observation intervals in which Inappropriate Behaviors occurred as a function of conditions is graphed in Fig. 1 and 2. Major changes in Inappropriate Behaviors occurred only when Praise or Approval for Appropriate Behaviors was emphasized in the experimental procedures. A *t* test, comparing average Inappropriate Behavior in conditions where Praise was emphasized with those where Praise was not emphasized, was significant at the 0.05 level ($df - 2$).

Before examining the results more closely, it is necessary to inspect the data on teacher behavior. Table 3 gives the frequency of

classes of teacher behaviors averaged within experimental conditions. Since day-to-day variability of teacher behavior was low for the measures used, these averages fairly reflect what went on.

Introduction of Rules into the classroom had no appreciable effect on Inappropriate Behavior.

Ignoring Inappropriate Behaviors produced inconsistent results. In Class A the children clearly became worse under this condition; in Class B little change was apparent. Both teachers had a difficult time adhering to this condition, and Teacher A found this phase of the experiment very unpleasant. Table 3 shows that Teacher A was only able to reduce critical comments from an average of one per 1 min to an average of three in 4 min. Teacher B cut her critical comments in half. In view of these difficulties, the present results cannot be taken as a clear test of the effects of responding with Disapproval to Inappropriate Behaviors.

The failure to eliminate Disapproval Reactions to Inappropriate Behaviors in Phase Three of the experiment, adds some ambiguities to the interpretation of the Phase Four data for Teacher A. The Rules, Ignore, and Praise condition for Teacher A involved both a reduction in critical comments (Ignoring) as well as a marked increase in Praise. As demonstrated previously (Becker *et al.*, 1967), this

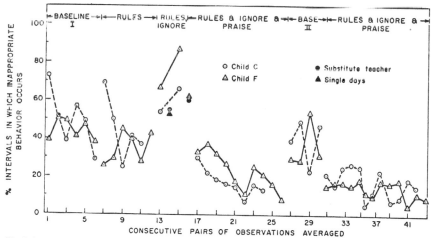

Fig. 1. Inappropriate behavior of two problem children in Classroom A as a function of experimental conditions.

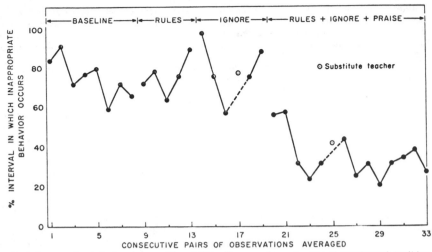

Fig. 2. Inappropriate behavior of one problem child in Classroom B as a function of experimental conditions.

Table 3

Teacher Behavior—Averages for Experimental Conditions (Frequency per 20-min Observation)

| Teacher A Behavior Classes | Experimental Conditions | | | | | |
|---|---|---|---|---|---|---|
| | Baseline I | Rules | Rules + Ignore | Rules + Ignore + Praise I | Baseline II | Rules + Ignore + Praise II |
| Approval to Appropriate | 1.2 | 2.0 | 0.0 | 18.2 | 2.5 | 12.5 |
| Approval to Inappropriate | 8.7 | 0.8 | 2.0 | 1.2 | 4.0 | 5.1 |
| Disapproval to Inappropriate | 18.5 | 20.5 | 15.7 | 4.1 | 9.8 | 3.5 |
| Disapproval to Appropriate | 0.9 | 0.7 | 1.0 | 0.3 | 0.9 | 0.0 |
| Timeout | 3.3 | 1.4 | 1.7 | 0.4 | 0.0 | 0.1 |
| Academic Recognition | 26.5 | 23.6 | 46.3 | 52.4 | 45.4 | 45.6 |
| Days observed | 15 | 8 | 3 | 11 | 4 | 9 |

| Teacher B Behavior Classes | Baseline | Rules | Ignore | Rules + Ignore + Praise |
|---|---|---|---|---|
| Approval to Appropriate | 19.2 | 14.1 | 19.3 | 35.2 |
| Approval to Inappropriate | 1.9 | 0.9 | 0.3 | 0.0 |
| Disapproval to Inappropriate | 16.9 | 22.1 | 10.6 | 10.8 |
| Disapproval to Appropriate | 0.0 | 0.0 | 0.0 | 0.0 |
| Timeout | 1.5 | 1.5 | 0.3 | 0.4 |
| Academic Recognition | 14.5 | 5.1 | 6.5 | 35.6 |
| Days observed | 8 | 6 | 6 | 10 |

combination of procedures is very effective in reducing inappropriate classroom behaviors, but we still lack a clear isolation of effects. The data for Teacher B are not confounded with a simultaneous shift in frequency of Disapproval and Approval Reactions, but they are made less interpretable by a marked shift in Academic Recognition (defined in Table 2) which occurred when the shift in Praise was made. Since Academic Recognition does not show any systematic relations to level of Appropriate Behaviors elsewhere in the study, we are not inclined to interpret this change as showing a causal effect. A best guess is that the effective use of Praise gave the teacher more time to focus on academic skills.

The reversal operation for Teacher A quite clearly shows that the combination of Praising and Ignoring exerts a strong control over Appropriate Behaviors.

As with Academic Recognition, no attempt was made to control how frequently the teacher used procedures labelled "Timeout" (defined in Table 2). The frequency data reported in Table 4 indicates that during Baseline, Teacher A, especially, used "Timeout" procedures to try to establish control (usually turning off the lights until the children were quiet). The changes in the frequency of use of "Timeout" procedures are not systematically related to the behavior changes graphed in Fig. 1 and 2.

In summary, the main results indicate: (a) that Rules alone had little effect in improving classroom behavior, (b) the functional status of Ignoring Inappropriate Behavior needs further clarification, (c) the combination of Ignoring and Praising was very effective in achieving better classroom behavior, and (d) Praise for Appropriate Behaviors was probably the key teacher behavior in achieving effective classroom management.

The effects of the experimental procedures on individual classes of behavior for the two children in Class A are presented in Table 4. The data in Table 4 illustrate that with a few exceptions the effects on individual classes of behavior are similar to those for Inappropriate Behavior as a whole.

## DISCUSSION

*Technical Considerations*

The problems of gaining good data and maintaining adequate experimental control in an ongoing classroom in a public school have not all been recognized as yet, much less solved. The greatest difficulty encountered was that of maintaining stable control over some important variables while others were being changed. When these variables involve aspects of teacher behavior, the problem becomes one of helping the teacher maintain discriminative control over her own behavior. Daily feedback

Table 4

Percentage of intervals in which behaviors occur: averages for two children in classroom A by experimental conditions.

| | Experimental Conditions | | | | | |
| Behavior Classes[1] | Baseline I | Rules | Rules + Ignore | Rules + Ignore + Praise I | Baseline II | Rules + Ignore + Praise II |
|---|---|---|---|---|---|---|
| Inappropriate Behavior[2] | 46.8 | 39.8 | 68.5 | 20.5 | 37.6 | 15.1 |
| Gross Motor | 13.9 | 11.3 | 32.7 | 5.9 | 15.5 | 4.1 |
| Object Noise | 3.5 | 1.4 | 1.3 | 0.5 | 1.9 | 0.8 |
| Disturbing Other's Property | 3.3 | 1.8 | 1.9 | 0.7 | 0.7 | 0.3 |
| Turning Around | 21.6 | 9.9 | 11.4 | 9.1 | 12.8 | 7.6 |
| Verbalizations | 12.0 | 16.8 | 21.8 | 6.5 | 8.0 | 3.5 |
| Other Inappropriate Behavior | 10.9 | 7.8 | 16.5 | 3.9 | 7.8 | 2.6 |
| Mouthing Objects | 5.5 | 2.9 | 3.5 | 0.7 | 0.2 | 0.1 |

[1]*Contact* occurred less than 1% of the time and is not tabulated here.

[2]The sum of the separate problem behaviors will exceed that for Inappropriate Behavior, since the latter measure does not reflect the possibility that more than one class of problem behaviors may occur in an interval.

from the experimenter, based on the observer ratings, can help in this task (*i.e.*, show the teacher the up-to-date graph of her behavior). Also, providing the teacher with a small counter to help monitor her own behavior can be helpful (Thomas, *et al.*, 1968). Most difficult to control in the present study was teacher's Disapproving Reactions to Inappropriate Behaviors during the Ignore Phase of the experiment. Teacher A became very "upset" as her classroom became worse. One solution to this problem might be a pre-study in which the teacher is trained in effective management techniques, and then taken through a series of short periods where both Approval and Disapproval are eliminated and one or the other reinstated. The teacher would then have confidence that she can effectively handle her class and be better able to tolerate short periods of chaos (if such periods did occur). She would also have had sufficient training in monitoring her own behavior to permit more effective control.

No attempt was made to program the frequency of various classes of Academic Recognition behaviors. Since such behavior may be important in interpreting results, and was found to vary with some experimental conditions, future work should strive to hold this behavior constant also.

The present study emphasized the importance of contingencies between student and teacher behaviors, but did not measure them directly. While producing similar effects on two children in the same classroom and one child in another classroom, and showing correlated changes in teacher behaviors (including a reversal operation), more powerful data are potentially obtainable with a different technology. Video-tape recordings could enable the use of present coding techniques to obtain contingency data on all classroom members over longer observation periods. Just as the children adapted to the presence of observers, a class could be adapted to the presence of a TV camera man. Costs could be trimmed by saving only some sample tapes and reusing others after reliability ratings are obtained. The current observation procedures (short of having an observer for each child) cannot readily be extended to include simultaneous coding of teacher and child behavior without over-taxing the observers. The present findings, and related studies in this series, are sufficiently promising to warrant an investment in more powerful recording equipment.

*Teacher Reactions*

*Teacher A.* Initially, Mrs. A generally maintained control through scolding and loud critical comments. There were frequent periods of chaos, which she handled by various threats.

When praise was finally added to the program, Mrs. A had these reactions: "I was amazed at the difference the procedure made in the atmosphere of the classroom and even my own personal feelings. I realized that in praising the well-behaved children and ignoring the bad, I was finding myself looking for the good in the children. It was indeed rewarding to see the good rather than always criticizing. . . . I became convinced that a positive approach to discipline was the answer."

*Teacher B.* During Baseline Mrs. B was dispensing a great deal of praise and approval to her classroom, but it was not always contingent on Appropriate Behavior. Her timing was wrong and inconsistencies were apparent. For example, on one occasion two children were fighting with scissors. The instigator was placed under a table away from the rest of the class and left there for 3 min. After 3 min Mrs. B took the child in her arms and brought her back to the group even though she was still emitting occasional loud screams. Mrs. B would also ignore behavior for a period of time and then would revert to responding to Inappropriate Behavior with a negative comment; she occasionally gave Approval for Inappropriate Behavior. The training given in seminar and discussions with the experimenter led to an effective use of contingencies. Teacher B was also able to use this training to provide instructions and training for her aide to eliminate problems which arose in the final phase of study when the aide was continuing to respond to Disruptive Behaviors.

*Changes in the Children*

Cliff showed little change until Mrs. A started praising Appropriate Behavior, except to get worse during the Ignore phase. He was often doing no academic work, talking to peers, and just fiddling away his time. It took considerable effort by Mrs. A to catch Cliff showing praiseworthy behavior. As the use of praise continued, Cliff worked harder on his assigned tasks, learned to ignore other children who were misbehaving, and would raise his hand to get teacher's attention. He participated more in class discussions. He was moved up to the fastest arithmetic group.

Frank showed little change in his "hyperactive" and "inattentive" behaviors until praise was introduced. Frank responded rapidly to praise. After just two days in the "praise" phase, Frank was observed to clean his desk quietly and quickly after completing a handwriting assignment. He was able to finish a task and study on his own until the teacher initiated a new activity. He began to ask for extra assignments and volunteered to do things to help his teacher. He had learned to sit quietly (when appropriate), to listen, and to raise his hand to participate in class discussion, the latter occurring quite frequently.

Stan slowly improved after contingent praise was instituted, but some of the gains made by Mrs. B were in part undone by the teacher aide. The aide was described as playing policeman and it took special efforts by the teacher to get her to follow the program. Mrs. B summarized the changes in Stan as follows: "Stan has changed from a sullen, morose, muttering, angry individual into a boy whose smile seems to cover his whole face." He became very responsive to teacher praise and learned to follow classroom rules, to pay attention to teacher-directed activities for long periods of time, and to interact with his peers in a more friendly way.

*Implications*

This replication and refinement of an earlier study by Becker, et al. (1967) adds further confidence to the assertion that teachers can be taught systematic procedures and can use them to gain more effective behaviors from their students. Unless teachers are effective in getting children "ready to learn", their technical teaching skills are likely to be wasted. Knowledge of differential social reinforcement procedures, as well as other behavioral principles, can greatly enhance teachers' enjoyment of the profession and their contribution to effective development of the students.

The reader should note that while we formally recorded the behavior of a few target children, teacher and observer comments indicated dramatic changes in the whole "atmosphere" of the classroom and in the teachers' enjoyment of their classes.

## REFERENCES

Allen, K. E., Hart, B. M., Buell, J. S., Harris, F. R., and Wolf, M. M. Effects of social reinforcement on isolate behavior of a nursery school child. In L. P. Ullmann and L. Krasner (Eds.), *Case studies in behavior modification.* New York: Holt, Rinehart, & Winston, 1965. Pp. 307-312.

Becker, W. C., Madsen, C. H., Jr., Arnold, Carole R., and Thomas, D. R. The contingent use of teacher attention and praise in reducing classroom behavior problems. *Journal of Special Education,* 1967, **1,** 287-307.

Bijou, S. W. and Baer, D. M. Some methodological contributions from a functional analysis of child development. In L. P. Lipsitt and C. S. Spiker (Eds.), *Advances in child development and behavior.* New York: Academic Press, 1963. Pp. 197-231.

Hart, Betty M., Reynolds, Nancy J., Baer, Donald M., Brawley, Eleanor R., and Harris, Florence R. Effect of contingent and non-contingent social reinforcement on the cooperative play of a preschool child. *Journal of Applied Behavior Analysis,* 1968, **1,** 73-76.

Thomas, D. R., Becker, W. C., and Armstrong, Marianne. Production and elimination of disruptive classroom behavior by systematically varying teacher's behavior. *Journal of Applied Behavior Analysis,* 1968, **1,** 35-45.

Madsen, C. H., Jr., Becker, W. C., Thomas, D. R., Koser, Linda, and Plager, Elaine. An analysis of the reinforcing function of "Sit Down" Commands. In Parker, R. K. (Ed.), *Readings in educational psychology* Boston: Allyn and Bacon (in press).

# EFFECTS OF TEACHER ATTENTION ON STUDY BEHAVIOR[1]

R. Vance Hall, Diane Lund, and Deloris Jackson

The effects of contingent teacher attention on study behavior were investigated. Individual rates of study were recorded for one first-grade and five third-grade pupils who had high rates of disruptive or dawdling behavior. A reinforcement period (in which teacher attention followed study behavior and non-study behaviors were ignored) resulted in sharply increased study rates. A brief reversal of the contingency (attention occurred only after periods of non-study behavior) again produced low rates of study. Reinstatement of teacher attention as reinforcement for study once again markedly increased study behavior. Follow-up observations indicated that the higher study rates were maintained after the formal program terminated.

A series of studies carried out in preschools by Harris, Wolf, and Baer (1964) and their colleagues demonstrated the effectiveness of contingent teacher attention in modifying behavior problems of preschool children. In these studies inappropriate and/or undesirable rates of isolate play (Allen, Hart, Buell, Harris, and Wolf, 1964), crying (Hart, Allen, Buell, Harris, and Wolf, 1964), crawling (Harris, Johnston, Kelley, and Wolf, 1964), and a number of other problem behaviors were modified by systematically manipulating teacher-attention consequences of the behaviors. Similarly, teacher and peer attention were manipulated by Zimmerman and Zimmerman (1962), Patterson (1965), and Hall and Broden (1967) to reduce problem behaviors and increase appropriate responses of children enrolled in special classrooms.

To date, however, there has been little systematic research in the application of social reinforcement by teachers in the regular school classroom beyond the successful case studies reported by Becker, Madsen, Arnold, and Thomas (1967) in which no attempt was made to evaluate the reliability of these procedures through experimental reversals.

The present studies analyzed experimentally the reliability with which teachers could modify the study behavior of children of poverty-area classrooms by systematic manipulation of contingent attention.

## GENERAL PROCEDURES

### Subjects and Setting

The studies were carried out in classrooms of two elementary schools located in the most economically deprived area of Kansas City, Kansas.[2] Teachers who participated were recommended by their principals. The teachers nominated pupils who were disruptive or dawdled. They were told that one or two observers would come regularly to their classrooms to record behavior rates of these pupils.

[1]The authors wish to express appreciation to Dr. O. L. Plucker, Ted Gray, Alonzo Plough, Clarence Glasse, Carl Bruce, Natalie Barge, Lawrence Franklin, and Audrey Jackson of the Kansas City, Kansas Public Schools and Wallace Henning, University of Kansas, without whose cooperation and active participation these studies would not have been possible. Special tribute is due to Dr. Montrose M. Wolf and Dr. Todd R. Risley for their many contributions in developing research strategy and for their continuing encouragement. We are also indebted to Dr. R. L. Schiefelbusch, Director of the Bureau of Child Research, and administrative director of the project, who provided essential administrative support and counsel.

[2]The research was carried out as part of the Juniper Gardens Children's Project, a program of research on the development of culturally deprived children and was partially supported by the Office of Economic Opportunity: (OEO KAN CAP 694/1, Bureau of Child Research, Kansas University Medical Center) and the National Institute of Child Health and Human Development: (HD-00870-(04) and HD 03144-01, Bureau of Child Research, University of Kansas).

JOURNAL OF APPLIED BEHAVIOR ANALYSIS, 1968, Vol. 1, pp. 1-12.

### *Observation*

The observers used recording sheets lined with triple rows of squares, as shown in Fig. 1. Each square represented an interval of 10 sec. The first row was used to record the behavior of the student. (The definition of study behavior was somewhat different for each student and depended on the subject matter taught. Generally, study behavior was defined as orientation toward the appropriate object or person: assigned course materials, lecturing teacher, or reciting classmates, as well as class participation by the student when requested by the teacher. Since each pupil was observed during the same class period, however, the response definition was consistent for each student throughout the course of an experiment.) Teacher verbalizations to the student were recorded in the second row. The third row was used to record occasions when the teacher was within a 3-ft proximity to the student.

## EXPERIMENTAL CONDITIONS

### *Baseline*

Rates of study were obtained for the selected pupils. Thirty-minute observations were scheduled at a time each day when the pupils were to be working in their seats. In most cases observations were made two to four times per week. After obtaining a minimum of two weeks of baseline, the students' study rates were presented graphically to the teachers. Then, selected studies (Hart *et al.*, 1964; Allen *et al.*, 1964; Hall and Broden, 1967) were presented to the teachers, the fundamentals of social reinforcement were discussed, and a pupil was selected for systematic study.

### *Reinforcement$_1$*

During reinforcement sessions the observer held up a small square of colored paper in a manner not likely to be noticed by the pupil whenever the pupil was engaged in study.

SECONDS ONE MINUTE

| 10 | 20 | 30 | 40 | 50 | 60 | | | | | | | | | | | | | | | | | | |
|---|---|---|---|---|---|---|---|---|---|---|---|---|---|---|---|---|---|---|---|---|---|---|---|
| N | N | N | N | N | N | N | S | S | S | N | N | S | S | S | S | N | N | N | N | N | N | N | N |
| | | T | T | T | | | | | | | T | | | | | | | | | | | T | T |
| | | | / | / | | | | / | | | / | | | | | | | | | | | | |

ROW 1 N Non-Study Behavior. S Study Behavior.

ROW 2 T Teacher Verbalization directed toward pupil.

ROW 3 / Teacher Proximity (Teacher within three feet).

Fig. 1. Observer recording sheet and symbol key.

These observations were made during each 10 sec interval of each session. The observers sat at the rear or the side of the classroom, and avoided eye contact or any other interaction with pupils during observation sessions.

Inter-observer agreement was analyzed by having a second observer periodically make a simultaneous observation record. Agreement of the two records was checked interval by interval. The percentage of agreement of the records [# agreements × 100 ÷ (# agreements + # disagreements)] yielded the percentage of inter-observer agreement.

Upon this signal, the teacher attended to the child, moved to his desk, made some verbal comment, gave him a pat on the shoulder, or the like. During weekly after-school sessions, experimenters and teachers discussed the rate of study achieved by the pupil and the effectiveness of attention provided by the teacher, and made occasional adjustments in instructions as required.

### *Reversal*

When a satisfactory rate of study had been achieved, the observer discontinued signaling and (as much as possible) the teacher returned to her former pattern, which typically consisted of attending to non-study behavior.

### Reinforcement₂

When the effect of the reversal condition had been observed, social reinforcement of study was reinstituted. When high study rates were achieved again, the teacher continued reinforcement of study behavior without the observer's signals.

### Post Checks

Whenever possible, periodic post-checks were made through the remainder of the year to determine whether the new levels of study were being maintained.

### Correlated Behavioral Changes

Where possible, other behavioral changes, including teacher reports, grades, and other records of academic achievement were recorded. Because such data are difficult to evaluate, their importance should not be unduly stressed.

## INDIVIDUAL EXPERIMENTS

### Robbie

Robbie was chosen because he was considered a particularly disruptive pupil who studied very little. Figure 2 presents a record of Robbie's study behavior, defined as having pencil on paper during 5 sec or more of the 10-sec interval. During baseline, study behavior occurred in 25% of the intervals observed during the class spelling period. The behaviors which occupied the other 75% of his time included snapping rubber bands, playing with toys from his pocket, talking and laughing with peers, slowly drinking the half-pint of milk served earlier in the morning, and subsequently playing with the empty carton.

During the baseline period the teacher would often urge Robbie to work, put his milk carton away, *etc.* In fact, 55% of the teacher attention he received followed non-study behavior. Robbie engaged in continuous study for 60 sec or more only two or three times during a 30-min observation.

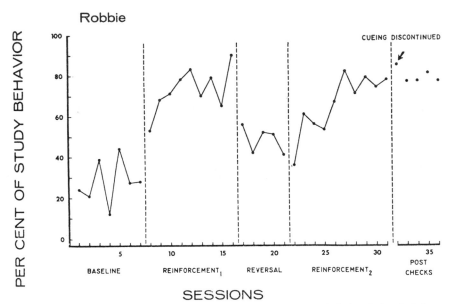

Fig. 2. A record of study behavior for Robbie. Post-check observations were made during the fourth, sixth, seventh, twelfth, and fourteenth weeks after the completion of Reinforcement₂ condition.

Following baseline determination, whenever Robbie had engaged in 1 min of continuous study the observer signaled his teacher. On this cue, the teacher approached Robbie, saying, "Very good work Robbie", "I see you are studying", or some similar remark. She discontinued giving attention for non-study behaviors including those which were disruptive to the class.

Figure 2 shows an increased study rate during the first day of the first reinforcement period. The study rate continued to rise thereafter and was recorded in 71% of the intervals during this period.

During the brief reversal period, when reinforcement of study was discontinued, the study rate dropped to a mean of 50%. However, when reinforcement for study was reinstituted, Robbie's study rate again increased, stabilizing at a rate ranging between 70% and 80% of the observation sessions. Subsequent follow up checks made during the 14 weeks that followed (after signaling of the teacher was discontinued) indicated that study was being maintained at a mean rate of 79%. Periodic checks made during each condition of the experiment revealed that agreement of observation ranged from 89% to 93%.

Robbie's teacher reported behavior changes correlated with his increased rate of study. During Baseline, she reported that Robbie did not complete written assignments. He missed 2 of 10, 5 of 10, and 6 of 10 words on three spelling tests given during Baseline. By the final week of Reinforcement$_2$, she reported that he typically finished his initial assignment and then continued on to other assigned work without prompting. Disruptive behavior had diminished and it was noted that he continued to study while he drank his milk and did not play with the carton when finished. He missed 1 of 10 words on his weekly spelling test.

*Rose*

Rose was a classmate of Robbie. Baseline observations were made during the math and/or spelling study periods. The mean rate of study during Baseline was 30%, fluctuating from 0% to 71%. Her non-study behaviors included laying her head on the desk, taking

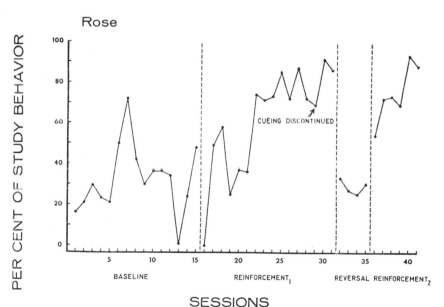

Fig. 3. A record of study behavior for Rose.

off her shoes, talking, and being out of her seat.

On the day her teacher was first to reinforce Rose's study behavior, Rose did not study at all, and the teacher was thus unable to provide reinforcement. Therefore, beginning with the second reinforcement session, the teacher attended to behavior that approximated study (*e.g.*, getting out pencil or paper, or opening her book to the correct page). Once these behaviors were reinforced, study behavior quickly followed, was in turn reinforced, and had risen to 57% by the third reinforcement session.

During the fourth session, however, study dropped to 25%. An analysis of the data indicated Rose had increased in out-of-seat behavior, to have her papers checked and to ask questions. Consequently her teacher thereafter ignored Rose when she approached but attended to her immediately if she raised her hand while seated. There was an immediate drop in out-of-seat behavior and a concurrent increase in study behavior. As can be seen in Fig. 3, during the last 10 sessions of Rein-

forcement₁, study behavior ranged between 74% and 92%, the mean rate for the entire period being approximately 71%. A high rate of study was maintained after the observer discontinued signaling after the thirteenth reinforcement session.

During the four reversal sessions, study was recorded in only 29% of the intervals. However, a return to attention for study immediately increased study behavior and during the second reinforcement period study was recorded in 72% of the observed intervals. Observer agreement measured under each condition ranged from 90% to 95%.

An analysis of the attention provided Rose by her teacher demonstrated that it was not the amount of attention, but its delivery contingent on study which produced the changes in this behavior. Figure 4 shows these amounts, and the general lack of relationship between amount of attention and experimental procedures.

In fact these data show that when teacher attention occurred primarily during non-study intervals there was a low rate of study.

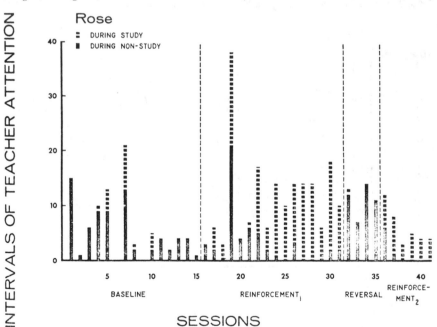

Fig. 4. A record of teacher attention for Rose.

158

When teacher attention occurred primarily during study intervals there was a higher rate of study. Figure 4 also shows that the mean rate of total teacher attention remained relatively stable throughout the various experimental phases, rising somewhat in the Reinforcement₁ and Reversal phases and declining to baseline levels in the Reinforcement₂ phase.

Rose's grades at the end of the baseline phase were D in arithmetic and D in spelling. Her grades for the reinforcement phase of the experiment were C— in arithmetic and B in spelling.

## Ken

Ken was one of the other 41 pupils in Rose's class. He had a wide range of disruptive behaviors including playing with toys from his pockets, rolling pencils on the floor and desk, and jiggling and wiggling in his seat. His teacher had tried isolating him from his peers, reprimanding by the principal, and spanking to control his behavior. These efforts apparently had been ineffective. Study behavior ranged from 10% to 60%, with a mean rate of 37%, as seen in Fig. 5.

Reinforcement of study behavior was begun at the same time for both Ken and Rose. The observer used different colored cards to signal when the behavior of each pupil was to be reinforced. Ken's study increased to a mean rate of 71% under reinforcement conditions. However, during his brief reversal, Ken's rate of study was again about 37%. The re-introduction of the reinforcement for study recovered study behavior in 70% of the observed intervals. Agreement between observers measured during each of the conditions ranged from 90% to 92%.

Ken's teacher reported several correlated behavior changes. Before the experiment she had stated that he rarely, if ever, finished an assignment. His grades for the baseline period included D in math, D in spelling and U (unsatisfactory) in conduct. After reinforcement was instituted his teacher reported a marked decrease in disruptive behavior and stated, "He's getting his work done on time now." Ken's report card grades subsequently

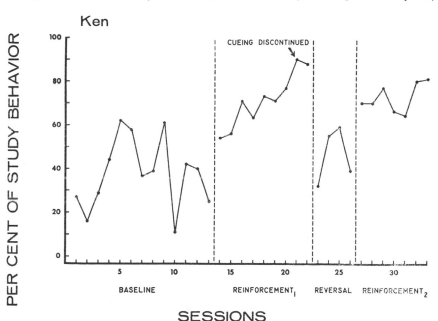

Fig. 5. A record of study behavior for Ken.

were C in spelling, C in arithmetic and S (satisfactory) in conduct.

## Gary

Gary, a third-grade boy in another classroom of 39 pupils was chosen as a subject because he failed to complete assignments. The course of Gary's program is shown in Fig. 5. Observations made during the 30-min morning math period indicated that Gary engaged in study during 43% of the 10-sec intervals observed. Non-study behaviors included beating his desk with a pencil, chewing and licking pages of books, moving his chair back and forth in unison with a classmate, banging his chair on the floor, blowing bubbles and making noises while drinking his milk, and punching holes in the carton so that milk flowed onto the desk. He would also gaze out the window or around the room and would say "This is too hard", "Shoot, I can't do this", and "How did you say to work it?"

Gary had been observed to engage in appropriate study for 60 sec or more at least one to three times during most study periods. The

observer thus signaled the teacher whenever Gary had engaged in study for six consecutive 10-sec intervals, and he was attended to by the teacher only on those occasions.

As shown in Fig. 6, reinforcement produced a marked increase in studying. With the rise, almost all disruptive behavior disappeared. He still talked out of turn in class but typically to say "I know how to do it", "He's wrong", "Can I do it, teacher?", "Oh, this is easy." Gary engaged in study during approximately 77% of the 10-sec intervals observed during Reinforcement₁.

After the twentieth session a reversal was programmed, and the teacher was signaled whenever Gary engaged in non-study behavior for 30 sec. When this occurred, the teacher gave Gary a reminder to get back to work. No attention was given for study behavior.

As can be seen, this resulted in a fluctuating but declining rate of study during the 30-min math period. At this point it was noted that Gary's rate of study was again rising, and that the teacher was in fact providing intermittent reinforcement for study. Therefore,

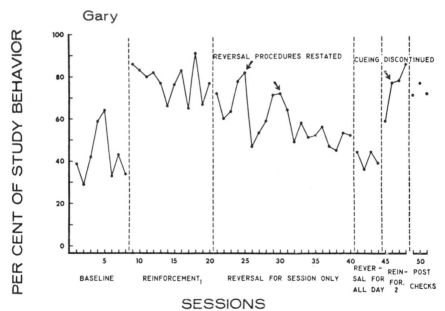

Fig. 6. A record of study behavior for Gary. Post-check observations were made during the first, fourth, and tenth weeks after completion of Reinforcement₂ condition.

on two occasions the procedures for reversal were gone over once again in conference with the teacher and a subsequent slow but steady decline in study rate was achieved. There also appeared to be an increase in disruptive behavior. The mean rate of study at this point of Reversal was about 60%.

It was then noted that a more rapid reversal effect had been brought about in the previous studies, probably because that teacher had carried out reversal procedures for the entire day whereas Gary's teacher practiced reversal only during the 30-min observation period. Reversal of reinforcement conditions was, therefore, extended to the entire day. The mean rate for these sessions was approximately 42%. However, resumption of reinforcement immediately recovered a study rate of 60% which increased as reinforcement continued. After the first day of this reinforcement phase the teacher expressed confidence in being able to work without cues from the observer. Signaling was therefore discontinued without loss of effect. Periodic checks made during subsequent weeks indicated study behavior was being maintained at a level higher than 70%. The reliability of observation measured during each condition ranged from 92% to 96%.

*Joan*

Joan, one of Gary's classmates, did not disrupt the class or bother other pupils but was selected because she dawdled. Typically, during arithmetic study period, she would lay her head on her desk and stare toward the windows or her classmates. At other times she would pull at or straighten her clothing, dig in her desk, pick or pull at her hair, nose or fingernails, draw on the desk top or play with her purse. During baseline her study rate was approximately 35%.

During the Reinforcement$_1$ phase, after the observer signaled that 60 sec of continuous study had occurred, the teacher made comments such as, "That's a good girl", and often tugged lightly at Joan's hair or patted her shoulder. As can be seen in Fig. 7 this resulted in an immediate increase in study behavior. The observer discontinued signaling after Session 20 when the teacher stated it was no longer necessary. Though the study rate fluctuated in subsequent sessions it generally remained higher than in Baseline. The lowest

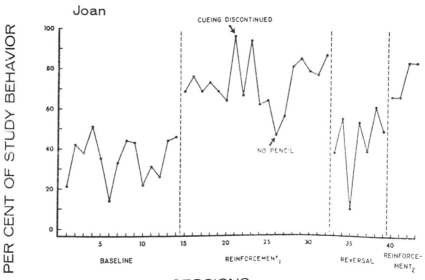

Fig. 7. A record of study behavior for Joan.

rate of study came in Session 26 when Joan was without a pencil through the first part of the session. Study was observed in 73% of the intervals of the Reinforcement₁ phase.

During Reversal, Joan's study rate declined markedly and play with clothes, pencils, and head on desk behaviors appeared to increase. The mean study rate for the reversal sessions was approximately 43%. Reinstatement of reinforcement for study, however, resulted in a rapid return to a study rate of approximately 73%. No post-checks were obtained because of the close of school. Observer agreement ranged from 93% to 97%.

Joan's arithmetic-paper grades provided interesting correlated data. During Baseline a sampling of her arithmetic papers showed an average grade of F. During Reinforcement₁ they averaged C. All her arithmetic papers graded during Reversal were graded F. In Reinforcement₂ the average grade on arithmetic papers was C−.

*Levi*

Levi was a first-grade boy who was selected because of his disruptive behaviors. Although he achieved at a fairly high level, he often disturbed the class by making loud noises, by getting out of his seat, and by talking to other students. The school counselor suggested using reinforcement techniques after counselling with the pupil and teacher brought about no apparent improvement in Levi's behavior.

The counselor was trained in the observation procedures and he obtained baseline rates of Levi's study and disruptive behaviors during seatwork time. A second observer was used to supplement data gathering. During Baseline, Levi's rate of study was approximately 68%, ranging from 34% to 79%. An analysis of teacher attention during baseline showed that although Levi had a relatively high rate of study, he received almost no teacher attention except when he was disruptive (*i.e.*, made noise or other behaviors which overtly disturbed his neighbors and/or the teacher).

During Reinforcement₁ the teacher provided social reinforcement for study and, as much as possible, ignored all disruptive behavior. No signals were used since Levi had a relatively high study rate and the teacher was confident she could carry out reinforcement without cues. Figure 8 shows that study

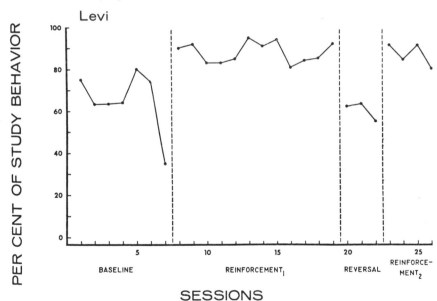

Fig. 8. A record of study behavior for Levi.

162

occurred in approximately 88% of the intervals of Reinforcement₁ and at no time went below that of the highest baseline rate. A brief reversal produced a marked decrease in study to a mean rate of 60%. However, when reinforcement for study was reinstated study again rose to above the baseline rate (approximately 85%).

Figure 9 presents the disruptive behavior data for the four periods of the experiment. Disruptive behavior was defined to occur when Levi made noises, got out of his seat or talked to other students and the response appeared to be noticed by the teacher or another student. During Baseline the mean rate of disruptive behavior was 7%. During Reinforcement₁ the mean rate declined to 2.2%. During the brief Reversal phase the mean rate rose to 3.2%. In Reinforcement₂ the rate declined to an almost negligible 0.25%. No follow-up data were obtained because of the close of the school year. Observer agreement measured under each condition was consistently over 80%.

The teacher and the school counselor re-

ported at the conclusion of the experiment that in their opinion Levi was no longer a disruptive pupil.

## DISCUSSION

These studies indicate clearly that the contingent use of teacher attention can be a quick and effective means of developing desirable classroom behavior. Effective teachers have long known that casually praising desired behaviors and generally ignoring disruptive ones can be useful procedures for helping maintain good classroom discipline. What may appear surprising to school personnel, however, is the degree to which student behavior responds to thoroughly systematic teacher attention.

One purpose of these studies was to determine whether the procedures could be carried out by teachers in public school classrooms. Although these teachers were initially unfamiliar with reinforcement principles and had had no prior experience with the procedures, they were clearly able to carry them

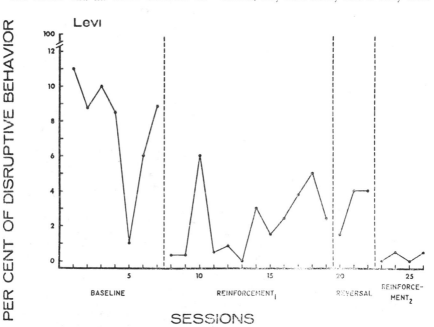

Fig. 9. A record of disruptive behavior for Levi.

163

out with important effect. The fact that they were carried out in crowded classrooms of schools of an urban poverty area underscores this point. In such areas one would expect a high incidence of disruptive behaviors and low interest in academic achievement, conditions generally conceded to make teaching and motivation for study difficult. Yet, with relatively slight adjustment of the social environment, it was possible to increase rates of study with comparative ease.

The teachers in these studies did not have poor general control of their classrooms. Most of their pupils seemed to apply themselves fairly well, although a few did not. When their baseline data were analyzed, it became clear that these pupils were in effect being motivated not to study. It became apparent that for these pupils, most teacher attention was received during non-study intervals rather than when they were studying. This was not surprising since many of the non-study behaviors were disruptive and thus seemed to the teacher to require some reprimand.

Several aspects of the teacher training program appear worthy of mention. During baseline, as far as the teacher was concerned, the primary purpose was to determine study rates. After baseline, a simple procedure designed to increase those study rates was emphasized (rather than the fact that the teacher had in all probability been reinforcing the very behaviors which were causing concern).

The teacher was constantly informed of the results of each day's sessions and its graphed outcome. These daily contacts, plus weekly conferences in which the procedures were discussed and the teacher was praised for bringing about the desired behavioral changes, may have been central to the process of a successful study.

The teachers readily accepted the advisability of carrying out a brief reversal when it was presented as a means of testing for a causal relationship between teacher attention and pupil behavior. All, however, felt reversal sessions were aversive and were glad when they were terminated.

These procedures did not seem to interfere greatly with ongoing teaching duties. For one thing they did not necessarily result in more total teacher attention for a pupil. In fact, the teachers had more time for constructive teaching of all pupils because of the decrease in disruptive behaviors in the classroom.

Two teachers reported they were able to utilize systematic attention to increase appropriate study of other pupils in their classrooms who were not included in these studies. No corroborative data were collected to verify their reports. Investigation of the degree to which this kind of generalization occurs should be a goal of further research, however, since such a result would be highly desirable.

In the first five subjects, cueing of the teacher was initially used to make certain that the teacher could discriminate when study behavior was occurring. Later, cueing was discontinued without loss of effectiveness. In the case of Levi, cueing was never used. Further research will be needed to determine how often cueing contributes to the efficiency of the procedures.

In one classroom, a teacher was unable to carry out the procedures in spite of the fact that the same orientation and training processes were used which had previously proved successful. Although the teacher seemed sincere in her efforts to reinforce study, she observably continued to give a high rate of attention for non-study behaviors. Observations indicated that the teacher gave almost no praise or positive attention to any member of the class. Virtually her entire verbal repertoire consisted of commands, reprimands, and admonitions. Consequently the teacher was instructed to provide positive verbal reinforcement for appropriate behavior of all class members. This did result in a measurable increase in the number of positive statements made to individuals and to the class. According to both the teacher and the observers, this greatly improved general classroom behavior. Only slight increases in study were recorded for the two pupils for whom data were available, however, and the close of the school year prevented further manipulations.

This failure prompted the authors to begin developing a system for recording appropriate behavior rates for an entire class. It also indicates that there may be certain teachers who need different or more intensive training to carry out these procedures effectively.

Finally, it should be noted that the pupils of this study did have at least a minimal level of proficiency in performing the academic tasks and thus seemed to profit from the increased time they spent in study. The teachers apparently assigned study tasks within the range of the pupils' skills, and correlated gains in academic achievement were noted. If teachers were to use the procedures but failed to provide materials within the range of the pupil's level of skill, it is unlikely that much gain in achievement would result.

## REFERENCES

Allen, K. E., Hart, B. M., Buell, J. S., Harris, F. R., and Wolf, M. M. Effects of social reinforcement on isolate behavior of a nursery school child. *Child Development*, 1964, **35**, 511-518.

Becker, W. C., Madsen, C. H., Jr., Arnold, R., and Thomas, D. R. The contingent use of teacher attention and praise in reducing classroom behavior problems. *Journal of Special Education*, 1967, **1**, 287-307.

Hall, R. V. and Broden, M. Behavior changes in brain-injured children through social reinforcement. *Journal of Experimental Child Psychology*, 1967, **5**, 463-479.

Harris, F. R., Johnston, M. K., Kelley, C. S., and Wolf, M. M. Effects of positive social reinforcement on regressed crawling of a nursery school child. *Journal of Educational Psychology*, 1964, **55**, 35-41.

Harris, F. R., Wolf, M. M., and Baer, D. M. Effects of adult social reinforcement on child behavior. *Young Children*, 1964, **20**, 8-17.

Hart, Betty M., Allen, K. Eileen; Buell, Joan S., Harris, Florence R., and Wolf, M. M. Effects of social reinforcement on operant crying. *Journal of Experimental Child Psychology*, 1964, **1**, 145-153.

Patterson, G. R. An application of conditioning techniques to the control of a hyperactive child, Ullman, L. P., and Krasner, L. (Eds.), *Case studies in behavior modification*, New York: Holt, Rinehart and Winston, Inc., 1966. Pp. 370-375.

Zimmerman, Elaine H. and Zimmerman, J. The alteration of behavior in a special classroom situation. *Journal of the Experimental Analysis of Behavior*, 1962, **5**, 59-60.

MARCIA BRODEN
R. VANCE HALL
ANN DUNLAP
ROBERT CLARK

# Effects of Teacher Attention and a Token Reinforcement System in a Junior High School Special Education Class

A SERIES of studies carried out in nursery schools (Harris, Wolf, & Baer, 1964), special education classes (Hall & Broden, 1967; Zimmerman & Zimmerman, 1962), and regular public schools (Hall, Lund, & Jackson, 1968; Hall, Panyan, Rabon, & Broden, 1968; Thomas, Becker, & Armstrong, 1968) have demonstrated that contingent teacher attention could be effective in increasing appropriate classroom behavior.

Similarly, token reinforcement systems backed up by food, field trips, toys, money, and grades were demonstrated to be effective in increasing academic behaviors of pupils in special education programs including classrooms for the retarded (Birnbrauer, Wolf, Kidder, & Tague, 1965), remedial classrooms for poverty area elementary age children (Wolf, Giles, & Hall, 1968), and for elementary special education pupils (McKenzie, Clark, Wolf, Kothera, & Benson, 1968; O'Leary & Becker, 1967).

With the exception of the study by Hall, Panyan, Rabon, and Broden (1968), however, these studies were carried out by experienced teachers and dealt with preschool and ele-

EXCEPTIONAL CHILDREN, January 1970, pp. 341-350.

mentary age children. Those using token reinforcement systems used reinforcers primarily extrinsic to the classroom, and most often there was more than one teacher available to conduct the class and carry out the experimental procedures.

In contrast, the present study was carried out in a public junior high school special education classroom by a first year teacher without prior teaching experience. When systematic teacher attention to appropriate behavior proved to be limited in its effect, a token reinforcement system backed by reinforcers available to most junior high school teachers was used to reduce extremely disruptive behavior and to increase appropriate study behavior.

## Subjects and Setting

The subjects were 13 seventh and eighth grade students, eight boys and five girls, in a special education class in Bonner Springs Junior High School, Bonner Springs, Kansas. All students were several years behind in at least one major academic area and had other problems, including severe reading deficits, almost incoherent speech, emotional instability, and acts of delinquency. Some specific problem behaviors involved cursing the teacher; refusing to obey teacher requests or to do assignments; throwing pencils, pens, or paper; fighting; chasing each other about the room; and eating a variety of snacks.

The inappropriate behaviors described had persisted through the first four months of school although the teacher had used generally accepted methods for maintaining classroom control, including some praise for appropriate behavior and reprimands or a trip to the counselor or principal's office for misconduct.

The class met for five periods of the eight period day. The entire class was present for the first, fifth, and eighth periods. Only the seven seventh graders were present for the second and sixth periods, and only the six eighth graders were present during the third and seventh periods.

*Observations.* The system used was essentially that developed by Broden (1968) for recording classroom study behavior. Daily

observations were made by an observer equipped with a recording sheet and stopwatch. Data were recorded on the recording sheet at 5 second intervals. At the 5 second mark the behavior of the first pupil was recorded, at the 10 second mark the behavior of a second pupil was recorded, at the 15 second mark that of the third student, and so on until every student had been observed once; then the sequence was begun again. Thus the behavior of a different pupil was recorded every 5 seconds on a consecutive rotation basis.

As is shown in Figure 1, the recording sheet was divided into triple rows of squares with a different pupil's name entered at the top of each column of three vertical squares. The middle row of squares was used to record whether or not the pupil was studying. An "S" (for study) was recorded if the pupil were attending to or oriented toward the appropriate book when he had been assigned reading to do, if he were attending to the teacher or another pupil who was speaking during class discussions, if he were writing spelling words during spelling period, or if he were otherwise engaged in a teacher assigned task. All other behaviors were designated as "N" except for the specific nonstudy behavior "out of seat" which was recorded as "O."

The top row of squares was used to record verbalizations by the teacher to a subject or to the class. A "T" designated teacher verbalization directed to an individual pupil during that 5 second interval.

The bottom row of squares was used to record pupil verbalizations. A "V" designated verbalizations recognized by the teacher.

Observations lasted from 30 to 40 minutes during any given period.

Computing the percentage of the total 5 second intervals in which "S" had been recorded revealed the class study rate. It was also possible to compute individual study rates by dividing the number of "S" intervals for the pupil by the total number of intervals that the individual pupil was observed and multiplying the result by 100. Thus both class and individual study rates could be obtained.

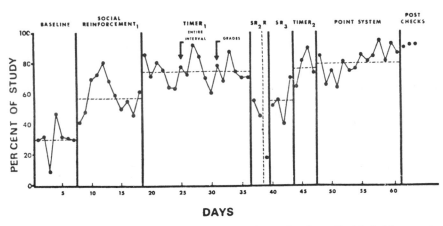

| | ROY | JOE | JACK | CLEM | LANNY | DIRK | DELLA | LULU | MARTA | FANNY | JODI | HOLT | ROB | ROY | JOE | JACK | CLEM | LANNY | DIRK | DELLA | LULU | MARTA | FANNY | JODI | HOLT | ROB |
|---|---|---|---|---|---|---|---|---|---|---|---|---|---|---|---|---|---|---|---|---|---|---|---|---|---|---|
| | | | T | | | | | | T | | | | | | | | | | T | | | | | T | | |
| | S | N | N | S | S | S | N | N | N | S | S | S | S | S | S | N | N | S | S | N | N | N | S | S | S | N |
| | | | V | | | | | | Ⓥ | | | | | | | | | V | V | | | | | | | |

Row 1  T = Teacher verbalization directed to pupil
Row 2  S = Study behavior, N = Nonstudy behavior
Row 3  V = Appropriate pupil verbalization, v = Inappropriate verbalization

FIGURE 1. Observer recording sheet and symbol key.

FIGURE 2. A record of fifth period study behavior during Baseline₁, Social Reinforcement₁, Timer₁, Social Reinforcement₂ (SR₂), Reversal (R), Social Reinforcement₃ (SR₃), Timer₂, Point System, and Postcheck conditions.

Reliability checks were made periodically throughout the study. A second observer made independent, simultaneous observations. This record was compared with that of the primary observer, interval by interval. The percentage of agreement was then computed. Observer agreement for this study ranged from 83 to 98 percent.

**Experiment I**

Initially, daily observations were begun during the fifth period when all 13 pupils were present. Assigned study tasks included reading, writing, and participation in class discussions.

During the first (baseline) 7 days of ob-

servation the teacher was asked to conduct class in her usual manner and to ignore the observer. Care was taken not to mention possible experimental procedures. Pupils were told someone would be coming in at various times to assist the teacher. All contact between the observer and teacher or pupils was avoided during class sessions.

Figure 2 presents the data for the seven baseline sessions. The broken horizontal line indicates that the mean rate of study behavior was 29 percent. During baseline sessions the teacher was observed giving attention to both study and nonstudy behaviors.

Prior to the eighth day of observation a conference was held with the teacher. She

168

was shown the baseline study data and was asked to begin giving attention to study behavior only and to ignore all nonstudying. During the next 11 days the teacher went to pupils who were studying and commented on their good study behavior and work, called only on pupils who raised their hands, and complimented the entire group when all were studying quietly.

As can be seen in the Social Reinforcement$_1$ phase of Figure 2, this procedure resulted in an increase in study behavior to a mean rate of 57 percent. Although an improvement over baseline rates, there were still frequent outbursts of inappropriate verbalizations, out of seat, and other disruptive behaviors. Therefore a new contingency for appropriate study was introduced.

During the next 18 sessions a kitchen timer was placed on the teacher's desk and set to go off at random intervals averaging 8 minutes. Pupils who were in their seats and quiet when the timer sounded were given a mark on a card taped to their desk tops. Each mark earned allowed them to leave one minute earlier for lunch. Teacher attention for study was continued during this phase.

As can be seen in the Timer$_1$ phase of Figure 2, an immediate increase in study behavior resulted. Beginning in the 25th session ("Quiet Entire Interval" in Figure 2) pupils were required to be quiet during the entire interval between timer rings in order to receive a mark. Beginning in the 31st session marks (grades) were continued as before, but a grade of E (excellent) was also given if the pupil had been engaging in study behavior. These conditions seemed to have little additional effect on study level.

The mean study rate for the entire Timer$_1$ phase was 74 percent, and according to the subjective judgments of the teacher and observer there was noticeably less disruptive behavior.

In order to see if the reinforcement procedures were the primary factors in increasing study, a brief return to prior conditions was made. For 2 days the timer early dismissal contingency was removed and only social reinforcement for study was given. This re-

sulted in a drop in study behavior to 55 percent the first day and to 45 percent the second (Social Reinforcement$_2$). The following day (session 39) social reinforcement for study was also withdrawn. The teacher attended only to nonstudy behavior and ignored study behavior. This complete reversal of procedures resulted in a breakdown of study behavior and almost complete disruption of the class. As can be seen in Figure 2 (R-Reversal) the study level during this one day reversal was only 18 percent.

During the next phase (Social Reinforcement$_3$) the teacher again attended to study behavior and ignored nonstudy. The level rose to 55 percent. During the next 4 days the timer and marks for early lunch dismissal plus grades for study were reinstituted. Under these conditions (Timer$_2$) the mean study level was 76 percent.

Beginning in session 48, the timer condition was discontinued and pupils were put on a token point system described in Experiment II. The data presented in the Point System phase of Figure 2 indicate that the higher study levels established with the timer were not only maintained but also slightly increased under the token point system. In fact, the mean study level rose to 90 percent.

Postchecks taken over the next month and a half after conclusion of daily monitoring indicated that the higher study levels were maintained through the remainder of the school year despite the fact the teacher was not informed prior to observation time when these checks would occur.

### Experiment II

After a few days of higher study levels achieved by the procedures described above, the teacher and principal concurred in their judgment that pupil behavior during fifth period was indeed under much better control. However, they reported that the higher study rates had not transferred to the other five daily class periods. Therefore, an attempt to increase study during these periods also was made.

First, observations were made in order to determine the actual level of study during these five other periods. Nineteen 30 minute

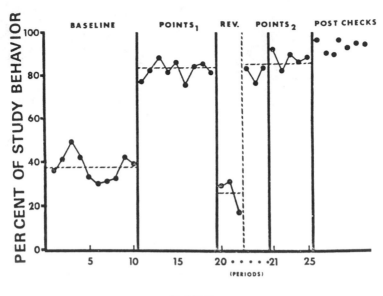

FIGURE 3. A record of study behavior during the entire day, under Baseline, Points, Reversal (Rev.), Points₂ and Post Check conditions. Post Checks were taken periodically during the final six weeks of school after termination of regular observations.

observations were made on 10 different days. Although the mean number of observations was a little less than 2 per day, the number on any one day ranged from 1 to all 5 (the number monitored on days 7 and 8). As can be seen in Figure 3 the mean levels of study for the 10 days of observation ranged from 33 to 47 percent. The mean baseline level as indicated by the dotted horizontal line was 39 percent.

Following baseline a token reinforcement system was instituted. A point system using a combination of available privileges and punishments was selected. (These periods were not followed by lunch and therefore earlier dismissal for lunch could not be utilized as it had been for period five.)

Each pupil was given a copy of the point system values similar to that shown in Table 1.

The "Earn Points" section was comprised of items suggested by the teacher, principal, and observer as desirable pupil behaviors. Earn Points were assigned so that a pupil could

accumulate about 20 points per class period by engaging in reasonably appropriate behavior such as remaining in his seat and being quiet. (Pupils were given the option of when and for what they would spend the points earned.)

The "Spend Points" section was comprised of activities and privileges which included those suggested by the pupils when they were asked, "What would you like to do if you had one free period?" Other Spend Point items were recommended by the teacher, principal, and the observer as probable reinforcers which could be administered within existing school policy. Spend Points were assigned so that behaviors thought to be highly desired were more costly than less desired ones.

The "Minus Points" section was comprised of undesirable pupil behaviors. Minus Points were assigned values so that the most disruptive behaviors cost the most. Pupils who accumulated 20 or more minus points were

170

## Table 1

### Point System

*Earn Points:*

- 5 in seat
- 5 quiet
- 5 doing assignment
- 2 extra credit (after regular assignment is complete)
- 3 an "A" on an assigned task
- 2 a "B" on an assigned task
- 1 a "C" on an assigned task
- 0 a "D" on an assigned task

*Minus Points:*

- 15 out of seat without permission
- 1 talking out of turn: hand is not raised, teacher hasn't called on you
- 20 out of the room without permission
- 5 incomplete assignment (per period)
- 3 namecalling, swearing
- 20 throwing, hitting
- 20 arguing with the teacher
- 20 teacher must tell you more than once to stop

*Spend Points:*

- 50 five minute pass to the rest room
- 50 permission to go five minutes early to lunch
- 10 permission to get out of your seat for one minute
- 50 permission to move your desk for one period
- 100 permission to move your desk for one day
- 300 permission to move your desk permanently
- 20 pass to get a drink of water
- 10 permission to talk to another person for five minutes
- 50 Friday snack
- 400 field trip
- 20 nonacademic activities approved by the teacher such as knitting, puzzles, games, records.

*To Earn Off Minus Points:*

- 1 stay after school (per minute)
- 1 five earned positive points (earns off one minus point)
- * teacher assigned academic task
- * the teacher determines the task and the point value

required to stay after school for 1 1/2 hours on Thursday afternoon, which was the school-wide detention period. Minus points could also be bought off by Earn Points at a ratio of 5 earned points to one minus point.

The teacher kept account of points during the period on a form at her desk which listed all pupils and had columns for posting point totals earned, spent, or lost. Point totals were posted on the chalkboard at the end of each period and pupils could see how many Earn Points and how many Minus Points each had acquired.

The results of instituting the point system were immediate and dramatic. As can be seen in the Points$_1$ phase of Figure 3, the mean class study rate rose to 83 percent on the first day. Study was maintained at high levels throughout the Points$_1$ phase of the experiment.

This increase in study level was recorded even though three pupils argued that it was childish, stated that they would refuse to cooperate, would quit school, and would complain to the principal and counselor. These remarks were largely ignored and the second day, two of the three showed increased study rates. Over the next 4 days the third objector, Rob, became extremely disruptive. He cursed the teacher, erased the board, tore up assignments, left the room, fought with other pupils, and said he wouldn't work and that no one could make him do it. When he was told to go to his seat or to the office he refused. Under the point system he soon accumulated 512 minus points and 19 positive points. By the fourth day other class members were spending increasing time watching Rob and laughing at his antics. Wolf, Risley, and Mees (1961) had demonstrated that isolation procedures could be used effectively to reduce tantrum behaviors in a preschool child. Since much of Rob's behavior resembled tantrums these procedures were explained to both the teacher and the principal and a modified version of isolation was decided upon. It was agreed that if Rob refused to obey the teacher's direction to be quiet or sit down he would be sent immediately to the office. Unlike other times he had been sent there, he was not to be allowed back into the classroom until he had stated that he would be quiet and stay in his seat.

During the first period of the fifth day Rob refused to obey a teacher direction to be quiet and was sent directly to the principal's office. To reduce the chance that office procedures would reinforce him, the principal had an area screened off so that the student could not see who entered the office or what they were doing. He was not given work to do. He remained there until the end of the school day. The next day when he arrived at school he requested that he be returned to class and stated that he would stay in his seat and be quiet. When he returned to class, his talking and out of seat behaviors decreased and his study behaviors increased. From that point on Rob presented no particular problem and obeyed the teacher. Though he refused to study for a time, he did begin to read a library book, then began to do individual work, and finally began to participate in group discussions. He began accumulating earn points and working off the minus points. He freely spent points, seldom accumulating enough for a field trip. By the end of school, however, he was able to participate in a field trip and an auction which was held to use up surplus earn points.

After 9 days of increased study under the point system a reversal procedure was instituted. The experimenters agreed to allow reinstitution of the point system immediately if class behavior deteriorated to former levels and the teacher seemed to be losing control. It was thought that the effect of reversal might be observable over a 3 or 4 day period.

Reversal conditions were begun during first period of day 20. The pupils were told that the point system was no longer in effect and the teacher discontinued giving attention for appropriate study although she provided verbal reprimands for nonstudy behaviors.

The data for day 20 are shown on a period by period basis in Figure 3 (Reversal). Study dropped to 29 percent in the first period. Second period it was 31 percent and third period it dropped to 16 percent. Because of the extremely chaotic situation and the prior agreement to discontinue reversal if control was lost, the point system was put back into effect during the fourth period. As can be seen in Figure 3 this resulted in a dramatic return to high study rates in the final three class periods of the day.

Period by period observations during the next 5 days showed that the mean study rate was above 80 percent.

Observations taken intermittently beginning 2 weeks later showed that over the next 1 1/2 months of the remainder of the school year, high study rates were being maintained under the point system (see Postchecks, Figures 2 and 3).

The high Postcheck rate (90 percent) was maintained even though the system was changed so that Minus Points were subtracted from earned points on a one to one basis in the interest of simplifying the record keeping system.

The data indicated that in addition to study behavior, inappropriate talking and the number of times pupils were out of their seats were affected by the experimental procedures. During baseline, inappropriate verbalizations were recorded in 84 percent of the observed intervals. Under Points$_1$ conditions inappropriate talking dropped to 10 percent. It rose to 44 percent during Reversal. It dropped to 5 percent when the point system was reinstated and was at 7 percent during the Postcheck period.

Pupils were out of their seats an average of 70 seconds per period during baseline. When the point system was instituted the mean rate was 10 seconds per period. In the brief and chaotic three period Reversal phase the time out of seats rose to mean rate of 215 seconds per period. Out of seats time returned to 10 seconds per period during the Points$_2$ and Postcheck phases. These data indicated that control of these specific inappropriate behaviors as well as increases in study had been achieved.

### Individual Data

Since a record was kept of which student was being observed during each 5 second interval it was possible to compute individual study rates for each experimental condition by dividing the number of study intervals by the total number of intervals that particular individual was observed and multiplying by 100.

An analysis of the data revealed that there was considerable individual variation in study rates and in the effects of the various experimental conditions on individuals. During the fifth period baseline phase, for example, study levels ranged from 11 to 62 percent. Although teacher attention was effective in increasing study for all pupils, it was much more effective for some than for others. For instance, one girl's study level increased from 14 to 64 percent while one boy's study increased only from 12 to 18 percent. Similarly, though the $Timer_1$ condition backed by early dismissal for lunch resulted in further increases in study for all other pupils, it resulted in an actual decrease in study level for one.

Reversal effects varied from pupil to pupil also. During the reversal phase all showed decreased study levels, although study for six students remained at levels substantially higher than baseline rates while almost no study was recorded for the three pupils who had the lowest baseline study rates.

An analysis of the data for the point system also showed variations in study levels. Marked increases in study levels over baseline were achieved for all pupils under the points system. All pupils showed a marked decrease in study during the brief reversal phase when the point system was withdrawn. In the $Points_2$ and Postcheck phases data indicated that even though the three pupils who had the lowest baseline study levels were still studying less than their classmates, all three were above the 70 percent level, higher than the highest study rate recorded for any pupil during baseline.

## Discussion

This study showed that systematic reinforcement procedures using contingencies available in most junior high school classrooms could be used by a beginning teacher to gain control of an extremely disruptive junior high school special education class. Systematic teacher attention increased study levels but was limited in its effect. For most pupils classroom privileges, including such activities as early dismissal to lunch, getting a drink, sharpening a pencil, and talking to another pupil for 5 minutes, were more powerful than teacher attention alone for motivating desired behavior. Reversal procedures demonstrated the functional relationship between the reinforcement contingencies and the increases in appropriate behaviors.

The data also revealed that the effectiveness of a given procedure varied from pupil to pupil. In the case of one pupil it was necessary to institute a time out procedure to gain participation in the point system. Once participation was gained increases in study were dramatic.

In discussing the point system it should be mentioned that there was no rationale for the number of points assigned for particular activities or for the selection of the activities other than a seemingly suitable balance between the behaviors required to earn points and the reinforcing value of the activities and privileges for which they could be spent. Another teacher would doubtless have to adjust the system to fit his particular classroom group and the resources available to him.

Evaluating the point system in terms of value and convenience to the teacher is necessarily subjective but relevant to a discussion of the overall worth of the system. In her evaluation the teacher stated that the system was helpful for it gave both the student and the teacher "a black and white list of what is allowed in the classroom." She also stated that it was easier for her to be fair, since the clearly stated penalties and rewards stopped arguments over the teacher's handling of misconduct. She also reported that pupils did a great deal more classwork and made better grades. At times she had difficulty keeping up with the amount of extra credit work since pupils would choose extra work over any other activities if they were working for a highly prized privilege. She reported further that most pupils indicated they liked the order the system helped provide.

According to the teacher the system could be improved by establishing a simpler system for computing point totals. She felt it was important to post the totals every hour so pupils would have more immediate feedback on their status, but daily instead of hourly computations would reduce the amount of teacher time needed to figure points. She also suggested that the pupils should be more involved in establishing the point system. Such involvement might reduce the initial resistance to the system. She reported that allowing the class to take part in modifying the system when problems arose had helped them accept it.

It is understood by the authors that the procedures used to bring about classroom control in this study are not new or startling. Good teachers have used teacher attention and access to privileges to motivate appropriate pupil behavior for many years. The results reported here are of interest, however, for they demonstrate a means by which a teacher who had not managed to do so was helped to organize the environmental consequences available to her and bring about desired classroom behavior. In essence the point system acted as a convenient means for the teacher and the pupils to link desired study behavior with participation in desired activities.

It is conceded that a point system may not be necessary or appropriate in many junior high school classrooms. It may, however, be a valuable aid to teachers who have difficulty in maintaining classroom control over children with highly deviant and disruptive behaviors.

## References

Birnbrauer, J. S., Wolf, M. M., Kidder, J. D., & Tague, E. Classroom behavior of retarded pupils with token reinforcement. *Journal of Experimental Child Psychology*, 1965, **2**, 219-235.

Broden, M. Notes on recording. Observer's Manual for Juniper Gardens Children's Project, Unpublished manuscript, Bureau of Child Research, 1968.

Hall, R. V., & Broden, M. Behavior changes in brain-injured children through social reinforcement. *Journal of Experimental Child Psychology*, 1967, **5**, 463-479.

Hall, R. V., Lund, D., & Jackson, D. Effects of teacher attention on study behavior. *Journal of Applied Behavior Analysis*, 1968, **1**, 1-12.

Hall, R. V., Panyan, M., Rabon, D., & Broden, M. Instructing beginning teachers in reinforcement procedures which improve classroom control. *Journal of Applied Behavior Analysis*, 1968, **1**, 315-322.

Harris, F. R., Wolf, M. M., & Baer, D. M. Effects of adult social reinforcement on child behavior. *Young Children*, 1964, **20**, 8-17.

McKenzie, H., Clark, M., Wolf, M., Kothera, R., & Benson, C. Behavior modification of children with learning disabilities using grades as token reinforcers. *Exceptional Children*, 1968, **34**, 745-752.

O'Leary, K. D., & Becker, W. C. Behavior modification of an adjustment class: token reinforcement system. *Exceptional Children*, 1967, **33**, 637-642.

Thomas, D. R., Becker, W. C., & Armstrong, M. Production and elimination of disruptive classroom behavior by systematically varying teacher's behavior. *Journal of Applied Behavior Analysis*, 1968, **1**, 35-45.

Wolf, M. M., Giles, D. K., & Hall, R. V. Experiments with token reinforcement in a remedial classroom. *Behaviour Research and Therapy*, 1968, **6**, 51-64.

Wolf, M. M., Risley, T. R., & Mees, H. L. Application of operant conditioning procedures to the behavior problems of an autistic child. *Behaviour Research and Therapy*, 1964, **1**, 305-312.

Zimmerman, E. H., & Zimmerman, J. The alteration of behavior in a special classroom situation. *Journal of the Experimental Analysis of Behavior*, 1962, **5**, 59-60.

K. DANIEL O'LEARY
KENNETH F. KAUFMAN
RUTH E. KASS
RONALD S. DRABMAN

# The Effects of Loud and Soft Reprimands on the Behavior of Disruptive Students

$A$ NUMBER of studies demonstrate that teacher attention in the form of praise can reduce disruptive classroom behavior (Becker, Madsen, Arnold, & Thomas, 1967; Hall, Lund, & Jackson, 1968; Madsen, Becker, & Thomas, 1968; Walker & Buckley, 1968). In these studies, praising appropriate behavior was usually concomitant with ignoring disruptive behavior. In addition, shaping appropriate behavior or reinforcing successive approximations to

some desired terminal behavior was stressed. Despite the generally positive results obtained when a teacher used these procedures, a closer examination of the studies reveals that (a) they were not always effective (Hall et al., 1968), (b) the teacher did not actually ignore all disruptive behavior (Madsen et al., 1968), and (c) in one class of disruptive children, praising appropriate behavior and igoring disruptive behavior resulted in classroom pandemonium (O'Leary, Becker, Evans, & Saudargas, 1969).

One might argue that where praising appropriate behavior and ignoring disruptive behavior prove ineffectual, the teacher is not appropriately shaping the children's behavior. Although such an argument is theoretically rational, it is of little solace to a teacher who unsuccessfully attempts to reinforce approximations to desired terminal behaviors. Furthermore, the supposition that the teacher is not appropriately shaping ignores the power of peers to rein-

K. DANIEL O'LEARY *is Associate Professor of Psychology, State University of New York, Stony Brook, and* KENNETH F. KAUFMAN, RUTH E. KASS, *and* RONALD S. DRABMAN *are Graduate Students in Psychology, State University of New York, Stony Brook.*
*The research reported herein was performed in part pursuant to Biomedical Sciences Support Grant No. 31-8200-C, US Public Health Service, 1967-69.*

EXCEPTIONAL CHILDREN, October 1970, pp. 145-155.

175

force disruptive behavior. Disregard of disruptive behavior is based on two premises —that it will extinguish if it is not reinforced and that praising appropriate behavior which is incompatible with disruptive behavior will reduce the frequency of the latter. However, even when a teacher ignores disruptive behavior, other children may reinforce it by giggling and smiling. These peer reactions may occur only occasionally, but they may make the disruptive behavior highly resistant to extinction. Thus, the teacher may ask what she can do when praise and ignoring are not effective. The present studies were designed to assess one alternative to ignoring disruptive behavior: reprimanding the child in a soft manner so that other children in the classroom could not hear the reprimand.

The effectiveness of punishment in suppressing behavior of animals has been amply documented (Solomon, 1964). Similarly, the effectiveness of punishment with children in experimental settings has been repeatedly demonstrated (Parke & Walters, 1967). However, experimental manipulations of punishment or reprimands with disruptive children have not often been investigated in applied settings. One attempt to manipulate teacher reprimands was made by O'Leary and Becker (1968) who varied aspects of teacher attention and found that soft reprimands were effective in reducing disruptive behavior of a class of first-grade children during a rest period. Since soft reprimands seemed to have no adverse side effects in the study and since ignoring disruptive behavior is not always effective, further analyses of the effects of soft reprimands seemed promising.

Soft reprimands offer several interesting advantages over loud ones. First of all, a soft reprimand does not single out the child so that his disruptive behavior is made noticeable to others. Second, a soft reprimand is presumably different from the reprimands that disruptive children ordinarily receive at home or in school, and, consequently, it should minimize the possibility of triggering conditioned emotional reactions to reprimands. Third, teachers consider soft reprimands a viable alternative to the usual methods of dealing with disruptive behavior. Two experiments are presented here which assessed the effects of soft reprimands.

### Experiment I

Two children in a second-grade class were selected for observation because of their high rates of disruptive behavior. During a baseline condition, the frequency of disruptive behaviors and teacher reprimands was assessed. Almost all reprimands were loud, i.e., many children in the class could hear them. During the second phase of the study, the teacher was asked to voice her reprimands so that they would be audible only to the child to whom they were directed. The third phase of the study constituted a return to the teacher's former loud reprimand. Finally, during the fourth condition, the teacher was requested to again use soft reprimands.

*Subjects.* Child D was described as nervous and restless. He bit his nails, drummed his fingers on his desk, and stuttered. He was often out of his seat talking and bothering other children. D avoided any challenging work. He was quick to argue and was known to get into trouble in the neighborhood.

Child S was described as uncooperative and silly. He paid little attention to his work, and he would often giggle and say things out loud. His teacher said that he enjoyed having other children laugh at him and that he acted in this manner to gain attention.

*Observation.* Before base period data were collected, college undergraduates were trained over a 3-week period to observe in the classroom. During this time, the observers obtained reliabilities of child observations exceeding 70 percent agreement. There were two undergraduate observers. One observed daily, and the other observed less frequently, serving as a reliability checker. The observers were instructed to neither talk nor make any differential responses in order to minimize their effect on the children's behavior.

Each child was observed for 20 minutes

a day during the arithmetic lesson. Observations were made on a 20-second observe, 10-second record basis: The observer would watch the child for 20 seconds and then record in 10 seconds the disruptive behaviors which had occurred during that 20-second period. The disruptive behaviors were categorized according to nine classes modified from the O'Leary and Becker study (1967). The nine classes of disruptive behavior and their associated general definitions are:

1. *Out-of-chair:* Movement of the child from his chair when not permitted or requested by teacher. No part of the child's body is to be touching the chair.

2. *Modified out-of-chair:* Movement of the child from his chair with some part of the body still touching the chair (exclude sitting on feet).

3. *Touching others' property:* Child comes into contact with another's property without permission to do so. Includes grabbing, rearranging, destroying the property of another, and touching the desk of another.

4. *Vocalization:* Any unpermitted audible behavior emanating from the mouth.

5. *Playing:* Child uses his hands to play with his own or community property so that such behavior is incompatible with learning.

6. *Orienting:* The turning or orienting response is not rated unless the child is seated and the turn must be more than 90 degrees, using the desk as a reference point.

7. *Noise:* Child creating any audible noise other than vocalization without permission.

8. *Aggression:* Child makes movement toward another person to come into contact with him (exclude brushing against another).

9. *Time off task:* Child does not do assigned work for entire 20-second interval. For example, child does not write or read when so assigned.

The dependent measure, mean frequency of disruptive behavior, was calculated by dividing the total number of disruptive behaviors by the number of intervals observed. A mean frequency measure was obtained rather than frequency of disruptive behavior per day since the length of observations varied due to unavoidable circumstances such as assemblies. Nonetheless, only three of the 27 observations for child D lasted less than 20 minutes and only four of the 28 observations for child S were less than 20 minutes. Observations of less than 10 minutes were not included.

*Reliability.* The reliabilities of child observations were calculated according to the following procedure. A perfect agreement was scored if both observers recorded the same disruptive behavior within a 20-second interval. The reliabilities were then calculated by dividing the number of perfect agreements by the number of different disruptive behaviors observed providing a measure of percent agreement. There were three reliability checks during the base period (Loud I) and one during the first soft period for child D. There were two reliability checks during the base period and one reliability check during the first soft period for child S. The four reliability checks for child D yielded the following results: 81, 72, 64, and 92 percent agreement; the three for child S resulted in: 88, 93, and 84 percent agreement.

The reliability of the observations of the teacher's loud and soft reprimands to the target children was also checked. On two different days these observations were taken simultaneously with the observation of the target children. One reliability check was made during the base period and one check was made during the first soft period. A perfect agreement was scored if both observers agreed that the reprimand was loud or soft and if both observers scored the reprimand in the same 20-second interval. The consequent reliabilities were 100 percent and 75 percent during the base period and first soft period respectively.

## Procedures

**Base Period (Loud I).** During the base period the teacher was asked to handle the children as she normally would. Since few, if any, soft reprimands occurred during the base period, this period was considered a loud reprimand phase.

**Soft Reprimands I.** During this phase the following instructions were given to the teacher:

1. Make reprimands soft all day, i.e., speak so that only the child being reprimanded can hear you.

2. Approximately one-half hour before the observers come into your room, concentrate on using soft reprimands so that the observers' entrance does not signal a change in teacher behavior.

3. While the observers are in the room, use only soft reprimands with the target children.

4. Do not increase the frequency of reprimands. Reprimand as frequently as you have always done and vary only the intensity.

5. Use soft reprimands with all the children, not just the target children.

**Loud Reprimands II.** During this phase the teacher was asked to return to loud reprimands, and the five instructions above for the soft period were repeated with a substitution of loud reprimands for soft ones.

**Soft Reprimands II.** During this final period, the teacher was asked to return to the soft reprimand procedures.

## Results

**Child D.** Child D displayed a marked reaction to soft reprimands. The mean frequency of disruptive behavior during the four conditions was: Loud I, 1.1; Soft I, 0.8; Loud II, 1.3; Soft II, 0.9. A reversal of effects was evident. When the loud reprimands were reinstated disruptive behavior increased while disruptive behavior declined during the second soft period (Figure 1). In addition, in order to more closely examine the effects of the two types of reprimands, there was an assessment of the frequency of disruptive behaviors in the two 20-second intervals after a reprimand, when another reprimand had not occurred in one of the two intervals. The results revealed that the average number of disruptive behaviors in these two intervals during the four conditions was: Loud I, 2.8; Soft I, 1.2; Loud II, 2.6; and Soft II, 1.6.

**Child S.** Child S also displayed a marked reaction to soft reprimands. The mean frequency of his disruptive behavior during the four conditions was: Loud I, 1.4; Soft I, 0.6; Loud II, 1.1; Soft II, 0.5. Again a reversal of effects was evident when the loud reprimands were reinstated. The average number of disruptive behaviors in the two 20-second intervals just after a reprimand was made was as follows during the four conditions: Loud I, 2.9; Soft I, 1.5; Loud II, 2.1; Soft II, 0.9.

**Teacher.** Although teacher A was asked to hold constant the incidence of her reprimands across conditions, the mean frequency of her reprimands to child D during the four conditions was: Loud I, 7; Soft I, 5; Loud II, 12; Soft II, 6. Similarly, she also had difficulty in holding constant her reprimands to child S across conditions as the following data show: Loud I, 6; Soft I, 4; Loud II, 8; Soft II, 3. Thus, there is some possibility that the increase in disruptive behavior during the second loud phase was a consequence of increased attention to the behavior per se, rather than a consequence of the kind of attention given, whether loud or soft. As the disruptive behavior increased, teacher A felt it impossible to use the same number of reprimands that she had used during the soft period.

Because the frequency of loud reprimands was greater than the frequency of soft reprimands, one could not conclude from Experiment I that the loudness or softness of the reprimands was the key factor in reducing disruptive behavior. It was clear, however, that if a teacher used

178

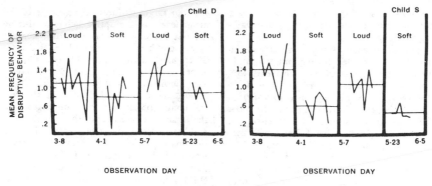

FIGURE 1. Disruptive behavior of children D and S in Class A.

soft reprimands, she could use fewer reprimands and obtain better behavior than if she used loud reprimands.

### Experiment II

Experiment II was conducted to assess the effects of loud and soft reprimands with the frequency held constant and to test whether all the children's disruptive behavior decreased when the teacher used soft reprimands. Experiment II is divided into three parts. Part I followed the same ABAB paradigm described in Experiment I (Loud, Soft, Loud, Soft), but Parts II and III involved variations which will be described later.

#### Part I

*Subjects.* Class B, Grade 2: Child Z was a large boy who said that he wanted to be a bully when he grew up. He was the only child in the class who deliberately hurt other children. He constantly called out answers without raising his hand and his work habits were poor. Child V was extremely talkative. He loved to be with other children and he was always bursting with something to say. He was also mischievous, but never intentionally hurt anyone. His work habits were poor and his papers were never completed.

Class C, Grade 3: Child E was an extremely nervous child. When she

directed all her energy to her studies she could perform well. However, she was very undependable and rarely did her work. She was in and out of her seat and talked endlessly. Child W was a disruptive child whose reaction to most situations was to punch, kick, throw things, and to shove others out of his way. He did little work and devoted his time to such activities as chewing his pencils and punching holes in his papers.

*Observation.* The observational procedures described earlier in Experiment I were identical to those used in Experiment II. Each target child was observed during a structured academic lesson for 20 minutes each day on a 20-second observe, 10-second record basis. The nine classes of disruptive behavior were the same as those in Experiment I with some definitial extensions and a slight change in the definition of aggression. The dependent measure was calculated in the same manner as described in Experiment I.

To minimize the possibility of distance as the key factor in reprimanding the children, the target children in both classes were moved near the front of the room so that the teacher could administer soft reprimands without walking a great distance. This seating arrangement made it easier for the teacher to reprimand the target children either loudly or softly and decreased

179

the possibility of the teacher's serving as a cue for appropriate behavior by her walking to the child.

The occurrence of loud and soft reprimands was recorded throughout the study by a teacher-observer. As mentioned previously, the teachers were asked to hold the frequency of reprimands constant both to the target children and to the class throughout the study. The teacher was also asked to hold other behaviors as constant as possible so that behaviors such as praise, "eyeing down" a child, and reprimands to the class as a whole would not confound the results. A graduate student observed almost daily and gave the teachers feedback to ensure adherence to these requirements.

In addition to observations on target children, daily observations of disruptive behavior were taken on all the other children by a sampling procedure for one hour each day. Each nontarget child was observed consecutively for 2 minutes. The observer watched the children in a predetermined order each day, looking for the disruptive behaviors that had been observed in the target children.

*Reliability.* The reliabilities of child observations for both the target children and the class samples were calculated according to the procedures discussed in Experiment I. There were three reliability checks during the base period for both target children and the class sample. The average reliability for the target children was 84 percent and for the class sample was 79 percent. Nine additional reliability checks of the observations averaged 79 percent for the target children and 82 percent for the class sample.

The reliability of the observations during the base period of loud and soft reprimands used by Teacher B was 79 percent and 80 percent respectively. The reliability of the observation of loud and soft reprimands used by Teacher C was 82 percent and 72 percent respectively.

*Results.* Because there were definite decreasing trends of disruptive behavior during both soft conditions for three of

the four target children, the average of the mean levels of disruptive behavior during the last five days of each condition for the target children are reported in Table 1. There were changes in children's behavior associated with changes in teacher behavior (see Figure 2). There was a decrease in the children's disruptive behavior in the soft reprimand phase and then an increase in the disruptive behavior of three of the four children during the reinstatement of loud reprimands. Finally, the second soft period was marked by a decrease in disruptive behavior. Although the disruptive behavior of child V did not increase during the reinstitution of loud reprimands, a reduction of disruptive behavior was associated with each introduction of soft reprimands—particularly during the second soft phase. Consequently, soft reprimands seemed to influence the reduction of disruptive behavior of each of the four children. A mean reduction of 0.4 and 0.7 disruptive behaviors was associated with each introduction of soft reprimands for these children.

In order to demonstrate that the reduction of disruptive behavior was not a function of changes in frequency of reprimands, the frequencies of loud and soft reprimands are provided in Table 2. Although there was some slight reduction of reprimands for individual children during the soft reprimand phases, the teachers were able to hold the frequency of reprimands relatively constant across days and conditions, despite an obvious change in the children's behavior. The mean total reprimands, loud and soft, during the four conditions were as follows: Loud I, 5.7; Soft I, 4.6; Loud II, 5.3; Soft II, 3.7. Also

#### TABLE 1

**The Average of the Mean Levels of Disruptive Behavior During the Last Five Days of Each Condition for the Target Children**

| Subjects | Condition | | | |
|---|---|---|---|---|
| | *Loud I* ($\bar{X} = 1.3$) | *Soft I* ($\bar{X} = 0.9$) | *Loud II* ($\bar{X} = 1.2$) | *Soft II* ($\bar{X} = 0.5$) |
| Child Z | 1.0 | 0.9 | 1.3 | 0.8 |
| Child V | 1.7 | 1.4 | 1.3 | 0.6 |
| Child E | 0.9 | 0.6 | 1.1 | 0.4 |
| Child W | 1.6 | 0.8 | 0.9 | 0.3 |

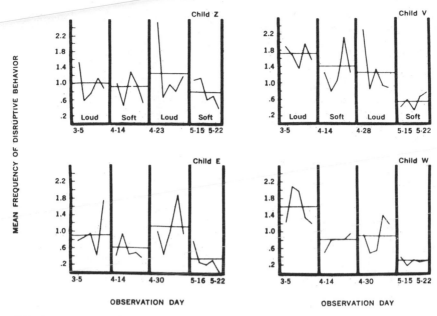

FIGURE 2. Disruptive behavior of children Z and V in Class B and children E and W in Class C.

of particular significance was the constancy of praise comments across conditions. There was an average of less than one

TABLE 2

Average Frequency of Loud and Soft
Reprimands Per Day

| Condition | Type of Reprimand to Child Z | | Condition | Type of Reprimand to Child V | |
|---|---|---|---|---|---|
| | Loud | Soft | | Loud | Soft |
| Loud I | 3.8 | 2.0 | Loud | 6.8 | 2.2 |
| Soft I | 0.6 | 2.6 | Soft | 0.5 | 6.7 |
| Loud II | 3.0 | 1.7 | Loud | 3.5 | 1.0 |
| Soft II | 0.1 | 2.6 | Soft | 0.1 | 3.6 |

| Condition | Reprimand to Child E | | Condition | Reprimand to Child W | |
|---|---|---|---|---|---|
| | Loud | Soft | | Loud | Soft |
| Loud I | 3.5 | 0.6 | Loud | 3.3 | 0.7 |
| Soft I | 0.4 | 5.0 | Soft | 0.4 | 2.3 |
| Loud II | 5.7 | 0.9 | Loud | 5.3 | 0.3 |
| Soft II | 0.2 | 3.4 | Soft | 0.1 | 4.6 |

praise comment per day given to each child in each of the four conditions. It can be inferred from these data that soft reprimands can be influential in modifying classroom behavior of particularly disruptive children.

The data from the class samples taken during the last five days of each condition did not show that soft reprimands reduced disruptive behavior for the whole class. Because of the variability within conditions and the lack of any clear relationship between type of reprimands and level of disruptive behavior, those data are not presented here. However, the changes in the behavior of the target children are evident when one considers that the mean frequency of disruptive behavior for the class sample B was .9 throughout the experiment and .8 during the second soft condition. The mean frequency of disruptive behavior for the class sample C was .6 throughout the experiment and .5 during the second soft condition. Thus one should note that the disruptive behavior of the four target children during the second soft period was less than the level of disruptive behavior for the class.

## Part II

Two target children and a class sample were observed in the class of a third-grade teacher. A baseline (Loud I) of disruptive behavior was obtained in this class during a structured academic lesson using the procedures described in Experiment I. In the second phase of the study (Soft I) the teacher was asked to use soft reprimands, just as the other teachers had done. Because of the infrequency of her reprimands in the second phase, the teacher was asked to double her use of soft reprimands in phase three (Soft II-Double). During phase four (Loud II), she was asked to maintain her more frequent use of reprimands but to make them loud. Both child and teacher observations were made in accord with the procedures described in Part I of Experiment II.

*Subjects.* Child B was reported to be a happy extrovert who was a compulsive talker. Child R was described by his teacher as a clown with a very short attention span.

*Reliability.* The reliability of child observations was obtained for the target children on seven occasions, and the reliability of the class sample on five occasions. The resultant average reliabilities were 87 percent and 87 percent, respectively.

The reliability of the observations of teacher behavior was checked on two occasions during the base period and once during the first soft period. The average reliability of the observations of loud and soft reprimands was 82 percent and 72 percent, respectively.

*Results.* Child B's disruptive behavior declined from 1.6 during the last five days of baseline (loud reprimands) to 1.3 during the last five days of soft reprimands. In contrast, child R's disruptive behavior increased from 1.5 in the last five days of baseline to 1.9 during the last five days of soft reprimands (see Figure 3). With the instructions to increase the use of soft reprimands during phase three (Soft II-Double), child B's disruptive behavior showed a slight drop to 1.1 while child R's increased slightly to 2.0. The return to loud reprimands was associated with an increase to 1.8 for child B and almost no change for child R.

The increase in child R's disruptive behavior from the loud to the first soft condition cannot be attributed to the soft reprimands. In fact, the change appeared to be due to a decrease in both loud and soft reprimands. Even with the instructions

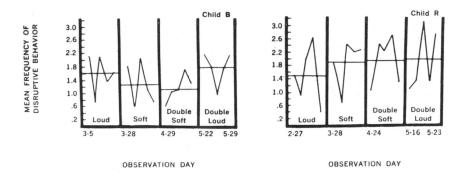

FIGURE 3. Disruptive behavior of children B and R in Class D.

to double the use of soft reprimands, the teacher observations reported in Table 3 indicate that the frequency of total reprimands during the double soft phase was less than during baseline. However, since child R's disruptive behavior did not increase with the return to loud reprimands, the experimental control over R's behavior was minimal or nonexistent. On the other hand, child B's disruptive behavior appeared to lessen with the use of soft reprimands.

## TABLE 3

### Average Frequency of Loud and Soft Reprimands Per Day

| Condition | Type of Reprimand to Child B | | Condition | Type of Reprimand to Child R | |
|---|---|---|---|---|---|
| | Loud | Soft | | Loud | Soft |
| Loud I | 2.0 | 0.4 | Loud | 1.5 | 0.2 |
| Soft I | 0.5 | 1.0 | Soft | 0.2 | 0.0 |
| Soft II | | | Double | | |
| (Double) | 1.8 | 1.1 | soft | 0.0 | 0.8 |
| Loud II | 3.1 | 2.3 | Loud | 2.5 | 0.0 |

| Condition | Reprimand to Child D | | Condition | Reprimand to Child J | |
|---|---|---|---|---|---|
| | Loud | Soft | | Loud | Soft |
| Loud | 4.5 | 1.3 | Loud | 1.3 | 0.2 |
| Soft | 0.2 | 3.2 | Soft | 0.0 | 2.2 |

Again, the data from the class sample did not show that soft reprimands reduced disruptive behavior for the whole class. Those data will not be presented here in detail. The mean frequency of disruptive behavior for the class sample throughout the experiment was .62.

*Discussion.* The failure to decrease child R's disruptive behavior by soft reprimands may have been due to his very deficient academic repertoire. He was so far behind his classmates that group instruction was almost meaningless for him. It is also possible that the teacher felt frustrated because of increases in child R's disruptive behavior when she used soft reprimands; teacher D found them particularly difficult to use. She stated, "It was difficult for me to give soft reprimands as I feared they were a sign of weakness. The walking and whispering necessary to administer soft reprimands to the disruptive child were especially strenuous for me. As the day wore on, I found that my patience became exhausted and my natural tendency to shout like a general took over." Also of particular note was an observer's comment that when verbal reprimands were administered, whether in a loud or soft phase, they were rarely if ever soft in intensity. In summary, teacher D's data showed that soft reprimands did reduce disruptive behavior in one child. Because of lack of evidence for any consistent use of soft reprimands to the second child, nothing can be said conclusively about its use with him.

## Part III

In a third-grade class of a fourth teacher, two target children and a class sample were observed during a structured academic activity. A baseline of disruptive behavior was obtained in the class with procedures identical to those of Experiment I. In the second phase of the study, the teacher was asked to use soft reprimands, just as the other teachers had done. Because of some unexpected results following this second phase, the general nature of the study was then changed and those results will not be presented here. Both child and teacher observations were made according to the procedures described in Part I of Experiment II.

*Subjects.* Child D was a very intelligent boy (135 IQ) who scored in the seventh-grade range on the reading part of the Metropolitan Achievement Test but he was only slightly above grade level in mathematics. His relations with his peers were very antagonistic.

Child J was occasionally considered disruptive by his teacher. However, he did not perform assigned tasks and would often pretend to be working while he actually was not.

*Reliability.* The reliability of child observations was obtained for the target children on 15 occasions, and the reliability of the class sample was obtained on

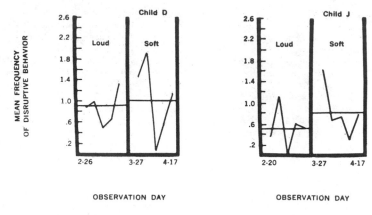

FIGURE 4. Disruptive behavior of children D and J in Class E.

three occasions. The resultant average reliabilities were 88 percent for the observations of the target children and 91 percent for the observations of the class sample.

The reliability of the observations of teacher behavior was checked on two occasions during the base period and once during the soft period. The average reliability of the observations of loud and soft reprimands on these three occasions was 78 percent and 79 percent respectively.

*Results.* Child D's disruptive behavior increased from .9 during the last five days of baseline (loud reprimands) to 1.0 during the last five days of soft reprimands. Child J's disruptive behavior increased from .4 to .8 from baseline to the soft reprimand period (see Figure 4). There was no change in the class sample from baseline to the soft reprimand period. The mean frequency of disruptive behavior for the class sample during the loud and soft phase was .6 and .5 respectively.

As can be seen in Table 3, teacher E's behavior with child D and child J did appear to have been influenced by the experimental instructions.

*Discussion.* The reasons that soft reprimands failed to decrease disruptive behavior in this class are not clear. Several factors may have been important. First of all, teacher E was always very skeptical about the possibility that soft reprimands could influence disruptive behavior whereas the other teachers were willing to acknowledge the probability of their influence. Second, it is possible that the children learned to control the teacher's behavior since a soft reprimand had to be made while the teacher was close to the child. That is, a child might realize that he could draw the teacher to his side each time he misbehaved during the soft reprimand period. In addition, this teacher tolerated more disruptive behavior than the other teachers, and her class was much less structured. Probably most important, she wished to investigate the effectiveness of various types of instructional programs rather than soft reprimands.

### Conclusions

These two experiments demonstrated that when teachers used soft reprimands, they were effective in modifying behavior in seven of nine disruptive children. Because of a failure to document the proper use of soft reprimands by one teacher (D) to one child, it is impossible to assess the effectiveness on that child. Of particular significance was the finding that soft reprimands seemed to be associated with an increase in disruptive behavior of one—and possibly two—target children in one teacher's class although the soft reprimands did not influence the level of disruptive behavior for the class as a whole. The results of Experiments I and II lead to the conclusion that with particularly disruptive children a teacher can generally use fewer soft reprimands than loud ones and obtain less disruptive behavior than when loud reprimands are used.

The authors wish to make clear that they do not recommend soft reprimands as an alternative to praise. An ideal combination would probably be frequent praise, some soft reprimands, and very occasional loud reprimands. Furthermore, it is always necessary to realize that classroom management procedures such as praise and types of reprimanding are no substitute for a good academic program. In the class where soft reprimands were ineffective for both target children, a type of individualized instruction was later introduced, and the disruptive behavior of both the target children and the class sample declined.

Because soft reprimands are delivered by a teacher when she is close to a child it is possible that a soft reprimand differs from a loud one in other dimensions than audibility to many children. Although observations of teachers in this study did not reveal that teachers made their soft reprimands in a less harsh, firm, or intense manner than their loud reprimands, it might be possible for a teacher to utilize soft reprimands in such a manner. If the latter were true, soft reprimands might require less teacher effort than loud reprimands. Ultimately soft reprimands might prove more reinforcing for the teacher both because of the relatively small expenditure of effort and the generally positive and sometimes dramatic changes in the children's behavior. The inherent nature of the soft reprimand makes its use impossible at all times, particularly when a teacher has to remain at the blackboard or with a small group in one part of the room. As one teacher mentioned, "I had to do more moving around, but there appeared to be less restlessness in the class."

In sum, it is the authors' opinion that soft reprimands can be a useful method of dealing with disruptive children in a classroom. Combined with praise, soft reprimands might be very helpful in reducing disruptive behavior. In contrast, it appears that loud reprimands lead one into a vicious cycle of more and more reprimands resulting in even more disruptive behavior.

### References

Becker, W. C., Madsen, C. H., Jr., Arnold, C., & Thomas, D. R. The contingent use of teacher attention and praise in reducing classroom behavior problems. *Journal of Special Education*, 1967, 1, 287-307.

Hall, R. V., Lund, D., & Jackson, D. Effects of teacher attention on study behavior. *Journal of Applied Behavior Analysis*, 1968, 1, 1-12.

Madsen, C. H., Becker, W. C., & Thomas, D. R. Rules, praise, and ignoring: Elements of elementary classroom control. *Journal of Applied Behavior Analysis*, 1968, 1, 139-150.

O'Leary, K. D., & Becker, W. C. Behavior modification of an adjustment class: A token reinforcement program. *Exceptional Children*, 1967, 33, 637-642.

O'Leary, K. D., & Becker, W. C. The effects of a teacher's reprimands on children's behavior. *Journal of School Psychology*, 1968, 7, 8-11.

O'Leary, K. D., Becker, W. C., Evans, M. B., & Saudargas, R. A. A token reinforcement program in a public school: A replication and systematic analysis. *Journal of Applied Behavior Analysis*, 1969, 2, 3-13.

Parke, R. D., & Walters, R. H. Some factors influencing the efficacy of punishment training for inducing response inhibition. *Monographs of the Society for Research in Child Development*, 1967, 32, (1, Serial No. 109).

Solomon, R. L. Punishment. *American Psychologist*, 1964, 19, 239-253.

Walker, H. M., & Buckley, N. K. The use of positive reinforcement in conditioning attending behavior. *Journal of Applied Behavior Analysis*, 1968, 1, 245-250.

## PRODUCTION AND ELIMINATION OF DISRUPTIVE CLASSROOM BEHAVIOR BY SYSTEMATICALLY VARYING TEACHER'S BEHAVIOR[1]

DON R. THOMAS, WESLEY C. BECKER, AND MARIANNE ARMSTRONG

Teachers are sometimes unaware of the effects of their actions on the behavior of their students. Many teachers assume that if a child performs disruptive acts in the classroom then the child must have a problem at home, or at the very least, must not have reached a stage of sufficient maturity to function adequately in the school situation. However, an increasing body of evidence indicates that many of the behaviors which teachers find disruptive are actually within their control. A teacher can modify and control the behavior of her students by controlling her own responses.

Contingent use of social reinforcement has been shown to control such motor behaviors as walking, standing, and running (Bijou and Baer, 1963), talking and crying (Kerr, Meyerson, and Michael, 1965; Hart, Allen, Buell, Harris, and Wolf, 1964), and classroom conduct (Becker, Madsen, Arnold, and Thomas, 1967; Zimmerman and Zimmerman, 1962).

Becker *et al.* (1967) worked in public schools with teachers who had problem children in their classes. Behaviors exhibited by the students were observed and the frequency of these behaviors was estimated for each child. Each teacher was taught to use praise, smiles, *etc.* to reinforce good behavior. The rate of appropriate classroom behaviors increased in most cases as soon as teacher approval and recognition were made contingent on such behavior.

The present study evolved from prior research showing the importance of social reinforcement, and Becker's work, which suggests that specific procedures, or definable classes of teacher behaviors can be used by the teacher to increase appropriate classroom behaviors. In order to provide more convincing data on the role of different teacher behaviors, the present study was designed to produce and remove problem behavior in students by systematically varying teacher behaviors in an initially well-behaved class.

### METHOD

#### Subjects

*Students.* A class of 28 elementary students at the middle-primary level was selected. According to the teacher her class was "a good class, with an above-average distribution of ability and no 'bad' kids." Most of the children were from upper-middle- and middle-

[1]The authors wish to thank Urbana School District #116 and the principal of Thomas Paine School, Mr. Richard Sturgeon, for their cooperation. The observers (Loretta Nielson, Barbara Goldberg, Marilyn Goldberg, and Darlene Zientarski) deserve thanks for their conscientious work. This research was supported, in part, by National Institute of Child Health and Human Development Grant HD-00881-05.

JOURNAL OF APPLIED BEHAVIOR ANALYSIS, 1968, Vol. 1, pp. 35-45.

186

income-range families. Ages at the beginning of the study ranged from 6 yr, 11 months to 7 yr, 11 months; I.Q. range (group test) was from 99 to 134.

*Teacher.* The teacher, age 23, obtained her student teaching experience with a class of "maladjusted" children. In addition, she had 1-yr experience with a class of "slow learners". Preliminary observations indicated that she rarely attended in an approving manner to children who behaved inappropriately, and rarely reprimanded children who were performing their assigned tasks. She volunteered to participate in the study because of its potential contribution to teacher training in the future.

*Observation Procedures*

The basic data for the study consisted of the relative frequency of occurrence of classes of child behaviors in relation to classes of teacher behaviors utilizing rating schedules to be described. One to three observers were placed in the classroom each morning from approximately 9:15 to 10:00 a.m. while the students were completing reading and reading workbook assignments. To insure obtaining a daily sample of both child and teacher behaviors during this 45-min work period, a 20-min observation time was decided on for both child and teacher observations. Thus, even if only one observer was present, the relevant information could be obtained. This time restriction limited the number of children who could be observed each day. Ten children were selected for observation each morning by drawing numbers from a hat. During Baseline₁ and the first No Praise condition a no-replacement procedure was used so that all children had to be observed before a child's number could be drawn a second time. At the start of Baseline₂ this restriction was removed. Through the use of a numbered seating chart, the observers recorded the behaviors of selected children in the order in which they were chosen. Five extra numbers were drawn each day to provide observation targets in case one or more of the first 10 subjects drawn were not available for observation. Target children were observed for 2 min each. Each minute was divided into six 10-sec intervals. Observers were trained to record classes of behavior which occurred in a given interval. Recordings were made during the first five intervals of each minute. During the sixth 10-sec interval the observers made notes, checked for synchronization, and/or prepared to switch to a new child. Thus, the daily child observation sample consisted of ten 10-sec observation intervals on each of 10 children.

Teacher behaviors were recorded on a similar schedule, the only difference being that for teacher behaviors each occurrence of a response in a specified class was recorded (frequency measure), whereas for child behaviors a given class of behavior could be rated only once in a 10-sec interval. This difference in procedure was necessitated by the greater difficulty in separating child behaviors into discrete response units. Observers used a clipboard, stopwatch, and a recording sheet which had spaces for 100 observation intervals, guides for computing reliability, and a place for comments.

Undergraduate university students were hired and trained to collect the data. Each observer memorized the definitions of classes of child and teacher behaviors. Pre-baseline training in recording of behavior was carried out in the experimental classroom to allow the children to become accustomed to the presence of the observers. The children were already well adapted to the classroom before observer training was started. Observers were instructed to avoid all interactions with the students and teacher while in the class or on the school grounds. At the scheduled time they would enter the class, walk directly to chairs provided for them, sit down, and begin the observations. A hand signal was used to insure synchronization of observation times. Initially two observers were scheduled to observe on Monday, Wednesday, and Friday, and two on Tuesday and Thursday. When a systematic difference developed between the two sets of observers, one of the Tuesday-Thursday observers was placed on a three-day-a-week schedule to tie the two sets of observations together with reliability checks. Thus, on some days there were as many as three observers in the classroom. The number of observers in the classroom varied from one to three. Due to illness or the need to obtain observations in other classroom, there were times when only one observer was available. Observers were not informed of changes in experimental conditions.

The behaviors emitted by the teacher were defined as belonging to three general classes: (1) Disapproving Behavior, (2) Approving Behavior, and (3) Instructional Behavior. Disapproving and Approving Behaviors were rated only when they immediately followed discriminable child behaviors falling into inappropriate or appropriate classes (see below).[2] Listings were made of the teacher behaviors that could occur within each class.

The general class of Disapproving Behaviors included Physical Contact, Verbal, and Facial subclasses. The subclasses of Physical behaviors included forcibly holding a child, grabbing, hitting, spanking, shaking, slapping, or pushing a child into position. The Verbal subclass of Disapproving Behaviors included yelling, scolding, raising voice, belittling, or making fun of the child, and threats. Threats included "if-then" statements of loss of privilege or punishment at some future time. For example, the teacher might say to the class, "If you don't remain quiet, you will have to stay in from recess." The Facial subclass of Disapproving Behaviors included frowning, grimacing, side-to-side head shaking, gesturing, *etc.*

The general class of Approving Behaviors also included Physical Contact, Verbal, and Facial subclasses. Approving Physical Contacts included embracing, kissing, patting, holding hand or arm of child, or holding the child in the teacher's lap. Approving Verbal comments included statements of affection, approval, or praise. Approving Facial response was rated whenever the teacher smiled, winked, or nodded at one or more of the children.

The general class of Instructional Behavior included any response from teacher to children which involved giving instructions, information, or indicating correct responses.

In addition to recording the above classes of teacher behavior, note was taken of those times when the teacher terminated social interaction by turning out lights and saying nothing, turning her back on the class and waiting for silence, or stopping talking and waiting for quiet.

As noted earlier, the observers recorded every teacher response falling in a given class. Thus, the measures of teacher behaviors are frequency counts.

*Child Behaviors: The Dependent Variable*

The classes of child behaviors were developed by categorization of behaviors occurring with some frequency in the repertoire of problem children (Becker *et al.*, 1967). It was assumed that certain behaviors, because of their common topography, could be grouped together. Five classes of Disruptive Behavior (Gross Motor, Noise Making, Orienting, Verbalizations, and Aggression) and one class of Appropriate Behavior (Relevant) were defined. Behaviors not specifically defined were rated in a separate category (Other Task). Disruptive Behaviors were essentially behaviors apparently incompatible with good classroom learning conditions.

Included in the category of behaviors labeled as Gross Motor activities were: getting out of seat, standing up, walking around, running, hopping, skipping, jumping, rocking chair, moving chair, sitting with chair in aisle, kneeling in chair, arm flailing, and rocking body without moving chair.

The category of Noise Making was rated with the stipulation that the observers must hear the noise as well as see the noise-making action, and included tapping feet, clapping, rattling papers, tearing papers, throwing books or other objects onto desks, slamming desk top, tapping objects on desk, kicking desk or chair, and scooting desk or chair.

The Verbalization category was rated only when the observer could hear the response. Lip movements alone were not rated. Carrying on conversations with other children, calling out teacher's name to get her attention, crying, screaming, singing, whistling, laughing, and coughing were included in the category.

The Orienting class of behaviors required that the child be seated. Turning of head or head and body toward another person, showing objects to another child, and looking at another child were rated. Looking behaviors

---

[2]As it turned out, approval following inappropriate behavior occurred only three times and disapproval following appropriate behavior did not occur. Also, this teacher did not make non-response-contingent approval or disapproval comments. Thus, we were dealing essentially with two response-contingent classes of teacher behavior.

of less than 4-sec duration were not rated except for any turn of more than 90 degrees from the desk. When an Orienting response overlapped two rating intervals, and could not be rated in the first interval, because it began too late in the interval to meet the 4-sec criterion, it was rated in the second interval.

Aggression was defined as hitting, pushing, shoving, pinching, slapping, striking with objects, poking with objects, grabbing objects or work belonging to another, knocking neighbor's property off desk, destroying another's property, throwing objects. No judgments of intent were made.

Appropriate behaviors were labeled Relevant and were made more easily identifiable by restricting the observations to a period in the morning when all of the children were preparing reading and workbook assignments. Specific Relevant Behaviors were: looking at the teacher when she was speaking to the entire class or to the child being observed, answering questions of the teacher, raising hand and waiting for teacher to respond, writing answers to workbook questions, looking at pages of text in which reading was assigned. It was required that the entire 10-sec interval be filled with on-task behavior before the Relevant rating was made.

When a child being observed performed a response not defined by one of the categories of Disruptive Behaviors or by Relevant Behavior, a rating of Other Task was made. The Other Task rating was incompatible with Relevant, but could be recorded in the same interval as any or all of the categories of Disruptive Behavior.

When rating the children, the observers were instructed to record each class of behaviors which appeared in an interval regardless of how many other classes had already been recorded in that interval. All five categories of Disruptive Behaviors and the Other Task category were compatible with each other. Relevant Behavior was incompatible with the other categories. No category of behavior was rated more than once in an interval. If a child was conversing with his neighbor, and he made two verbal responses in one interval, this class of behaviors was recorded only once. Thus, each child-behavior measure was a record of intervals in which the response occurred, rather than a count of the number

of discrete responses as in the recording of teacher's behavior.

The overall level of Disruptive Behaviors was defined as the percentage of intervals in which one or more Disruptive Behaviors occurred.

*Reliability*

Two types of reliability were calculated. Reliability I reflects simply the degree to which two observers obtained the same score for each category of behavior during a 20-min observation period. The smaller score is divided by the larger. Reliability I most appropriately applies to the data as reported in Fig. 1, since these are averages for an observation period. Random errors tend to cancel each other out when a score is based on a series of observations and a reliability measure should reflect the gain in accuracy obtained by averaging. For training purposes, and for greater confidence in the accuracy of the observation procedure, a second type of reliability was also calculated (Reliability II). Reliability II required that the same behavior category be recorded in the same interval by each observer to define an agreement. Reliability II was calculated by dividing the number of agreements by the number of agreements plus disagreements.

During the pre-baseline observer training, reliability checks were required for every observation. Before baseline observations were started, consistent reliabilities (Type II) above 80% were required. Reliability I data based on a weighted average of the reliabilities of the child-behavior codes are reported in Fig. 1, as are the average reliabilities by conditions for teacher behaviors. Comparable Reliability II data averaged 82.6% for child behaviors and 83.2% for teacher behaviors. Reliabilities for individual categories are well represented by these averages.

*Sequence of Conditions*

The first phase of the study (Baseline$_1$) consisted of measuring both teacher and child behaviors. No attempt was made to manipulate teacher behavior.

The second phase (No Approval$_1$) was defined by the absence of Approval Behaviors. The teacher discontinued the use of praise statements and used only contingent Disapproving Behaviors to control the children.

189

These phases were then repeated (Baseline$_2$, No Approval$_2$). At the beginning of No Approval$_2$ and throughout the rest of the study, the teacher carried a small "supermarket" adding machine with her to count the frequency of Disapproval Behaviors so that she could better monitor her behavior.

The fifth phase of the study, Frequent Disapproval, involved increasing the level of Disapproving Behaviors to approximately three times that given during Baseline$_1$ while continuing to withhold Approving Behaviors.

Phase 6 returned to the lower level of Disapproval (No Approval$_3$) and Phase 7 again returned to the baseline conditions (Baseline$_3$).

The teacher was instructed to maintain experimental conditions throughout the day, not just during the observation period. During the periods when praise was withheld beginning with No Approval$_2$, checks of the daily counts of Disapproving Responses obtained by the teacher with her counter corresponded closely to those which would have

been predicted by extrapolation from the observation periods.

## RESULTS

The relationships of greatest interest are the effects of presence and absence of Approval Behaviors on Relevant Behaviors and the effects of levels of Disapproval Behaviors on Disruptive Behaviors. Because of a systematic rater bias which entered into the data for Other Task Behavior (discussed later), and therefore also affected Relevant Behaviors incompatible with Other Task, greater emphasis is given to the analysis of Disruptive Behaviors in presenting the results.

### Average Level of Disruptive Behavior

In Baseline$_1$ Disruptive Behaviors occurred in an average of 8.7% of the intervals observed. When Approving Behaviors were discontinued (No Approval$_1$), Disruptive Behavior increased to an average of 25.5% (Fig. 1). Approving Behaviors were again provided

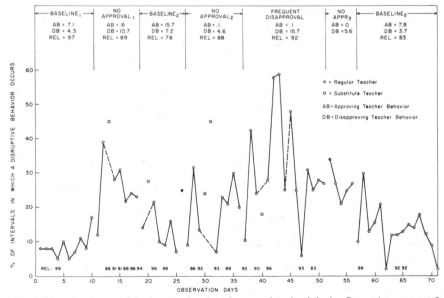

Fig. 1. Disruptive classroom behaviors as a function of nature of teacher behavior. Data points represent 2-min samples on 10 children each day. Dotted lines cross observations where the regular teacher was absent due to a recurrent illness, including a 10-day hospitalization between Days 39 and 41. The dotted line connecting days 44 and 45 represents the Easter vacation break. The data for Day 26 were taken with the teacher out of the room.

190

(Baseline$_2$) and Disruptive Behavior dropped to an average of 12.9%. In order to show more conclusively that the changes in Disruptive Behavior were related to the changes in teacher behavior, Approving Behaviors were again discontinued (No Approval$_2$) and the level of Disruptive Behaviors stabilized near the same level as in No Approval$_1$ condition (average 19.4%). When the Disapproving Behaviors (critical comments) were tripled (Frequent Disapproval), while Approving Behaviors were still withheld, Disruptive Behavior increased to an average of 31.2% with high points far above any observed before. The behavior stabilized, however, near the level at which the two previous No Approval phases had stabilized. When the rate of disapproval was lowered (No Approval$_3$), no great reduction in Disruptive Behavior occurred. The average level of Disruptive Behaviors over No Approval$_2$, Frequent Disapproval, and No Approval$_3$ was 25.9%. At the end of No Approval$_3$, Approval was again added to the low level of Disapproving Behaviors, and Disruptive Behavior dropped to an average of 13.2%, with the trend indicating a level far below this average.[3]

*Analysis of Classes of Behavior*

*Discontinuation of approving behaviors.* In reviewing the changes in the individual categories of behavior through the first two withdrawals of Approving Behavior, the majority of the increase in Disruptive Behaviors could be attributed to changes in Verbalization and Orienting categories (Table 1). The mean of Verbalization in No Approval$_1$ was 22.6% due to one extremely high observation on the second day of the condition; however, these behaviors stabilized between 9% and 17% (Fig. 2). Orienting showed a slight decrease across No Approval$_1$ (Fig. 2). The second time Approval was discontinued, Orienting increased across the condition while Verbalization remained relatively stable except for two high observations. Gross Motor behaviors followed the same pattern as Orienting and Verbalization through No Approval (1 and 2), increasing each time Approving Behavior was discontinued and decreasing when Approving Behaviors were present (Fig. 2).

Noise Making and Aggression followed a pattern through No Approval$_1$ and $_2$ which was distinctly different from the other categories of disruptive behavior. Both of these categories of behavior were already occurring at a low frequency in the Baseline condition (Table 1), but they occurred even less often when only Disapproving Behavior was given.

*Increase of disapproving behaviors.* In the Frequent Disapproval condition, Noise Making, Gross Motor, and Orienting all increased (Table 1). Verbalizations showed a decline

[3]A conservative statistical analysis was performed ($F$ test) to compare those three conditions where approval responses were available with those two conditions where approval responses were withdrawn. For this test the Frequent Disapproval and No Approval$_{2+3}$ conditions were collapsed into one condition. In order to insure independence of observations, the average values within each condition were used, thus providing four degrees of freedom. Significant differences were found for Relevant Behavior ($p < 0.01$), Noise Making ($p < 0.05$), Gross Motor ($p < 0.025$), and for the overall level of Disruptive Behavior ($p < 0.01$).

Table 1
Average Percentages for Specific Behavior Classes for Each Experimental Phase

| Behavior Classes | Baseline$_1$ | No Approval$_1$ | Baseline$_2$ | No Approval$_2$ | Frequent Disapproval | No Approval$_3$ | Baseline$_3$ |
|---|---|---|---|---|---|---|---|
| Disruptive Behaviors[a] | 8.7 | 25.5 | 12.9 | 19.4 | 31.2 | 26.8 | 13.2 |
| Gross Motor | 2.7 | 6.7 | 2.0 | 4.8 | 12.3 | 10.4 | 2.4 |
| Noise | 0.9 | 0.1 | 0.7 | 0.09 | 4.1 | 4.4 | 0.9 |
| Verbalization | 4.6 | 22.6 | 7.7 | 9.6 | 7.9 | 6.0 | 3.9 |
| Orienting | 1.4 | 6.5 | 4.1 | 7.1 | 11.5 | 10.2 | 7.6 |
| Aggression | 0.25 | 0.01 | 0.2 | 0.01 | 0.04 | 0.04 | 0.1 |
| Other Task | 7.0 | 10.4 | 5.9 | 10.7 | 5.9 | 4.2 | 1.2 |
| Relevant | 84.1 | 65.3 | 83.9 | 72.1 | 64.3 | 69.4 | 85.6 |

[a]The addition of percentages for the five classes of Disruptive Behaviors will usually lead to a sum higher than that reported as percentage of Disruptive Behaviors, since the latter does not reflect the occurrence of more than one subclass of Disruptive Behaviors in a given 10-sec interval.

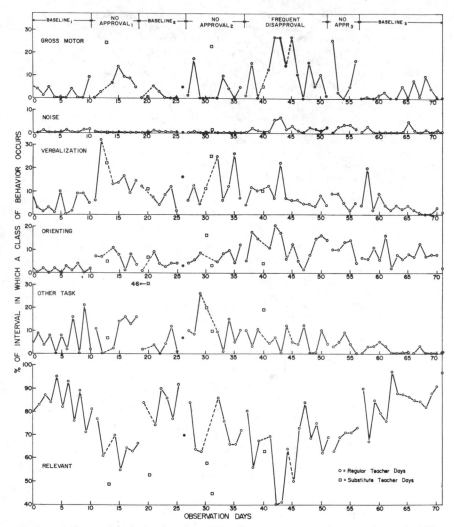

Fig. 2. Analysis of specific behavior classes by condition. Data points represent 2-min samples on 10 children each day. See notes under Fig. 1.

over this condition and continued to decline through the rest of the study.

Changing from a high level of Disapproving Behaviors to a lower level did not markedly change the frequency of the various categories of Disruptive Behaviors relative to their terminal level under the Frequent Disapproval condition.

When Approving Behaviors were again used by the teacher (Baseline₃), the frequency of Gross Motor, Noise Making, and Orienting behaviors decreased noticeably (Fig. 2). Verbalization continued to show the steady decrease in frequency which had started in the Frequent Disapproval condition. In Baseline$_3$ Aggression again occurred, but rarely. All Disruptive Behaviors except Orienting dropped to the level of the initial Baseline (or below) during the final Baseline.

*Relevant behavior.* Appropriate behaviors were initially high in the classroom (Fig. 2). Behaviors such as getting out of seat to move to a reading group or to check a completed workbook assignment were rated in the Gross Motor category. The requirements for such behaviors, however, remained constant through all conditions so changes in the level of Relevant Behaviors cannot be attributed to changes in classroom requirements. Relevant Behavior decreased each time Approving Behavior was discontinued and increased each time the Approval was reinstated. Relevant Behavior was at a slightly higher level during the final Baseline than during the initial Baseline.

*Other task: Behavior not specifically defined.* As indicated earlier, a systematic rater difference was encountered early in the study in rating Other Task behaviors. In Fig. 2 this bias can be seen by contrasting data collected on Days 2, 4, 6, 8, and 10 from one set of observers with that collected on Days 1, 3, 5, 7, and 9 by another set of observers. While an attempt was made to correct this bias by interlocking reliability checks, it is apparent that the bias continued to some extent throughout the study. Since Other Task is by definition incompatible with Relevant Behavior, Relevant Behavior shows the same bias. By looking at Disruptive Behavior, defined so as to exclude Other Task behaviors, the systematic bias was largely eliminated from the data presented in Fig. 1.

### Teacher Behaviors

The behavior of the teacher remained under good control throughout the study. Averages by conditions for Approving and Disapproving Behaviors are given in the upper part of Fig. 1. As the conditions were changed, little difficulty was found in withholding behaviors in the Approving category. Some difficulty was reported by the teacher in regulating the frequency of Disapproving Behaviors while withholding Approving Behaviors, but a partial solution to this problem was found. The teacher found that by carrying a small hand-counter (mentioned earlier) she could more accurately judge the frequency of her critical comments. In the Frequent Disapproval Phase there were days when the children were not emitting enough Disruptive Behaviors for critical comments to be appropriate at the programmed frequency. Rather than make inappropriate comments, the rate of Disapproving comments was adjusted to the frequency of the Disruptive Behaviors. When enough Disruptive Behaviors were available, Disapproving Behaviors were dispensed at a maximum rate of one per minute throughout the day; thus, many of the responses of the children were reprimanded very quickly.

General frequency of instructional comments did not change appreciably across conditions. However, the teacher did increase the frequency with which she would say in a neutral tone whether responses were correct or incorrect in the phases where Approval was not given.

The behaviors characterized as Terminating Social Interaction occurred only twice during the study and were, therefore, not subject to further analysis.

*Substitute teachers.* Observations taken on the days when a substitute teacher was in charge of the classroom appear in four conditions of the study. The frequency of Disruptive Behaviors increased in the presence of a temporary teacher as long as the regular teacher was in either Baseline or No Approving Behavior phases. When the Disapproving Behavior was being dispensed at a high rate, however, the level of Disruptive Behaviors decreased in the presence of a temporary teacher (Fig. 1).

*Day 26.* The data for this day were taken while the teacher was out of the room. Since the experimental conditions were not operative, this point should have been omitted altogether.

## DISCUSSION

The results indicate that some aspects of the behaviors included in the category of Approving Behaviors were reinforcing for task-appropriate behaviors. The frequency of Relevant Behaviors was high whenever Approving Behaviors followed Relevant child

Behavior, and decreased whenever Approving Behaviors were discontinued.

In each change of conditions that involved discontinuation of Approving Behaviors, there appeared a reliable transition effect (observation Days 11 and 27). This effect may be an example of the typical increase in rate found when a positive reinforcer is removed. In support of this explanation, the teacher reported, "When I stop praising the children, and make only negative comments, they behave very nicely for three or four hours. However, by the middle of the afternoon the whole classroom is chaotic." Since observations were taken during a study period in the morning, the periods of good behavior show up in the data each time a condition was changed. A similar low deviant behavior point occurred at the transition to Frequent Disapproving Behaviors (day 37), but it is not clearly explained. "The children seemed stunned."

Reviewing the individual classes of Disruptive Behaviors brings out certain similarities and differences among the classes. During the first alternations of Baseline with discontinuation of Approving Behaviors, Gross Motor, Orienting, and Verbalization Behaviors increased with discontinuation of Approval, while Noise Making and Aggressive Behaviors remained at their already low frequency. The increases are interpreted as suggesting that some responses in the disruptive classes may be reinforced by peer attention or other environmental circumstances when control through approving teacher responses to incompatible behaviors is withdrawn. For example, Orienting behaviors, such as looking around the room or out the window may be reinforced by seeing other children playing, by observing a custodian cleaning up the schoolyard, or by seeing any of numerous events which have no relationship to the classroom. Observational evidence for this inference was clearest in the Frequent Disapproval phase (below). It is also possible to attribute the increases in Disruptive Behaviors during No Approval$_1$ to the increase in use of Disapproval. However, the data for No Approval$_2$, where Disapproval was held to the Baseline level, would argue that the effect was primarily related to the withdrawal of approval.

Increasing Disapproving Behaviors to a high level produced four days where Disruptive

Behaviors were above 40%. Several individual categories of behavior also showed marked changes. The increase in Gross Motor Behaviors was related to an increase in interactions with other students. During the Frequent Disapproval condition, two or three children would make alternate trips to check their workbooks at a table provided for that purpose. Only one child was permitted at the table at a time. During Baseline and No Approval phases, it was rare to see a child make more than one trip to the table; in the Frequent Disapproval phase, some of the children would check their papers several times. Others responded by pushing their papers off of their desks and then getting up to get them. There was a noticeable "pairing off" with two or more children exhibiting the same behaviors.

Another consequence of the Frequent Disapproval phase was a marked increase in the noise level in the room. A majority of the noises during this period were created by children scooting their desks and chairs. One observer reported, "I waited for a few minutes after the regular observation period was over and counted the noises. During one 40-sec period, I counted 17 separate chair scraping noises. They came in bursts of two or three at a time. It looked as though the kids were trying to irritate the teacher." The noises in "bursts of two or three" seemed similar to the "pairing off" of children noted with the Gross Motor behaviors, and strengthens an hypothesis that reinforcement from peers is one of the elements which accounts for the increase in Disruptive Behaviors during this time. Peer attention cannot be the only element affecting the behavior of the children, however, because the Verbalization category of behaviors showed a constant decrease throughout the Frequent Disapproval condition. The inhibition of Verbalization could be due to interfering emotional responses being elicited by the high level of critical comments by the teacher. More probable, however, is that the children simply talked more quietly to avoid being caught by the teacher. Observers' reports indicate that a substantial number of verbalizations would have been recorded during the Frequent Disapproving Behaviors condition if there had been no requirement that the responses be heard by the observers. The children could be seen to turn their heads, and lip movements could be seen frequently, but the verbalizations could not be heard.

Work by Lövaas, Freitag, Kinder, Rubenstein, Schaeffer, and Simmons (1964) suggests that for some children any adult attention may be reinforcing. Some of the present findings under the Disapproval conditions could also be interpreted as indicating that teacher behavior of the Disapproving variety was positively reinforcing. The level of Disruptive Behaviors during each of the conditions when only Disapproving and Instructional attentions were available does appear to vary with the level of Disapproving Behaviors dispensed by the teacher. Unfortunately, the illness-caused absences and Easter break make the results less clear than hoped. It should be apparent that the effect of Frequent Disapproval on the behavior of the children is not subject to a simple interpretation. Some criticized behaviors decreased, some increased, and several possible controlling stimuli could have been operating with contradictory effects on behavior. It is obviously difficult in a field-experimental study of this complexity to maintain control of all the possibly relevant variables at once.

Another limitation of the present design should be noted. Because of a shortage of observation time under the desired classroom conditions, a sample of 10 children was observed daily. A procedure which included all children each day would have provided a stronger basis for analysis of effects on individuals. A rough analysis of individuals with the present data confirms, however, that an average of 76% of the students made changes in the same direction as the group changes. From Baseline, to No Approval, 81% of the students showed increases in Disruptive Behavior. When Approving Behavior became available, 75% of the students improved within two weeks. Discontinuing Approving Behavior a second time resulted in 78% of the students being more disruptive, while the final addition of Approving Behavior showed an increase in appropriate behavior for 71% of the children. Across condition changes, 5% of the children showed no change on the average, and 19% showed change (usually minor) in an opposite direction. Procedures which permitted specifications of which children were praised or criticized for which be-

haviors would be needed to clarify fully individual effects. It is quite possible that the children who changed opposite to the group trend were being responded to differently. Of course, there are many ways one can speculate here. In an as yet unpublished study we have shown that praising some children but not others leads to changes in the behavior only for the children who are praised. Results of this sort emphasize the importance of looking at individual contingencies.

Brief mention should be made of the possible ethical considerations involved in producing disruptive behaviors. One needs to weigh the potential gains in knowledge against the short-term or long-term deleterious effects on the children or teacher. On the basis of prior research and the return to baseline after the first No Approving Behaviors condition, the teacher and the experimenters were confident that appropriate behaviors could be readily reinstated at any time it was felt necessary. It may also be reassuring to know that this accelerated middle primary class did achieve well academically during the year. The children completed all second and third grade work and were all performing on a fourth grade level by the end of the year.

## IMPLICATIONS

This further demonstration of the importance of specific teacher behaviors in influencing classroom behavior has a double implication. First, the teacher who uses her Approving Behaviors as immediate consequences for good behavior should find that the frequency and duration of appropriate behaviors increase in her classroom (at least for most children). On the other hand, the teacher who cuddles the miscreant, tries pleasantly to get a child to stop behaving disruptively, talks with a child so that he "understands" what he was doing wrong, or who pleasantly suggests an alternative activity to a child who has been performing inappropriately, is likely to find an increase in the very behaviors she had hoped to reduce. This view of the functional importance of teacher's behavior in creating, maintaining, or reducing classroom behavior problems contrasts sharply with that generated by psychodynamic models of problem behaviors and what to do about them. Work of this sort also suggests a need to re-evaluate the popular cliche about the importance of the interaction of the "personality" of the teacher with that of the child in looking at classroom management procedures.

The suggestive evidence that peer reinforcement (among other stimuli) takes over when social reinforcement is not provided by teacher is given support by the recent work of Wahler (1967). Wahler has shown how preschool children can systematically control the behavior of their peers by differential use of social reinforcement. The more general implication for the teacher is this: unless an effort is made to support desirable classroom behaviors with appropriate consequences, the children's behavior will be controlled by others in ways likely to interfere with the teacher's objectives.

Finally, the possibility that critical comments may actually function to increase some behaviors upon which they are contingent cannot be overlooked. A recent study (Madsen, Becker, Thomas, Koser, and Plager, 1967), gives clear evidence that some forms of critical comment do function to strengthen behavior. The more often a teacher told first graders to "sit down", the more often they stood up. Only praising sitting seemed to increase sitting behavior.

## REFERENCES

Becker, W. C., Madsen, C. H., Jr., Arnold, Carole R., and Thomas, D. R. The contingent use of teacher attention and praise in reducing classroom behavior problems. *Journal of Special Education*, 1967, 1, 287-307.

Bijou, S. W. and Baer, D. M. Some methodological contributions from a functional analysis of child development. In L. P. Lipsitt and C. S. Spiker (Eds.), *Advances in child development and behavior*. New York: Academic Press, 1963. Pp. 197-231.

Hart, Betty M., Allen, K. Eileen; Buell, Joan S., Harris, Florence R., and Wolf, M. M. Effects of social reinforcement on operant crying. *Journal of Experimental Child Psychology*, 1964, 1, 145-153.

Kerr, Nancy; Meyerson, L., and Michael, J. A procedure for shaping vocalizations in a mute child. In L. P. Ullman and L. Krasner (Eds.), *Case studies in behavior modification*. New York: Holt, Rinehart, & Winston, Inc., 1965. Pp. 366-370.

Lövaas, O. I., Freitag, G., Kinder, M. I., Rubenstein, D. B., Schaeffer, B., and Simmons, J. B. Experimental studies in childhood schizophrenia—Establishment of social reinforcers. Paper delivered at Western Psychological Association, Portland, April, 1964.

Madsen, C. H., Jr., Becker, W. C., Thomas, D. R., Koser, Linda, and Plager, Elaine. An analysis of the reinforcing function of "sit down" commands. In R. K. Parker (Ed.), *Readings in educational psychology*. Boston: Allyn and Bacon, 1968 (in press).

Wahler, R. G. Child-child interactions in free field settings: Some experimental analyses. *Journal of Experimental Child Psychology*, 1967, 5, 278-293.

Zimmerman, Elaine H. and Zimmerman, J. The alteration of behavior in a special classroom situation. *Journal of the Experimental Analysis of Behavior*, 1962, 5, 59-60.

# EFFECTS OF TEACHER ATTENTION ON DIGIT-REVERSAL BEHAVIOR IN AN ELEMENTARY SCHOOL CHILD[1]

JOSEPH E. HASAZI AND SUSAN E. HASAZI

Teacher attention was systematically manipulated to modify digit-reversal behavior in an elementary school child. Almost invariably, the child reversed the order of digits (*e.g.*, writing 21 as the sum of 5 + 7) when adding numbers yielding a two-digit sum. The child, along with classmates, was given 20 addition problems a day for the duration of the study, and the number of reversals was recorded. During an initial baseline period, the teacher responded to digit reversals by marking them as incorrect and then giving the child "extra help" until all sums were correctly ordered. The child's present and previous teacher had both responded to reversals in this manner for approximately one year before the present study began. An experimental period followed during which the rate of reversals decreased sharply. During this period, all sums were marked as correct (whether reversed or not); "extra help" with reversals was discontinued; and correct, *i.e.*, non-reversed, response forms were responded to with a smile, a pat on the back, and a brief comment. A reversal period followed, during which the teacher responded to reversals as she had in the first baseline period. An increase in the rate of reversals to baseline level occurred within three days. A final period, replicating the first experimental period followed, and was characterized by a sharp decrease in the rate of reversals.

The failure to acquire academic behaviors at a rate commensurate with that of one's peers has long been recognized as a significant problem by parents, educators, and the social community in general. Kessler (1966) estimated that three-fourths of all elementary school-age students are referred for individual study and treatment because of academic behavior problems. If this estimate is accurate, then certainly the problem is one of considerable scope. Unfortunately, the problem has been approached from limited perspectives. One approach has been to view the problem as a technical one, although only in the sense of materials and methods of presenting them. Another approach, frequently taken in the face of repeated failures at modification, has been to attribute the problem to some characteristic of the student, such as stubborness, retardation, or a learning disability. Seldom have such problems been approached from the viewpoint of an experimental analysis of behavior.

An experimental analysis of academic behavior problems would necessitate consideration of all of the components of the reinforcement contingencies operative in the classroom. Hence, such an analysis would pay a good deal of attention to the consequences provided for student behavior and would attempt to identify and control reinforcing events. Certainly, such an analysis should address itself not only to the arrangement of reinforcement contingencies that will facilitate the development of academic behavioral repertoires, but should examine as well the role of mismanaged or accidental contingencies in the etiology of academic behavior problems.

[1] Portions of this paper were presented to the Florida Psychological Association, May, 1970, Miami Beach, Florida. The authors are indebted to Mr. Richard Gunther, Principal of Lehigh Elementary School, Ontario-Montclair School District, Ontario, California, for his encouragement and cooperation.

JOURNAL OF APPLIED BEHAVIOR ANALYSIS, 1972, Vol. 5, pp. 157-162.

197

One class of reinforcing events, likely to be operative in any classroom, involves aspects of the teacher's behavior. The reinforcing effects of teacher attention, for example, have been demonstrated in a number of recent studies. Teacher attention has been systematically manipulated to modify classroom behavior problems (Becker, Madsen, Arnold, and Thomas, 1967; Thomas, Becker, and Armstrong, 1968; Thomas, Nielsen, Kuypers, and Becker, 1968) and to increase the rate of "academic" behaviors (Hall, Lund, and Jackson, 1968; Zimmerman and Zimmerman, 1962). Given the results of these studies, it would seem advisable to analyze other classroom situations that typically involve contingent teacher attention.

One classroom situation likely to involve contingent teacher attention occurs when a student has difficulty learning some set of responses, such as are involved in adding a column of numbers. The teacher may give such a student individual attention until the responses in question are made appropriately. Differential reinforcement of incorrect response forms might occur in such a situation, particularly if they became discriminative stimuli controlling the teacher's attending behavior to the child. Zimmerman and Zimmerman (1962) reported on such a situation in the area of spelling behavior. The child in their study made repeated errors when called upon to spell a word that had been studied and drilled previously. As a consequence of this behavior, the teacher gave considerable time and attention to the child in an attempt to modify this behavior. While this procedure was ineffective, appropriate spelling behavior did develop when incorrect responses were ignored and correctly spelled responses were differentially attended to by the teacher. Thus, the study demonstrated a situation in which inappropriate academic behavior was maintained by the establishment of an accidental reinforcement contingency between incorrect spelling responses and teacher attention. The present study reports on a similar situation. In the study, the effects of teacher attention on maintaining and modi-

fying digit-reversal behavior in an elementary school child were analyzed.

## METHOD

*Subject*

Bob, an 8-yr-old boy, was enrolled in a Basic Skills class in the Ontario-Montclair (California) School District. While considered by his teacher to be one of her most capable students, Bob had specific difficulty in adding numbers yielding a two-digit sum. Almost invariably, he would reverse the order of digits in the sum, *e.g.*, writing 21 as the sum of 5 + 7. He had exhibited this behavior for approximately 1 yr before the present study began. As a result of this behavior, Bob received several neurological and visual examinations, and was given considerable "extra help" by his present and previous teacher. The failure of this extra help to modify the behavior led his present teacher to consider her role in maintaining the behavior.

Several factors suggested that teacher attention might be reinforcing Bob's digit-reversal behavior. First, Bob was able to discriminate easily between numbers containing the same but reversely ordered digits, such at 12 and 21. Second, he often pointed out reversals on his own paper to the teacher when she failed to notice them. Finally, he was observed on several occasions erasing correctly ordered sums and reversing the order of the digits contained.

*Procedures*

The basic datum of the study was the number of digit reversals made by Bob each day. For the duration of the study, Bob (along with other class members) was given 20 addition problems at the same time each morning. It was common classroom procedure to do a number of such problems daily, and hence, the study necessitated few deviations from normal classroom routine. All problems were designed to yield two-digit sums. Numbers yielding a sum of 10 or sums composed of two identical digits such as 11 or 22, were not used. This left a population of 80 sums composed of different digits. Addition problems were designed by first dividing these 80 sums into four groups: 12 to 32, 34 to 54, 56 to 76, and 78 to 98. Five sums from each group were chosen to comprise the problems for a given day. By choosing five different sums from each group on consecutive days, over a four-day period all 80 sums were used and none were repeated. Over the four weeks of the study, each sum was thus used seven times. On a given day, sums were chosen from each group such that no reversely ordered sums, such as 18 and 81, appeared. For any sum, the possible permutations of numbers yielding that sum is equal to the sum minus one. Thus, even for the lowest sum used, that of 12, eleven permutations of numbers exist that will yield that sum when added. By randomly selecting permutations without replacement, it was thus possible to provide 20 different addition problems each day, even though each sum was repeated seven times in the course of the study.

On each day of the study, Bob would raise his hand as soon as he had completed all 20 problems. The teacher would then proceed to Bob's desk and check his worksheet. For the first seven days of the study, the teacher marked all correct responses with a "C". All digit-reversals were marked as incorrect with an "X", and were pointed out to Bob by the teacher with the comment: "This one is incorrect. You see (pointing), you reversed the numbers in the answer." After all 20 problems had been scored in this manner, all digit reversals were returned to, and Bob was provided with "extra help" in solving each problem. This "extra help" had two basic components: one, Bob was taken through the adding processes involved in each problem, using a variety of teaching aids, such as counters and number lines; and two, verbal and physical prompting of correct response forms for those problems was provided. This constituted Baseline Period 1 of the study.

For the next seven days, all digit reversals were marked as correct with a "C". This procedure was adopted in consideration of the fact

that marks for incorrect responses might have developed conditioned reinforcing properties. No other comments were made concerning the reversals, no "extra help" was given with them, and statements pointing out such errors were ignored. Correctly written sums were likewise marked as correct with a "C", but were also followed by characteristic teacher consequences, consisting of a smile, a pat on the back, and the comment: "This one is *very* good." This combination of procedures had the effect of withholding all teacher attention for digit reversals (other than marking item as correct) and making more attention contingent upon correct response forms. After each problem had been scored and responded to, the teacher returned to her desk without further comment to Bob. This constituted Experimental Period 1 of the study.

Baseline Period 2 and Experimental Period 2 followed. Each was seven days in length and replicated the previous baseline or experimental period.

It should be emphasized that throughout the study, Bob's daily performance was evaluated and responded to only after all 20 problems were completed. Hence, any change in the digit-reversal behavior would not be evident until the day(s) following a change in the teacher-attention contingency.

## RESULTS

All of Bob's worksheets were rescored by an independent judge on each day of the study. Before rescoring, all of the teacher's marks were removed from the worksheets. Worksheets were then scored for correctly and reversely ordered sums. Two other scoring categories were possible, but were never used. These categories were for correctly and reversely ordered, inappropriately added sums. Reliability was computed by dividing the number of agreements between teacher and judge in scoring correctly and reversely ordered sums by 20, the number of possible agreements. This fraction was then multiplied by 100% to determine the percentage of agreement between scores. In all cases, the percentage of agreement was 100%.

The number of digit reversals made by Bob on each day of the study is graphed in Figure 1. It can be seen that in the first baseline period, digit reversals were made at a significantly high rate, varying between 18 and 20 and averaging 19.4 per day.

When the teacher-attention consequences of this behavior were discontinued, Bob continued to make reversals at a high rate for three days (Days 8 through 10 in Figure 1). The rate then dropped off dramatically, varying between 0 and 5 and averaging 2.5 reversals per day for the next four days (Days 11 through 14 in Figure 1). It should be noted that on Days 8 and 9, Bob failed to order any digits correctly. Consequently, the teacher was unable to respond differentially to correct response forms until Day 10. The significant drop in rate on Day 11 is thus indicative of the sensitivity of the behavior to the consequences provided by the teacher.

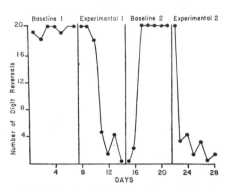

Fig. 1. Number of digit reversals per day under baseline and experimental conditions.

After the sixteenth day, when teacher attention was again made contingent upon digit reversals, the number of digit reversals jumped to 20 and remained at that level for the duration of the second baseline period. The average number of reversals per day for the last five days of this period was thus slightly higher than the daily average observed during the first baseline period.

The second experimental period (Days 22 through 28 in Figure 1) was also characterized by a drop in the rate of reversals. By the second day of this period, the number of reversals had dropped to three. The average number of reversals per day for the last six days of this period was two, slightly lower than during the final four days of the first experimental period. The significant changes in the rate of reversals occurring in the second baseline and experimental periods provide further evidence of the strong control exerted over this behavior by teacher attention.

DISCUSSION

The results indicate clearly that Bob's digit-ordering behavior was under the control of teacher attention. This finding closely parallels that of Zimmerman and Zimmerman (1962) with spelling behavior. In both studies, inappropriate academic behaviors were maintained, modified, and perhaps developed by teacher-controlled consequences. While many studies testify to the role of teacher attention in the modification of behavior problems, and in the development of appropriate classroom behavior, the present findings and those of Zimmerman and Zimmerman suggest that teacher attention may also be implicated in the development of learning difficulties in the classroom. It is not suggested that all such academic problems are developed in this manner or that the procedures used in this study should be applied to all children experiencing similar problems. However, it is a typical teaching practice to give a student individual attention when learning problems develop, and hence, the possibility of reinforcement of inappropriate academic behaviors exists. The teacher should remain aware of this possibility and attempt to determine which student behaviors are discriminative for her attending behavior.

The present findings take on additional significance when the typical ways of conceptualizing the determinants of academic problems, such as seen in this study, are considered. Given exposure to some standard set of teaching procedures, difficulties in learning to read, write, *etc.*, are likely to be attributed to intra-organismic factors. The student is said to be suffering from mental retardation, brain damage, a learning disability, or some other abnormal organic condition. The term "learning disability" is used when the difficulty is specific, and/or the response is unusual in form, *e.g.*, reversed or backwards. The digit-reversal behavior of the child in this study would thus qualify as a learning disability. It is appealing to attribute such behavior to some organically based process that interferes with normal information processing, input assimilation, *etc.*, as if what is "perceived" is also reversed or backwards. Conceptualizations of this sort discourage investigation of the role of environmental events in determining such behavior. Teaching, when attempted, is typically restricted to the manipulation of stimulus events (note the components of the extra help given to the child in this study), presumably, to help the student overcome information processing problems.

The results of this study demonstrate the advantages of viewing behavior as a function of contingencies of reinforcement and teaching as the arranging of such contingencies. Should a student display behavior of the type reported here, it is due presumably to the fact that the contingencies of reinforcement have not been arranged properly. Any explanation of such behavior should therefore take into account all of the variables composing the contingencies of reinforcement. Learning difficulties and disabilities, such as the subject's digit-reversal behavior, are probably related in many cases to an inappropriate presentation of stimulus events, but the present results demonstrate how reinforcement variables can also be involved. The present results suggest then that further research in the area of learning disabilities might find it profitable to adopt the viewpoint of an experimental analysis of behavior. Further research on the relationship of reinforcement variables to the development and modification of learning disabilities certainly seems warranted. Additionally, experimental analyses of the various methods and materials developed for use in learning disabilities, of the "extra help" which special education teachers provide, *etc.*, might provide a useful starting point for extending the principles and techniques of applied behavior analysis to an area of obvious need.

It should be clear that further analyses of the phenomena reported in this study are also needed. Obvious constraints are placed upon the data by having a single subject. Additionally, the functional relationship of teacher attention to the subject's behavioral change is not entirely clear. Baseline and experimental conditions differed in more than one respect. In the baseline conditions, little attention was provided for correct responses, while reversals resulted in a good deal of attention. In the experimental periods, reversals were ignored, and the amount of attention provided for correct responses was increased. Hence, the decrease in digit reversals during the experimental periods may reflect the reinforcement of correct response forms, the extinction of digit reversals, or a combination of these effects.

While the present design did not allow for systematic analysis of the effects of differential marking procedures, the results raise some interesting questions concerning the effects of such procedures. Certainly, differential marking procedures had been in effect for some time before the present study began without eliminating digit reversals. Given the results of the study, it is quite possible that marking a response as incorrect may even have developed conditioned reinforcing properties by virtue of being discriminative for the teacher's attending behavior. That the teacher's marks developed discriminative stimulus properties is also suggested by the data from Experimental Periods 1 and 2. During the first experimental period, no changes in

Bob's digit-reversal behavior were observed until a correctly ordered sum was differentially attended to, even though changes in the marking procedure had been in effect for two days. On the other hand, the rapid change in the subject's behavior in the second experimental period occurred simply as a function of the change in marking procedures before a correctly ordered sum had been differentially attended to. What this suggests then is that the effects of marking procedures may be variable depending on the contingencies that exist between marks and other reinforcing events. While further investigation of the effects of marking procedures is called for, the present findings point out, at the very least, the dangers inherent in assuming what is reinforcing or punishing for a particular student. In fact, any teacher attention seemed to be reinforcing. Similar findings have been reported by Thomas, Becker, and Armstrong (1968) with other student behaviors. Hence, whenever a teacher attends to a student, it is possible that some behavior is being reinforced.

## REFERENCES

Becker, W. C., Madsen, C. H., Jr., Arnold, R., and Thomas, D. R. The contingent use of teacher attention and praise in reducing classroom behavior problems. *Journal of Special Education,* 1967, **1**, 287-307.

Hall, R. V., Lund, D., and Jackson, D. Effects of teacher attention on study behavior. *Journal of Applied Behavior Analysis,* 1968, **1**, 1-12.

Kessler, J. W. *Psychopathology of childhood.* Englewood Cliffs, N.J.: Prentice-Hall, 1966.

Thomas, D. R., Becker, W. C., and Armstrong, M. Production and elimination of disruptive classroom behavior by systematically varying teacher's behavior. *Journal of Applied Behavior Analysis,* 1968, **1**, 35-45.

Thomas, D. R., Nielsen, L. J., Kuypers, D. S., and Becker, W. C. Social reinforcement and remedial instruction in the elimination of a classroom behavior problem. *Journal of Special Education,* 1968, **2**, 291-302.

Zimmerman, E. H. and Zimmerman, J. The alteration of behavior in a special classroom situation. *Journal of the Experimental Analysis of Behavior,* 1962, **5**, 59-60.

HUGH S. McKENZIE
MARILYN CLARK
MONTROSE M. WOLF
RICHARD KOTHERA
CEDRIC BENSON

# Behavior Modification of Children with Learning Disabilities Using Grades as Tokens and Allowances as Back up Reinforcers

*Abstract: The modification of academic behaviors of children in a learning disabilities class was undertaken by arranging for events such as amount of teacher attention, recess, and quality of weekly grade reports to be consequences for academic progress. As academic behaviors achieved with these consequences stabilized at less than an optimal level, the children's parents agreed to have the children earn their allowances on the basis of the weekly grade reports. This token reinforcement system, with grades as tokens and with allowances as added back up reinforcers, significantly increased the children's academic behaviors.*

A NUMBER of investigations have indicated that behavior modification techniques can be highly effective in the beneficial change of social and academic behaviors of both normal and exceptional children. Recent research has applied these techniques to bright, preschool children (Bushell, Wrobel, and McCloskey, 1967); to school dropouts (Clark, Lackowicz, and Wolf, in press); to emotionally disturbed children (O'Leary and Becker, 1967); and to low achieving culturally deprived children (Wolf, Giles, and Hall, in press). More extensive reviews of this growing body of experimental literature may be found in Anderson (1967) and Whelan (1966). The approach that these investigations have taken has been to employ token reinforcers such as colored chips or point cards to improve and maintain improvement of social and/or academic behaviors.

EXCEPTIONAL CHILDREN, 1968, Vol. 34, pp. 745-752.

Items such as candy, gum, toys, and money have served as back up reinforcers to these tokens, since tokens are exchanged for them.

The problems which can be created, even by an effective token reinforcement system, may be numerous. Not only can token systems be costly in terms of teacher time, but they also may involve an additional burden to already strained school budgets. The administration of tokens such as colored chips and the overseeing of the exchange of tokens for back up reinforcers such as toys may be an unfamiliar role for teachers. Also, parents may be given no function in a token system, although it is recognized that parents can play an integral part in an effective program for children with special needs (Cruickshank, 1967).

These considerations mean that a token system must make a contribution to the amelioration of the children's learning difficulties which is significantly greater than that possible with less costly procedures. As O'Leary and Becker (1967) have indicated, the rationale usually offered for employing token systems is that other incentives available to the school, such as teacher attention and grades, have not been effective, since the children involved still exhibit a high frequency of asocial and nonacademic behaviors.

The primary goal of the present research was to assess whether a pay for grades token reinforcement system could increase academic behavior to levels higher than those achieveable with the usually available school incentives. Another aim was to reduce the problems often associated with token systems. By employing grades as tokens, the teacher was not subjected to an unfamiliar role. With weekly allowances as back up reinforcers for grades, parents were able to administer the exchange aspect of the system and were consequently involved in the program. Because parents managed the exchange of tokens for back up reinforcers, and because corrections and some form of grades are an integral part of almost any instructional program, the teacher spent little extra time in the execution of this system. Since the parents of the children of the present study were accustomed to giving their children allowances, neither parents nor school assumed added costs.

**Method**

*Subjects.* The subjects were ten students in a learning disabilities class which was held in Skyline Elementary School, Roesland School District #92, Shawnee Mission, Kansas, during the 1966-1967 school year. This class was one of several special classes operated by the Northeast Johnson County Cooperative Program in Special Education, Johnson County, Kansas.

These ten students, eight boys and two girls, ranged in age from ten to 13 years and were selected for a learning disabilities class on the basis that although their ability levels were above the educable mentally retarded range, their achievement levels were retarded by at least two years in one or more academic areas. All students had received medical and/or psy-

chological evaluations which had suggested minimal brain damage with accompanying emotional disturbance. Case histories reported all students to be highly distractible and prone to engage in disruptive behaviors.

Data are reported on eight of the ten students, as data were incomplete on two students who returned to regular classes after the first week of the pay for weekly grades period.

*Teacher.* Prior to teaching the Skyline special class, the teacher had had five years of full time teaching and five years of teacher substitute work in grades K-8. She had obtained her M. Ed. in Special Education from the University of Kansas, with the major part of the academic work for this degree involving courses in behavior modification and operant psychology. Her master's thesis dealt with a basic education program for school dropouts employing a token reinforcement system (Clark, Lackowicz, and Wolf, in press).

Volunteers from a women's service organization also participated in the program as teacher aides. These aides served mainly to correct and grade the children's academic work.

*Classroom.* The skyline special classroom is similar to self contained classrooms found in many elementary schools. With the exception of desk shields extending about 20 inches above and on three sides of a desk's writing surface, no effort was made to reduce stimuli in the room to a bare minimum, as is sometimes recommended (Cruickshank, 1967). Decorative curtains served as window drapes; different colors surfaced walls, floor, and ceiling; books, teaching materials, and art supplies were always in full view. Walls served as display areas for the children's art work and construction projects. The room often had a festive air as the children decorated it for the various seasons.

*Instructional Materials and Programing.* The commercially available academic materials used were those which might be found in any elementary classroom. Where possible, the children worked on programed instructional materials (e.g., the SRA reading series). Otherwise, children did workbook assignments (e.g., Ginn's arithmetic workbooks). Such materials were used because they require overt responses.

204

Prior to the beginning of school and during the first two days of school, the teacher tested the children with the Durrell Analysis of Reading Difficulty and the SRA Achievement Tests. On the basis of these measures, children were placed at academic levels in each of the five instructional areas of the class: reading, arithmetic, spelling, penmanship, and English composition and grammar.

Children were given weekly assignments in each of these five instructional areas, with one assignment sheet for each area. Assignment sheets listed the materials to be worked on each day and the total number of responses assigned, and provided space for the child to record his starting and finishing time and for the teacher (or aide) to record daily the number of responses completed, the number correct, and the child's grade. In each academic area, children were required to complete all previous assignments before going on to new work. If any work was not completed by the week's end, it was assigned for the following week as a new assignment.

*Observations and Recording Procedures.* Children were observed by a research assistant through the one way mirror of a room adjacent to the classroom. A sound system was arranged so that the assistant could hear what occurred.

Observation time covered the first three hours of every morning: the reading and arithmetic periods, together with a short break between these periods in which the children had physical education or recess. Attending was defined as direct orientation toward work materials, i.e., a child was scored as attending if he was sitting at his desk with materials open and before him, and eyes directed toward these materials. Any contact with teacher or aide (raising hand for teacher help or discussion of assignment) was likewise scored as attending. In group work, a child was scored as attending if he was oriented toward work materials, to a reciting fellow student, or to the teacher, or if he himself was responding orally to a lesson. All behaviors other than those specified above were scored as nonattending.

An attending score was obtained for each child once every three minutes. From 90 to 120 seconds were required to observe and score the entire class. The remaining 60 to 90 seconds of the three minute period were used to note teacher and aide behaviors and prepare for the next group of observations.

The reading period lasted about 80 minutes and the arithmetic 60, so that approximately 26 and 20 measures of attending to reading and arithmetic, respectively, could be made on each child on each school day. A child would at times finish an assignment early, resulting in fewer observations of that child for that assignment period. The observer stopped recording the behavior of a child when he had turned his materials in to the teacher or aide and these materials had been certified as complete.

Although the observer was aware of the general orientation of the investigation, he was informed neither of the details of the pay for grades procedure, nor of when it was put into effect.

*Baseline Period.* Incentives available in the school were employed as described below.

1. *Recess.* The children earned recess by the successful completion of all of their assignments for the given assignment week up to the point of a given recess period. Children were required to work through recess if their work was not complete.

2. *Free Time Activities.* When a child had completed all of his assigned work before a given academic period had ended, he was free to go to a free time table to draw, paint, or construct, or he could read a book of his choice at his seat. Free time activities were not available to children until all work was complete.

3. *Special Privileges.* School errands were run by those children who were working hard and well, or who had shown recent improvement in the quality of their work. Line leaders and monitors were chosen on the same basis.

4. *Group versus Individual Lunch.* Children who had all of their work complete by lunchtime earned the privilege of eating in the school cafeteria with the rest of the school. Those whose work was incomplete ate at their desks, in silence.

5. *Teacher Attention.* The attention of the teacher was contingent upon appropriate working behaviors of the children. For ex-

ample, the teacher would say to a hard working child, "Good for you, you're working well, and that's the way you'll become smart in arithmetic and return to regular class sooner." Inappropriate behavior was either ignored or, if disruptive, was punished.

6. *Weekly Grades.* Every week children were given grades to take home to their parents. The parents signed the grade sheets, which the children then returned to the teacher. Both daily and weekly grades were included on these grade sheets. *A* grades indicated that a child had finished his work with 90 percent correct, *B* indicated 80 to 90 percent, *C* indicated 79 percent and below, and *Incomplete* indicated that a child had failed to finish his assigned work.

The teacher conducted group parent conferences once a month at the school, during which time the parents were instructed to praise grades of *A* and *B* and to compliment children for their hard work. Grades of *C* were acceptable, while brief expressions of sorrow were to be paired with grades of *Incomplete* (e.g., "That's too bad you didn't finish all your work in reading this week"), and children were to be encouraged to finish all work for the next week.

Discussions about academic behaviors and their reinforcers were undertaken by the teacher with individual children as well as with the entire group. These discussions were kept brief and never were held when a child was emotionally upset. Through these discussions it was hoped that the children would gain a further awareness of how they could succeed academically and what rewards would accompany such achievement.

To be maximally effective, reinforcers must be consistently applied. In this case, academic behaviors were consistently reinforced, while nonacademic behaviors were extinguished (not reinforced) or punished (resulting in the removal of some reinforcer). To ensure consistency, both the observer and the first author observed the teacher (and aides, where appropriate) and made at least one report a day to the teacher concerning her application of behavior modification techniques. For example, a tally sheet was kept of the number of times the teacher attended to academic behaviors during the school day and of the number of times she incorrectly attended to inappropriate, nonacademic behaviors. By daily discussion of this tally sheet, the teacher was able to increase her frequency of attending to good behaviors and could virtually ignore the unacceptable ones.

The teacher was likewise informed if a child had earned but not been awarded the opportunity to run a school errand, and if a child should not have been allowed recess because of incomplete work. With this information feedback, the teacher appeared to increase her behavior modification skills.

*Pay for Weekly Grades Period.* All procedures employed during the baseline period were continued in identical fashion during the pay period. However, the weekly grades of the baseline period now acquired an additional back up reinforcer: the payment of a weekly allowance to children by their parents on the basis of the children's grades for all subject areas. All the children had received some allowance previous to this period, but the amount received had not depended on their weekly grades. Children were paid for the average weekly grade of each subject area.

At a parent teacher conference toward the end of the baseline period, parents were instructed in the pay for grades procedures. As an example, parents were told that a child might be paid ten cents for *A's*, five cents for *B's*, and one cent for *C's*, while *Incompletes* would lead to a subtraction of the *A* amount, or minus ten cents. The parents determined the precise amounts on the basis of how much money their child was accustomed to having and the cost of the items he would be expected to purchase from his earnings. Amounts actually paid by parents for the weekly grades ranged from the values in the above example up to five times each grade amount in the example. Thus, with the five areas of the special class, plus physical education and music which the children took with the other children in the school, children's maximum earnings varied from $.70 to $3.50. With *Incompletes* being subtracted from earned allowance, it was possible for a child to owe his parents money. Toward this eventuality, parents were told to allow such an indebted child to perform some household chores over the weekend to square his debt. No money beyond the debt was to be earned, however. One indebted child, during the early part of the pay period, settled the debt by cleaning the garage.

Parents were asked to sit down with their child each Friday afternoon when the child brought home his weekly grades, calculate with the child the amount earned, and then pay him this amount. This was to be made an important weekly event. Parents were also asked to see that a large portion of the allowance be immediately consumed, and that the child be expected to pay with his earnings for all items he valued highly. Such things as movies, sweets, models, dolls, horseback riding, the purchase and care of pets, makeup, and inexpensive clothes were to be the children's financial responsibility. The children were not allowed to earn other money about the home, and any added money which came as presents or which was earned outside the home was to be banked. Such procedures helped to maintain the child's need and desire for money at high levels so that money would continue to serve as an effective reinforcer for academic behavior.

Parents informed their children of the pay procedure on the day before the start of the week which would lead to the first payment for weekly grades. Parents also told their children what items the child would be expected to purchase with his earned allowance.

The pay procedure was continued for the remainder of the year for all children, including children who returned to regular classes. Regular classroom teachers were instructed to give these children grades of D and F, as well as higher grades, when their work was at these levels. A grade of D substracted the B amount from a child's allowance, while a grade of F subtracted the A amount. When a child had successfully made the transition to regular class and had performed well for an extended period of time, the length of grade periods was increased, e.g., from once a week to once every two weeks, with appropriate increases in amounts paid for grades. In this way it was hoped to strengthen the child's academic behavior further and to prepare him for the longer grading periods he would encounter in his future schooling.

## Results

A marked increase in attending to reading occurred in the pay period compared with the baseline period (see Figure 1). Overall medians increased from 68 percent in the baseline period to 86 percent in the pay period.

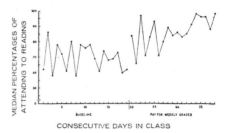

**Figure 1. Patterns of Medians in Attending to Reading**

It is necessary to be certain that the increases in the pay period cannot be attributed to progressive, though perhaps gradual, increases during the baseline period, since the consequences employed during the baseline period may have been increasing attending. Since the most powerful test for such trends was desired, an analysis of variance, rather than a nonparametric test, was performed on the baseline data, yielding an F ratio of less than one (see Table 1) which allows the retention of the hypothesis that the baseline procedures had no tendency to increase attending to reading. By computing eta square, it was estimated that trends accounted for only 6 percent of the variance of the baseline period.

#### TABLE 1
#### Analysis of Variance for Baseline Trends of Percentages of Attending to Reading

| Source | SS | df | MS | F |
|---|---|---|---|---|
| Between Subjects | 32345.368 | 7 | | |
| Within Subjects | 36351.684 | 144 | | |
| Trends | 4337.302 | 18 | 240.96 | $< 1$ |
| Residual | 32014.382 | 126 | 254.08 | |

The increase in attending to reading from the baseline period to the pay period was significant (see Table 2); $p < .005$, one tailed Wilcoxon Matched Pairs Signed Ranks Test (Siegel, 1956). The data for each student conformed very closely to the pattern of medians shown in Figure 1. Thus, it can be inferred that the token reinforcement system led to substantial gains in attending to reading for all students.

**TABLE 2**

**Subjects' Median Percentages of Attending to Reading**

| Subjects | Baseline | Pay | Increase |
|---|---|---|---|
| S1 | 71 | 89 | 18 |
| S2 | 82 | 95 | 13 |
| S3 | 23 | 77 | 54 |
| S4 | 83 | 93 | 10 |
| S5 | 72 | 83 | 11 |
| S6 | 72 | 79 | 7 |
| S7 | 75 | 83 | 8 |
| S8 | 62 | 75 | 13 |

*Note:*—Wilcoxon $T = 0$; $p < .005$ (one tailed test)

**TABLE 3**

**Analysis of Variance for Baseline Trends of Percentages of Attending to Arithmetic**

| Source | SS | df | MS | F |
|---|---|---|---|---|
| Between Subjects | 36957.158 | 7 | | |
| Within Subjects | 51337.684 | 144 | | |
| Trends | 7265.842 | 18 | 403.678 | 1.154* |
| Residual | 44071.842 | 126 | 349.776 | |

*$p > .25$

Similar results were obtained in arithmetic (see Figure 2). Overall medians increased from 70 percent in the baseline period to 86 percent in the pay period. The analysis of variance for trends during the arithmetic baseline period also yielded an insignificant F ratio (see Table 3; $F = 1.154$, $p > .25$). Through eta square, it was estimated that only 8 percent of the baseline arithmetic variance could be accounted for by trends.

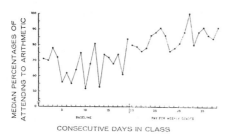

CONSECUTIVE DAYS IN CLASS

**Figure 2. Patterns of Medians in Attending to Arithmetic**

Attending to arithmetic also showed significant increases for the pay period over the baseline period (see Table 4; $p < .005$, one tailed Wilcoxon Test). Six subjects' graphs showed the same general form as the median graph in Figure 2. Thus, it can be inferred that the token system led to substantial gains in attending to arithmetic for these six subjects. The remaining two subjects (Subjects 2 and 7) showed gradual but steady increases in attending to arithmetic for the last ten days of the baseline period. Consequently, it cannot be concluded that the increases in attending to arithmetic shown by these two subjects for the pay period over the baseline period can be attributed solely to the pay for weekly grades procedure.

**TABLE 4**

**Subjects' Median Percentages of Attending to Arithmetic**

| Subjects | Baseline | Pay | Increase |
|---|---|---|---|
| S1 | 67 | 88 | 21 |
| S2 | 89 | 94 | 5 |
| S3 | 36 | 79 | 43 |
| S4 | 80 | 94 | 14 |
| S5 | 83 | 88 | 5 |
| S6 | 63 | 76 | 13 |
| S7 | 64 | 81 | 17 |
| S8 | 53 | 68 | 15 |

*Note:*—Wilcoxon $T = 0$; $p < .005$ (one tailed test)

Percentages of attending were determined in the following way: if a total of 20 observations were made on a child in arithmetic, and if, of these, ten were scored as attending, the child's percentage of attending to arithmetic on that day was $10/20 \times 100$ or 50 percent. Reliability checks were made between the first author and the observer on four occasions, two for reading and two for arithmetic. Reliability coefficients, estimated by the Pearson product moment formula and calculated across subjects with day and academic area held constant, were .91 and .95 for reading and .88 and .90 for arithmetic.

The attending data were obtained during October, November, and part of December, 1966. The month of September was used to refine the observational techniques and to ensure that instructional procedures and materials were adequate to meet each child's needs.

Although the observations were stopped after Christmas vacation, the number of *Incompletes* (with the exception of Subject 8) and the percentages of correct responses indicated that subjects maintained for the remainder of the school year the level of academic behavior attained during the pay period. Students' earnings varied from week to week and ranged from 30 to 85 percent of maximum possible earnings.

As the working efficiency of the students increased, larger assignments were given. At the end of the school year, all ten students were working successfully one to four levels above their starting levels in all academic areas. Six of the ten students were returned full time to regular classes to one grade higher than the ones they had been in during the previous school year. For two of these six, grading periods were extended to four weeks and for one, to two weeks, while the other three remained on the one week period since they were returned to regular classes with only two months of the school year left. In spite of the fact that regular classroom teachers were instructed to give grades of *D* and *F* when appropriate, half of the returned students consistently earned *B* averages and half earned *C* averages. At the close of the school year, all six of the returned students were again promoted, this time by their regular classroom teachers.

## Discussion

The present study demonstrated that a token reinforcement system with grades as tokens and allowances as back up reinforcers can significantly increase levels of academic behavior beyond those maintained by the systematic application of other reinforcers available to a school.

All students, with the exception of Subject 8, maintained these increased levels of academic behavior. This subject, with the pay still in effect, would alternate several weeks of complete work and high grades with several weeks of incomplete work. His parents reported that they had never reached agreement on the proper administration of the pay procedures and were, consequently, very inconsistent in its application. The subject was originally required to purchase his weekly movie and a construction model, yet his parents said that they gave him these rewards even when his earnings were insufficient to purchase them. One parent, on several occasions, had claimed all of his earnings as payment for misdemeanors committed at home. In the spring of the year he acquired a high level of social and academic behavior which was maintained for the remainder of the school year. This change in his behavior was coincidental with the death of one of his parents.

Grades have long been the token reinforcement system of schools. But as a reinforcer's effectiveness is directly proportional to its immediacy of presentation (Bijou and Baer, 1961), an apparent weakness of this grade system has been that grade reports are presented to children every six to nine weeks, a long delay of reinforcement for a child of elementary school age.

Teachers must correct children's work to ensure learning, and it is but a small step from corrections to grades. Although the teacher of the present study had volunteer aides to assist in the grading, the teacher felt that she could carry out the daily grading and weekly reports, and actually did for the many days that aides were absent.

No test was made to test the effect of the allowance back up reinforcer in the maintenance of high levels of academic behavior for the remainder of the school year. This effect could have been tested by paying the children their allowances independently of their weekly grades. If attending to academic materials had decreased significantly with this change, evidence would have been provided for a maintaining effect for this back up reinforcer. The risk of returning students to their less efficient levels of the baseline period overruled the possible gains in scientific information, and this analysis was not made.

## Conclusion

The token reinforcement system used in the present study increased levels of academic behavior with highly distractible and disruptive children. Several additional advantages are inherent in this token system. First, teachers need not spend valuable time in overseeing the

209

exchange of tokens for back up reinforcers. Parents can manage this task at home. Secondly, parents are frequently able to bear the cost of the allowance back up reinforcer, as many parents provide allowances for their children anyway. For parents unable to bear this cost, it seems likely that a service organization could be found which would contribute funds which parents could then pay to their children on the basis of weekly grades. Finally, the present system can open, as it did in this case, an effective channel of communication and cooperation between parents and teachers of children with special educational needs.

## References

Anderson, R. C. Educational psychology. In P. R. Farnsworth (Editor), *Annual Review of Psychology*. Volume 18. Palo Alto, California: Annual Reviews, 1967. Pp. 129-164.

Bijou, S. W., and Baer, D. M. *Child development*. Volume 1. New York: Appleton-Century-Crofts, 1961.

Bushell, D., Wrobel, P. A., and McCloskey, M. L. Some effects of normative reinforcement on classroom study behavior. Unpublished manuscript, Webster College, 1967.

Clark, M., Lackowicz, J., and Wolf, M. A pilot basic education program for school dropouts incorporating a token reinforcement system. *Behavior Research and Therapy*, 1968, 6 (2), in press.

Cruickshank, W. M. *The brain-injured child in home, school, and community*. Syracuse, New York: Syracuse University Press, 1967.

O'Leary, K. D., and Becker, W. C. Behavior modification of an adjustment class: a token reinforcement system. *Exceptional Children*, 1967, 33, 637-642.

Siegel, S. *Nonparametric statistics*. New York: McGraw-Hill, 1956.

Whelan, R. J. The relevance of behavior modification procedures for teachers of emotionally disturbed children. In P. Knoblock (Editor), *Intervention approaches in educating emotionally disturbed children*. Syracuse, New York: Syracuse University Press, 1966. Pp. 35-78.

Wolf, M. M., Giles, D. K., and Hall, V. R. Experiments with token reinforcement in a remedial classroom. *Behavior Research and Therapy*, 1968, 6, 51-64.

# MODIFICATION OF SOCIAL WITHDRAWAL
## THROUGH SYMBOLIC MODELING[1]

### ROBERT D. O'CONNOR

Recent years have witnessed increasing applications of principles of learning to psychopathology. Ample evidence has accumulated to indicate that behavioral approaches hold considerable promise for the treatment of diverse psychological conditions (Bandura, 1969; Eysenck, 1964; Krasner and Ullmann, 1967; Wolpe and Lazarus, 1967) Many of these applications, however, have been concerned with the treatment of highly circumscribed disorders. Only recently have researchers begun to investigate the modifications of interpersonal modes of behavior.

Social interaction, an obviously important factor in personality development, has become the focus of much attention among social-learning theorists, developmentalists, and therapists. There are several reasons for highlighting the role of interpersonal behavior in personality development. First, a child who is grossly deficient in social skills will be seriously handicapped in acquiring many of the complex behavioral repertoires necessary for effective social functioning. Second, children who are unable to relate skillfully to others are likely to experience rejection, harrassment, and generally hostile treatment from peers. Such negative experiences would be expected to reinforce interpersonal avoidance responses which, in turn, further impede the development of competencies that are socially mediated. Current theories concerning the determinants of personality patterns (Bandura, 1969; Bandura and Walters, 1963; Mischel, 1968; Peterson, 1968) emphasize social variables and underscore the general importance of social interaction.

Several attempts have been made to enhance the social behavior of isolate children (Allen, Hart, Buell, Harris, and Wolf, 1964; Hart, Reynolds, Baer, Brawley, and Harris, 1968; Hartup, 1964; Patterson and Anderson, 1964) through differential reinforcement. These studies have shown that if peer interaction is reinforced, either socially or otherwise, and isolate play is either punished or ignored, children eventually display a higher level of social behavior. The utilization of a treatment program based solely on reinforcement procedures may encounter difficulties in the development of social responsiveness in extreme isolates. However, while a series of preliminary observations which served as a pilot for the present study found 20% or more of nursery school children exhibiting rela-

[1]This research was supported by Public Health Research Grant M-5162 from the National Institute of Mental Health to Albert Bandura, and by the Louis Haas Research Fund, Stanford University. The author is grateful to Professor Bandura, whose enthusiastic assistance and many suggestions were invaluable during all phases of this project, and to Professor Eleanor E. Maccoby, who provided support and helpful comments during the initial stages of the experiment. Professors Robert R. Sears and Edith Dowley generously assisted in the design and implementation of observational procedures, and Marian O'Connor collaborated on numerous resources which insured the success of the program.

JOURNAL OF APPLIED BEHAVIOR ANALYSIS, 1969, Vol. 2, pp. 15-22.

tively low levels of social responsiveness, many of whom could be helped by arranging favorable response consequences; a smaller percentage of children either perform no social interaction response or provide only rare opportunities for the application of reinforcement. When such gross deficits exist, the reinforcing agent must either introduce a rather laborious set of "shaping" procedures, which requires waiting for the emission of a reinforceable social response, or resort to more active means for establishing the desired behavior.

Lovaas (1966) showed that relatively complex repertoires can be established to replace gross deficits through a combination of modeling and reinforcement procedures. Of greater interest and relevance to the approach used in the present study is evidence that children can acquire new patterns of behavior on the basis of observation alone (Bandura and Huston, 1961; Bandura and McDonald, 1963; Bandura and Mischel, 1965; Bandura, Ross, and Ross, 1963; Hicks, 1965). Since repertoires can thus be learned on a non-response basis, with no reinforcement to the observer, a modeling program may be particularly effective in the case of gross behavior deficits.

It was noted earlier that in most cases, severe withdrawal reflects both deficits in social skills and avoidance of interpersonal situations. An optimal treatment, therefore, should transmit new social competencies and also extinguish social fears. Modeling procedures are also ideally suited for this purpose. A series of studies by Bandura (1968a) demonstrated that various patterns of avoidance behavior can be successfully eliminated through modeling, and that such procedures are readily applicable to therapeutic situations.

By devising a carefully constructed film sequence, the therapist can stage rather complicated situations and events in a dramatic manner that controls the viewer's attention to relevant cues. While the exclusion of extraneous events provides much of this attention control, the enthusiastic and emotionally expressive behavior of models can further enhance attention and vicarious learning in the viewer (Bandura, 1962; Berger, 1962; Berger and Johansson, 1968). Once the observer's attention has thus been directed toward the filmed events, the therapist may introduce repeated exposure to clearly defined stimuli.

Positive response consequences to the model, such as social praise or material reinforcements for modeled behaviors, which have been shown to increase the performance of similar behavior in observers (Bandura, 1965; Bandura, 1968b), can also be incorporated into filmed events. Symbolic modeling processes employing such principles have effectively extinguished severe avoidance behavior in children (Bandura and Menlove, 1968).

The present experiment sought to extend the use of symbolic modeling to the modification of social withdrawal. This approach appears particularly well suited for achieving both of the desired outcomes indicated in the pathology described above; i.e., the transmission of social skills and the extinction of social fears. These two modeling processes, along with the facilitation of interpersonal behaviors which may exist in the observers' repertoire, provided the rationale for the manipulation of social interaction behavior, which in fact comprised the focus of the experimental change assessment.

Children who displayed extreme social withdrawal were shown a sound-film depicting peers engaged in progressively more active social interaction. The viewers were children who not only had very low base-rates of social interaction, according to the dual assessment procedure (below), but whose frequent retreats into corners, closets, and lockers gave observers and teachers a similar impression of active, purposive withdrawal in many instances. The filmed behavior of peers presented to these "isolates" was actively followed by reinforcing outcomes such as peer approval, either verbal or expressional (smiling, nodding, etc.); peer acceptance of the model into a game or a conversation, i.e., invitations to join or offering play materials or reaching out to take the model's hand, etc.; in most scenes the model behavior resulted in some tangible reinforcement such as a block or other toy, a book to read together with the peers, a dish to wash or dry in a cooperative homemaking activity; and so on. A second group of equally withdrawn children viewed a film that contained no human characters. After exposure to their respective films, the children's social behavior was observed in the nursery school situation. It was predicted that children having the benefits of symbolic mod-

212

eling would display a significant increase in social interaction with their peers.

## METHOD

*Selection of Isolates*

Head teachers in each of nine nursery school classes were asked to choose from their enrolment lists the five most socially withdrawn children in their class. Each teacher was to rank order these five children "who interact the least with their peers". Of the 365 children enrolled, the 45 nominated in this preliminary selection and 26 children randomly chosen from the remaining non-isolates were then observed in the nursery school setting at randomly selected times throughout the day.

Each child was observed for a total of 32 intervals, each interval consisting of 15 sec, over a period of eight days (with the time of day counterbalanced on consecutive days). During each 15-sec interval, the children's behavior was scored in terms of five separate response categories; one every 3 sec. These included physical proximity, verbal interaction, "looking at", "interacting with", and the size of the group involved in any interaction sequence. Although the first three response categories, considered social orienting responses, were scored, the measure of social behavior was based entirely on the frequency with which the children interacted with their peers (*i e.*, category four). The three categories of "orienting" responses and the "size of group" category were included in the observations for intra-sample reliability checks and for possible assessment purposes in case the primary "interacts" category had not reflected such notable change in the children's behavior. Obviously, a score in the "interaction" category necessitated "proximity and looking at" responses, and increases in the less critical "verbalizes" and "number in group" categories had to accompany most interactions performed by these former isolates. The major emphasis of the experimental manipulation, therefore, was on the interaction scores, and the changes assessed were in this category alone, although changes in the other behavioral categories were at least as significant as those reported in the response class of interest here. A social interaction was defined as any behavior directed toward another child which involved a reciprocal quality. Neither parallel play nor solitary verbalizations qualified. The two-way nature of a scorable interaction necessitated not only the output of the subject child, but some indication of recognition and attention from the second child in the interaction. Thus, if a subject spoke to or otherwise directed his behavior to another child, but the second child did not respond in any way, at least appearing to be aware of the intended interaction, no score was given for an interaction.

Six trained observers performed the ratings. During a randomly chosen 50% of the sessions, these observers were paired and observed a given child independently but simultaneously. Inter-scorer reliability on each of these sessions was $r = > 0.92$. (# of agreements/the 32 possible agreements on a given child's interactions), which allowed for matched observer correlations across subjects of $r = 0.90 +$ (product-moment) in all pairs of observers.

Children who scored fewer than five of 32 possible interactions and who had been rated by teachers as isolates were selected as subjects and randomly assigned to either the modeling or the control film conditions. Thus, to qualify for the experiment, children had to meet the dual criteria of having exhibited extreme withdrawal over a long period of time as judged by their teachers, and to have displayed isolate behavior as measured by objective behavioral observations. Of the 20 "isolates" who met these criteria, 13 were included in the experiment; four of the remaining seven were omitted because they were frequently absent from school; and three of the children vigorously refused to leave the nursery room.

The 26 non-isolate children were primarily included to furnish an additional baseline for evaluating any changes produced by the treatment program. These children displayed a mean of 9.1 social interactions, while the means for children assigned to the modeling and control conditions were 1.75 and 1.50 respectively, with the scores in both groups ranging from 0 to 5. The modeling group contained four girls and two boys and the control group, four girls and three boys.

*Treatment Conditions*

Children in both conditions were brought individually to the experimental room where they were told they could watch a television program. Each child was seated before a large TV console while the experimenter plugged in the set and ostensibly tuned in the picture. The films were shown on a glass lenscreen by means of a rear projector arrangement. As the apparatus was plugged in, the hidden projector and tape recorder were activated simultaneously. An extension speaker directed the sound through the TV set.

The experimenter left the child alone in the room to view the film on the pretext that he had some work to complete and would return before the film had ended. The experimenter then observed the session through a one-way mirror from an adjoining room. All children appeared to be highly attentive to the "TV show" throughout the film. The attention apparently commanded by the television presentation was quite impressive and obviously advantageous to the experimental procedure.

Children in the modeling condition saw a sound-color film lasting approximately 23 min. The film portrayed a sequence of 11 scenes in which children interacted in a nursery school setting. In each of these episodes, a child is shown first observing the interaction of others and then joining in the social activities, with reinforcing consequences ensuing. The other children, for example, offer him play material, talk to him, smile and generally respond in a positive manner to his advances into the activity. The scenes were graduated on a dimension of threat in terms of the vigor of the social activity and the size of the group. The initial scenes involve very calm activities such as sharing a book or toy while two children are seated at a table. In the terminal scenes, as many as six children are shown gleefully tossing play equipment around the room.

Multiple modeling has been shown to be more efficacious than single modeling (Bandura and Menlove, 1968). Also, a second pilot study conducted as a preliminary to the present experiment suggested a powerful effect on social behavior of subjects as a result of multiple, live peer-modeling; the child displaying the social approach behavior was varied from scene to scene in terms of age and sex, including a total of six different models, four girls and two boys, with their ages ranging from 4 to 7 yr.

To accent further the modeling cues and the positive consequences associated with the social behavior of the approaching child, a narrative sound track was prepared in which a woman's voice, judged by the experimenter to be very soothing, described the actions of the model and the other children in the ongoing sequence. The script consisted entirely of descriptions of ongoing social responses and outcomes and was a further attempt to focus the viewers' attention to relevant cues.

The control film depicted 20 min of the acrobatic performances of Marineland dolphins and was accompanied by a musical soundtrack. Since the film contained no human characters, it provided a control for any effects which might have been derived solely from the presentation of a film in the experimental procedure and contact with experimenters. The control group further provided a basis on which to measure any change in the social behavior of isolate subjects which might have occurred as a result of nursery school participation during the course of the project.[2]

*Post-Treatment Assessment*

Immediately after being shown their respective films, the children were returned to their regular classrooms. They were given 2 min to adapt to the classroom situation, after which they were observed for 32 consecutive intervals, each lasting 15 sec, according to the same observation procedure employed in the pretreatment assessment. The social interaction score was again the number of 15-sec intervals in which the child displayed a direct social interchange (defined according to the "reciprocal quality" criteria mentioned earlier) with one or more children. In order to control for any bias in ratings, observers were kept unaware of condition assignments, and each observed a random combination of treated and control subjects. Aside from the usual "blind assessment" control, this randomizing technique was thought to reduce further any possible observer bias.

## RESULTS

Figure 1 represents the mean number of social interaction responses performed by chil-

[2]A copy of the 400 ft super-8-mm film and soundtrack can be obtained from the author for approximately $66.00 (cost) plus $6.00 for packing and mailing.

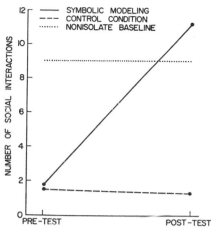

Fig. 1. Mean number of social interactions displayed by subjects in the modeling and control conditions, before and after the experimental sessions. The dotted line represents the level of interactions manifested by 26 non-isolate children who were observed at the pretest phase of the study.

dren in the modeling and control conditions during the pretest and immediately after the experimental session.

An analysis of within-group changes showed that the seven control children remained essentially unchanged, whereas the six children who had viewed the modeling film markedly increased their level of social interaction ($t = 2.29$; $p < 0.03$). The post-test interaction scores of treated subjects were in fact similar to those of non-isolates who had been observed during the pretest period.

A between-groups analysis revealed the change in social interaction to be significantly greater for subjects in the modeling treatment than for controls ($t = 2.53$; $p = 0.015$) A between-groups comparison of the levels of social interaction achieved at post-test indicated significant differences as evaluated by either the t-test ($t = 2.70$; $p = 0.01$) or the Mann Whitney U-test ($U = 3.0$; $p < 0.004$).

Having measured the powerful effects of the modeling film in terms of the group comparisons above, data for the individual subjects in the modeling condition were found to indicate consistent positive changes across subjects. All six children in the modeling condition exhibited increased social interaction behavior in the post-film assessment. Children in the control condition performed essentially the same number of interactions before and after viewing the control film, with only slight increases or decreases in the behavior.

## DISCUSSION

The present results established symbolic modeling as a highly efficacious procedure for modifying social withdrawal. Children who did not receive the modeling treatment remained socially withdrawn, whereas those who observed a systematic filmed presentation of peer interactions associated with reinforcing consequences displayed a significant increase in social responsiveness.

Follow-up observations could not be made because the nursery school term was completed. However, a second set of teachers' ratings was obtained at the end of the school year. The teachers, who were kept uninformed as to which conditions children had been assigned, again rated the five most withdrawn children from their enrollment lists as they had done in the preliminary selection. Only one of the six subjects who had been in the modeling condition was still rated as an isolate. It is interesting to note that this child, who also improved the least as measured by behavior observation, viewed the modeling film with the sound track 20-sec behind the picture due to a mechanical failure. Four of the seven control subjects were again judged to be extreme isolates. Although these findings have some suggestive value, they should be accepted with reservations because of the global nature of the ratings and the fact that changes in classroom enrollment may affect their comparability.

Immediate treatment effects achieved by symbolic modeling may produce lasting changes in social interaction without the need of additional procedures, provided that the children's initial social behavior is favorably received by peers. However, the application of systematic reinforcement of appropriate social responses would ensure the maintenance of the induced behavioral changes. Bandura has suggested "the combined use of modeling and reinforcement procedures" as the most efficacious mode of therapy in "eliminating severe behavioral inhibitions" (Bandura, Grusec, and Menlove, 1967). In order to substan-

215

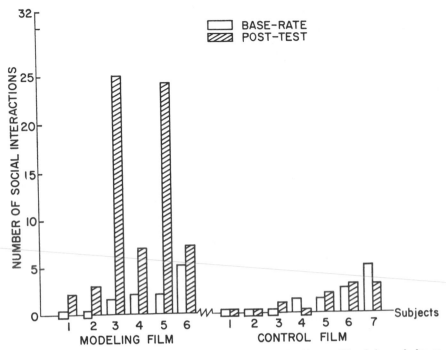

Fig. 2. Actual number of social interactions displayed by each child in either condition, before and after exposure to the modeling or control film.

tiate this hypothesis a study needs to be conducted which extends the design of the present experiment to include durational (follow-up) assessment periods, as well as a comparison of modeling, shaping, and combined treatment procedures. In the present study, social inhibitions were reduced and appropriate social responses were facilitated through symbolic modeling with built-in reinforcement to the model. New responses to familiar social stimuli which were formerly assumed to have elicited avoidance behavior were acquired vicariously within one treatment session.

The subsequent performance of these newly acquired behaviors is seen as primarily resulting from the facilitation and extinction effects which derive from the observation of models performing the target behaviors with no aversive consequences ensuing. This theoretical explanation of the modeling effects achieved

is based on the same set of experimental data which guided the construction of the treatment film (an important point in the comparison of differential treatment outcomes). A distinction is drawn between response *acquisition* and response *performance* according to experimental data derived from a recent experiment (Bandura, 1965b) which suggested that novel behaviors may be acquired by observers, even though the models are punished, but that these responses may not be performed readily without the addition of strong incentives beyond those of the situational stimuli in the modeling presentation. The conclusion from this study is theoretically relevant to the present discussion, in that it suggests that a model's reinforcement contingencies may be negative enough to inhibit performance of newly acquired responses, but have little or no effect on their acquisition. Other data, such as the Berger (1962, 1968) studies mentioned earlier and a recent demonstration of arousal reduction in snake phobics through live modeling (Blanchard, 1968), provide support for the additional modeling effects of disinhibition and the facilitation of responses existing in the observer's repertoire, which complete the three-fold theory of modeling effects incorporated into the design of the present film and the theoretical explanation of its effects.

An alternative explanation for the increased social behavior of children who observed the modeling film might be based strictly on the principles of reinforcement theory. Since the data here indicate only changes in the rate of social interaction responses, it might be argued that the simplest behavioral description would identify the filmed presentation as a discriminative stimulus for appropriate matching responses. (Baer and Sherman, 1964; Baer, Peterson, and Sherman, 1967; Peterson, 1968). This approach would be based upon what is often considered the most parsimonious behavioral analysis of observable events, i.e., the performance of measurable behaviors and a description of the stimulus situation in which the matching behaviors, as a "functional response class", occurred. The rationale for such a description might be based upon the observer's prior history of reinforcement for matching models' behavior, or similar conceptions of "imitation", per se, with emphasis on the change in reinforcement value of models' behavior, the controlling power of modeled behavior as a discriminative stimulus, etc. (Staats, 1963, 1968). Aside from recent suggestions concerning the presumptive nature of these "heavyweight" reinforcement-theory explanations (Glucksberg, 1968); the parsimony deriving from reinforcement approaches, in terms of therapeutic efficiency, has not yet been demonstrated in instances where gross behavior deficits are identified as the change worthy phenomena. The expense of "shaping time" must be compared to a treatment which may provide for the acquisition of possibly novel skills according to principles of associative learning (contiguous presentation of modeling stimuli), as well as facilitating the performance of modeled responses and other appropriate behaviors in the observer's repertoire (discriminative stimulus function of non-aversive modeled behavioral outcomes), while reducing negative arousal responses to feared

stimuli, all in one treatment session. The explanatory value of reinforcement principles may thus be relevant to performance variables, while an approach that is intended to effect input (learning) variables as well may provide treatment procedures with markedly greater applicability to behavior deficit conditions. The allowance for possible *learning deficits* in treatment strategies designed to modify *behavior deficits, i.e.,* attention to input as well as output deficits, may be much more than a theoretical distinction. The powerful effects of the modeling presentation reported here underscore what appears to be a very practical, therapeutically useful reason to allow for the notion of mediational processes as well as reinforcement principles when these factors may be relevant to the therapeutic strategy.

This brief discussion of two possible explanations of the modeling effects achieved in the present study may serve to direct the reader's attention to further analyses of the modeling process in general. Thoroughly detailed presentations may be found in more appropriate publications (Bandura, 1968c; Bandura, 1969; Mischel, 1968; O'Connor, 1969; Staats, 1968; Ullmann, 1968).

It should be noted in passing that the present experiment achieved significant changes in social behavior among children with relatively severe deficits without developing a therapeutic relationship. Until recently, a fairly intimate client-therapist relationship and the attainment of insight have been considered necessary conditions for personality change. In contrast, the results and discussion above indicate that the social behavior of children can be effectively enhanced by efforts to arrange social stimulus conditions which may ensure the acquisition of requisite competencies, the reduction of inhibiting fears, and the facilitation of appropriate responses. It should also be apparent that attention to learning variables provides for treatment procedures which can optimistically be applied to any program of behavior change. Teachers and other social agents might greatly increase the efficacy of their work with individual children, as well as in group procedures, by employing some of the principles of social learning and symbolic modeling presented here. The use of carefully designed therapeutic films in classroom and experimental situations alike may provide significantly more efficient modification of various behavior deficits and other deviant behaviors.

## REFERENCES

Allen, K. E., Hart, B. M., Buell, J. S., Harris, F. R., and Wolf, M. M. Effects of social reinforcement on isolate behavior of a nursery school child. *Child Development*, 1964, **35**, 511-518.

Bandura, A. Influence of models' reinforcement contingencies on the acquisition of imitative responses. *Journal of Personality and Social Psychology*, 1965, **1**, 589-595. (*b*)

Bandura, A. Modeling approaches to the modification of phobic disorders. *Ciba Foundation symposium: The role of learning in psychotherapy.* London: Churchill, 1968. (*a*)

Bandura, A. *Principles of behavior modification.* New York: Holt, Rinehart & Winston, 1969, (in press).

Bandura, A. A social learning interpretation of psychological dysfunctions. In P. London and D. Rosehan (Eds.) *Foundations of abnormal psychology.* New York; Holt, Rinehart & Winston, 1968. Pp. 293-344.

Bandura, A. Social learning theory of identificatory processes. In D. A. Goslin (Ed.), *Handbook of socialization theory and research.* Chicago: Rand McNally, 1968. Pp. 213-262 (*b*)

Bandura, A. Social learning through imitation. In M. R. Jones (Ed.), *Nebraska Symposium of Motivation: 1962.* Lincoln: University of Nebraska Press, 1962. Pp. 211-269.

Bandura, A. Vicarious processes: A case of no-trial learning. In L. Berkowitz (Ed.), *Advances in experimental social psychology.* Vol. II. New York: Academic Press, 1965. Pp. 1-55.

Bandura, A., Grusec, J., and Menlove, F. L. Vicarious extinction of avoidance behavior. *Journal of Personality and Social Psychology*, 1967, **5**, 16-23.

Bandura, A. and Huston, Aletha C. Identification as a process of incidental learning. *Journal of Abnormal and Social Psychology*, 1961, **63**, 311-318.

Bandura, A. and McDonald, F. J. Influence of social reinforcement and the behavior of models in shaping children's moral judgments. *Journal of Abnormal and Social Psychology*, 1963, **67**, 274-281.

Bandura, A. and Menlove, F. L. Factors determining vicarious extinction of avoidance behavior through symbolic modeling. *Journal of Personality and Social Psychology*, 1968, **8**, 99-108.

Bandura, A. and Mischel, W. Modification of self-imposed delay of reward through exposure to live and symbolic models. *Journal of Personality and Social Psychology*, 1965, **2**, 698-705.

Bandura, A., Ross, D., and Ross, S. A. Transmission of aggression through imitation of aggressive models. *Journal of Abnormal and Social Psychology*, 1961, **64**, 575-582.

Bandura, A. and Walters, R. *Social learning and personality development.* New York: Holt, Rinehart & Winston, 1963.

Baer, D. M. and Sherman, J. A. Reinforcement control of generalized imitation in young children. *Journal of Experimental Child Psychology*, 1964, **1**, 37-49.

Baer, D. M., Peterson, R. F., and Sherman, J. A. The development of imitation by reinforcing behavioral similarity to a model. *Journal of the Experimental Analysis of Behavior*, 1967, **10**, 405-416.

Berger, S. M. Conditioning through vicarious instigation. *Psychological Review*, 1962, **69**, 450-466.

Berger, S. M. and Johansson, S. L. Effect of model's expressed emotions on an observer's resistance to extinction. *Journal of Personality and Social Psychology*, 1968, **10**, 53-58.

Blanchard, E. B. *Relative contributions of modeling, informational influences, and physical contact in the extinction of phobic behavior.* Unpublished doctoral dissertation. Stanford University, 1968.

Eysenck, H. J. *Experiments in behavior therapy.* New York: Macmillan, 1964.

Glucksberg, S. A self-made straw man. *Contemporary Psychology*, 1968, **13**, 624-625.

Hart, B. M., Reynolds, N. H., Baer, D. M., Brawley, E. R., and Harris, F. R. Effect of contingent and non-contingent social reinforcement on the cooperative play of a preschool child. *Journal of Applied Behavior Analysis*, 1968, **1**, 73-76.

Hartup, W. W. Peers as agents of social reinforcement. *Young Children*, **20**, 1965.

Hicks, D. J. Imitation and retention of film-mediated aggressive peer and adult models. *Journal of Personality and Social Psychology*, 1965, **2**, 97-100.

Krasner, L. and Ullmann, L. P. *Research in behavior therapy.* New York: Macmillan, 1964.

Lovaas, I., Berberich, J. P., Perlof, B. F., and Schaeffer, B. Acquisition of imitative speech by schizophrenic children. *Science*, 1966, **151**, 705-707.

Mischel, W. *Personality and assessment.* New York: Wiley & Sons, 1968.

O'Connor, R. D. *Modeling treatment of non-behavior disorders.* Paper presented at 41st annual meeting of the Midwestern Psychological Association, Chicago, March 1969.

Patterson, G. R. and Anderson, D. Peers as social reinforcers. *Child Development*, 1964, **35**, 951-960.

Peterson, D. R. *The clinical study of social behavior.* New York: Appleton, Century, Crofts, 1968.

Peterson, R. F. Some experiments on the organization of a class of imitative behaviors. *Journal of Applied Behavior Analysis*, 1968, **3**, 225-235.

Staats, A. W. *Learning, language, and cognition.* New York, Holt, Rinehart & Winston, 1968.

Staats, A. W. and Staats, C. K. *Complex human behavior.* New York, Holt, Rinehart & Winston, 1963.

Ullmann, L. P. Making use of modeling in the therapeutic interview. Paper read at A.A.B.T. meetings, San Francisco, 1968.

Wolpe, J. and Lazarus, A. A. *Behavior therapy techniques.* London: Pergamon Press, 1966.

PAUL S. GRAUBARD

# Utilizing the Group in Teaching Disturbed Delinquents to Learn

IT HAS been demonstrated that the use of teacher praise and attention can effectively modify the behavior of low achieving and obstreperous children (Hall, Lund, & Jackson, 1968). Other studies report that token reinforcement productively changes behavior with the emotionally disturbed (O'Leary & Becker, 1967), the retarded (Bijou, 1966), the culturally deprived (Wolf, Giles, & Hall, 1968), and with a culturally deprived juvenile delinquent (Staats & Butterfield, 1965).

The Staats and Butterfield study was limited in that only a single subject was worked with and the teacher did not have to contend with antisocial behavior being reinforced by peers. Peers are, however, present in school situations. A study by Zimmerman and Zimmerman (1962) in a special education class found, in contrast to the Hall study, that teacher praise acted to decrease academic performance. Peer reinforcement might account for the different results of the two studies, for in certain subcultures the peer group can be a more

PAUL S. GRAUBARD is Associate Professor, Department of Special Education, Ferkauf Graduate School of Humanities and Social Sciences, Yeshiva University, New York.

EXCEPTIONAL CHILDREN, December 1969, pp. 267-272.

powerful reinforcer than the teacher. Nevertheless, the effect of the peer group is largely unexplored in the educational literature, and clinical experience and sociological theory suggest that many learners are caught up in the battle between peer and school values. These students probably comprise a sizable proportion of the educational casualties in schools. Enough theory has been generated to warrant attacking this problem directly.

## The Culture of the Delinquent

Cloward and Ohlin (1960) suggested that the school represents a value system and a way of life that is unacceptable to urban delinquents. Thus, a delinquent who is successful in school according to school norms risks losing status in his group. Cloward and Ohlin also argued that because of differential opportunities, certain rewards of society are denied to many youngsters. These individuals then band together to form a delinquent subculture which is capable of developing its own reward system. Parsons (1954) maintained that school and academic learning are perceived as unmasculine by delinquents and predelinquents. The group is formed to consolidate a masculine front as imposing as the demands of the schools. Parsons maintained that this is particularly true in urban areas where the female centered household is more common.

In the face of this, the general pattern of schools is to attempt to win individual students over to the traditional social values of success and reward. This has been called the "artichoke technique," because the teacher attempts to peel the child away from the group just as one peels the artichoke leaves off the stem. This technique is not universally successful because of the limited battery of rewards available to the teacher, as well as the relatively low power and status of the school when compared with the peer group. Clinical evidence has been found (Minuchin, Chamberlain, & Graubard, 1967) that with disturbed delinquents, rewards and teaching coming from peers are more effective than rewards and teaching associated with authority figures, such as teachers.

The primary purpose of this project was to ascertain whether the delinquent peer culture could explicitly be enlisted in the acquisition of academic skills and the diminution of antischool behavior, and to determine if children could learn more effectively and efficiently by utilizing the peer group as the reinforcing agent rather than the teacher. Another purpose of the study was to examine the process of managing and teaching disruptive groups by a clearly explicated teaching method.

**Method**

*Subjects.* The subjects were eight boys in residential treatment through court order for antisocial behaviors. They formed a natural group in that they comprised the residential population of an agency and made up a delinquent subculture within the agency. The boys had lived together for approximately one year. They ranged in age from 10 to 12. Their psychiatric diagnoses varied although the label "undifferentiated" is the most descriptive (Auerswald, 1964). IQ scores ranged from 74 to 112. Reading levels ranged from third to sixth grade. The referring agency was asked to select their most aggressive children for inclusion in the experimental classroom. Each subject had an extensive history of disruptive behavior in school situations.

*Setting.* Sessions were held at a university classroom 4 days a week for a one month period during the summer. The room, which was similar to public school classrooms in New York City, was a self contained unit, equipped with a one way vision mirror and closed circuit television.

*Instructional program.* The teaching day was divided into several segments: a reading period in which SRA and Sullivan materials were used, an arithmetic period in which teacher-made worksheets were completed, a dramatics period, a social studies discussion period, and free time if work had been completed and no antisocial conduct had been displayed during the school day. During this free time the boys were allowed to play games, but the children generally elected to bring their own records and phonograph and dance.

*Data recording.* Subjects were observed directly. Observers, stationed behind the one way mirror, observed the class for two 24 minute periods each hour. The subjects did not know when they were being observed although they were fully aware that there was an observer. The observer checked off the behavior of each subject by going down the list of names every 10 seconds for a 3 minute period. Each boy was observed approximately 36 times per hour, or 108 times per school morning. Using an observation schema adapted from Becker (1967), the subjects were given an "A" for appropriate behavior, which was defined as following directions, eyes on work, writing, speaking to the teacher or to peers about school matters, or following school routines and/or teacher instruction. The boys received an "I" for inappropriate behavior, which was defined as disrupting the class, cursing, throwing objects, hitting, being out of seat without permission, or talking without permission. The subjects received an "E" for excused absence, which was defined as going to the bathroom with permission, going for a drink with permission, etc. A finer breakdown of both appropriate and inappropriate behaviors was kept to help plan programs for individual boys, but these different behaviors can be subsumed under "A" or "I" for this report. The only school rules which were put into effect were that (a) attendance was mandatory (an agency requirement), (b) subjects could not destroy property, and (c) subjects could not use physical force. Infraction of these rules meant that the boys had to leave school for the day.

The observer ratings were checked by two other judges at least three times each week and agreement never fell below 92 percent. Reliability was calculated by total numbers of agreement over total numbers of observation times 100.

### Design

The class was taught under three different conditions. In each case the teacher's performance was continually monitored by two judges to make sure that she followed the required, predetermined teaching conditions. In the first condition (A) a group consensus determined reinforcers. The subjects selected kites, goldfish, shirts, baseball bats, marbles, and money. Points were assigned to each of these given items and the acquisition of these reinforcers was contingent upon *each* subject in the group achieving a minimum number of points. Points could be earned for following school rules and achieving specified outputs of academic work explicitly defined for each subject area. Rules dealing with attendance, destruction of property, and use of physical force in the classroom were given to the subjects and not open to discussion. Other rules dealing with talking out, standards for work, rules for discussions, procedures for working with the teacher, etc., were evolved by the teacher and pupils. The teacher then explained that she would not insist that children follow the rules, but would instead devote all her energy to assisting with academic work, keeping records, and giving out points for appropriate behavior. If the class engaged in inappropriate behavior the teacher would tolerate it, but the subjects would not receive their reinforcers.

Management of the class was then given to the subjects. No formal structure was established for this. Instead, the subjects would spontaneously remind transgressors that inappropriate behavior affected them all. A frequency count showed that these reminders usually came from the children who scored highest on a class sociometric device and were judged by the adults to be the group leaders.

The teacher did not react to inappropriate behavior (except when it involved destruction of property or use of physical force). To achieve appropriate behavior she rang a bonus bell at which time she would dispense bonus points. The bonus bell was rung at variable intervals; at first it was rung frequently (once every 4 minutes or less) on a random schedule, and later at longer intervals. If everyone were behaving appropriately when the bell rang, each subject earned 10 bonus points.

The bonus bell was based on the assumption that the more that the subjects displayed appropriate behavior the more likely they were to be rewarded. This assumption was predicated on the fact that since the boys could never be sure when the bonus bell would ring, and since acting appropriately when the bell rang resulted in achieving desired rewards, it was to their own advantage to act appropriately most of the time to increase the probability of being "caught" acting appropriately. The bonus bell was used for each contingency period although it was used less and less as the project progressed.

The group consensus period was followed by the noncontingent (B) reward condition. During this condition the same academic routines and work were followed as in the A period but points were given at the beginning of the day and thus were not contingent on the subjects' behaviors. Teacher praise, grades, and exhortation were used to help the boys complete academic tasks and follow school regulations. In addition, the teacher intervened during periods of obstreperous behavior, whereas under group consensus, obstreperous and inappropriate behaviors were ignored and left for the group to handle.

After the noncontingent teaching condition, the A group consensus condition was reinstated. (See A[1] in Figure 1 and Table 1.) Then the last condition (C) was initiated. During this condition (group and individual contingencies), each subject still had to achieve minimum behavior and academic points to win group prizes, but the prizes were changed

221

to snacks such as chicken, cake, and pizza. Individuals were then allowed to work for self selected prizes which were again made contingent upon achieving additional specified numbers of academic points. During the beginning of the project, behavior points were worth twice as much as academic points, but as the sessions progressed, these procedures were reversed.

## Results

The dependent variables in this study were appropriate and inappropriate classroom behaviors and reading levels. Reading gains were measured by progression from lower level SRA material to SRA material of a higher grade level. Each subject was able to read and comprehend material at least two color cards above his own entry point or baseline during the course of the 20 session project. SRA programs are divided into different levels of difficulty which are shown by a color code. These levels of difficulty roughly correspond to grade level.

Figure 1 shows how subjects performed during each condition. Since conditions were run for different lengths of time and since subjects were absent for varying lengths of time because of dental visits, etc., the most meaningful comparison seemed to be percent of behaviors based on total number of observations for each teaching condition.

The probability values of the changes in behavior have been calculated by the median test (Siegal, 1956) and are shown in Table 1.

Two things must be said about the results:

1. As the sessions progressed, the subjects had to complete increasingly longer assignments to achieve the same number of points and the behavior points decreased in value.

2. For purposes of this study, cursing was considered an inappropriate behavior. During the group conditions the majority of "I's" were received for cursing, an act which appeared to receive tremendous group reinforcement. Given a teacher with a high tolerance level for vulgar words, the "I" behaviors would have decreased to practically zero.

In addition the subjects had to leave school for infraction of rules regarding destruction of property and/or using physical force four times during the B condition, one time during the A condition, and no time during C.

## Discussion

The data show that the procedures used in this classroom were effective in increasing academic output of the group, in shaping appropriate classroom behaviors, and in eliminating disruptive behaviors. In fact, during the individual reward condition, for 3 days of the 6 day period, there were only two or fewer disruptive incidents observed in students who had been especially picked for aggressive behavior and who had a long history of failure in and expulsion from public schools. The group was able to move from a 24 percent inappropriate behavior level (approximately once in every 4 minutes) to 10 percent (once in 10 minutes), a much more tolerable level. In addition, subjects showed substantial progress in reading achievement as measured by completed frames of programed instruction and completion of teacher produced arithmetic worksheets. While the design of this study does not allow us to gauge the relative ef-

### TABLE 1

#### Probability Levels of Change in Behavior During Different Teaching Conditions

| Conditions | | Appropriate | Excused | Inappropriate |
|---|---|---|---|---|
| Noncontingent (B) vs. Group Consensus | (A¹) | .04 | NS | .02 |
| (A¹)  Group Consensus vs. Group + Individual (C) | | .01 | NS | .01 |
| (C)  Group + Individual vs. Noncontingent  (B) | | .005 | .02 | .005 |

*Note:*—Due to the small number of days during A, significance between A and B is not possible to obtain by the median test and therefore no statistical analysis was made, but inspection of Figure 1 shows the trend of the direction of the changes.

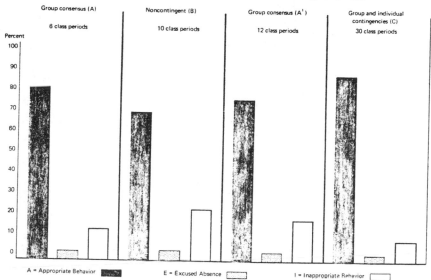

FIGURE 1. Subjects' behaviors during different teaching conditions.

Group consensus (A)    Noncontingent (B)    Group consensus (A¹)    Group and individual contingencies (C)

6 class periods    10 class periods    12 class periods    30 class periods

A = Appropriate Behavior        E = Excused Absence        I = Inappropriate Behavior

ficiency of this method compared to other approaches, such as going directly from noncontingent to individual rewards, the fact that this group was able to learn and behave in school is important in and of itself.

The process by which this occurred is worth analyzing, albeit speculatively. The fact that the group gave its consensus for rewards appears to be an important part of the process. Academic prowess and classroom conformity are not values that are highly admired by this population (Brown, 1965, Parsons, 1954). Great pressure is put on children not to conform to rules of authority (Polsky, 1962), and severe punishment is meted out by their peers to those children who do violate peer values. It is felt by the author that the group must consciously legitimize learning so that the individuals in the group do not have to concern themselves with loss of status for learning. This is not unlike family therapy where explicit permission must be given by the more powerful family members before a given topic can be discussed by individuals. In the group reward condition, learning is reinforced by the group since the group benefits from the performance of the individual. While there is no direct evidence from this study, it is doubtful

if many individuals are strong enough to resist the mores of the delinquent group regarding school achievement, and this might help to explain the low achievement of so many delinquent youth (Prentice & Kelley, 1963).

Once the group had sanctioned learning there was a sudden shift in the performance of individuals and disruptions began to decrease. While group rewards appear to be considerably better than noncontingent payoff, Condition C, group and individual rewards, was introduced because the eventual goal was to bring these subjects into the mainstream of education and to have them work with only minimal dependence on the group. In addition, there was a concern about a least effort effect where subjects would only work to achieve the group minimum.

Individual rewards were then introduced so the subjects could receive rewards in excess of those achieved by the group, contingent on the subject's own effort. Under this condition, after they had received the group's permission to learn, a dramatic increase in learning was noted with a simultaneous decrease of disruptive behavior.

The fact that the group took responsibility

223

for itself, gave individual members permission to learn, and could concretely achieve its own goals and rewards appears to have been the paramount factor in the success of this project.

The group's managing itself is not unlike aspects of the civil rights struggle in which groups and communities manage themselves, but will not be told what to do. It is recognized that this study was of short duration, used a small number of subjects, and took place in a laboratory setting rather than a public school. In other settings and over longer periods of time the boys might have reverted to former patterns of behavior or been more intractable regarding change. Only longer term studies which are now underway in public school settings can answer these questions. Nevertheless, the subjects were capable of shifting behavior when the environment shifted so that the teacher was able to teach and guide academic learning for most of the school day, and the group appeared to be instrumental in this process. To date, there has been little consonance between the world of disturbed delinquent children and the school. Instead of being cognizant of, negotiating with, and enlisting the support of the group, educators have traditionally ignored it and usually this has been done at the expense of the teacher and especially the children.

# References

Auerswald, E. Developmental effects of poverty in children of hard core urban families: Implications for nosology and treatment. Paper presented at the American Orthopsychiatric Association, Chicago, 1964.

Becker, W. C., Madsen, C. H., Jr., Arnold, C. R., & Thomas, D. R. The contingent use of teacher attention and praise in reducing classroom behavior problems. *Journal of Special Education*, 1967, **1**, 287-307.

Bijou, S. W. Functional analysis of retarded development. In N. R. Ellis (Ed.), *International review of research in mental retardation*. Vol. 1. New York: Academic Press, 1966. Pp. 1-19.

Brown, C. *Manchild in the promised land*. New York: MacMillan, 1965.

Cloward, R., & Ohlin, L. *Delinquency and opportunity: A theory of delinquent gangs*. Glencoe, Ill.: Free Press, 1960.

Hall, V., Lund, D., & Jackson, D. Effects of teacher attention on study behavior. *Journal of Applied Behavior Analysis*, 1968, **1**, 1-12.

Minuchin, S., Chamberlain, P., & Graubard, P. A project to teach learning skills to disturbed delinquent children. *American Journal of Orthopsychiatry*, 1967, 37, 558-567.

O'Leary, K. D., & Becker, W. C. Behavior modification of an adjustment class: A token reinforcement system. *Exceptional Children*, 1967, 33, 637-642.

Parsons, T. *Essays in sociological theory* (Rev. ed.). Glencoe, Ill.: Free Press, 1954.

Polsky, H. *Cottage six—The social system of delinquent boys in residential treatment*. New York: Russell Sage Foundation, 1962.

Prentice, N., & Kelley, F. J. Intelligence and delinquency: A reconsideration. *Journal of Social Psychology*, 1963, 60, 327-339.

Siegal, S. *Non-parametric statistics in the behavioral sciences*. New York: McGraw-Hill, 1956.

Staats, A., & Butterfield, W. Treatment of nonreading in a culturally deprived juvenile delinquent: An application of reinforcement principles. *Child Development*, 1965, 36, 925-942.

Wolf, M., Giles, D., & Hall, V. Experiments with token reinforcement in a remedial classroom. *Behavior Research and Therapy*, 1968, 6, 51-64.

Zimmerman, E., & Zimmerman, J. The alteration of behavior in a special classroom. *Journal of Experimental Analysis of Behavior*, 1962, 5, 159-160.

# ACHIEVEMENT PLACE: MODIFICATION OF THE BEHAVIORS OF PRE-DELINQUENT BOYS WITHIN A TOKEN ECONOMY[1,2,]

## ELERY L. PHILLIPS, ELAINE A. PHILLIPS, DEAN L. FIXSEN, AND MONTROSE M. WOLF

The "pre-delinquent" behaviors of six boys at Achievement Place, a community based family style behavior modification center for delinquents, were modified using token (points) reinforcement procedures. In Exp. I, point losses contingent on each minute late were effective in producing promptness at the evening meal. During the reversal phase, threats (which were not backed up with point losses) to reinstate the point consequences initially improved promptness but the last two of five threats were ineffective. In Exp. II, point consequences effectively maintained the boys' room-cleaning behavior and, during a fading condition where the percentage of days when the contingency occurred was decreased, the point consequences remained effective for over six months, even when they were delivered on only 8% of the days. Experiment III showed that the boys saved considerable amounts of money when point consequences were available for deposits but saved little money when no points were available. Also, when points were given only for deposits that occurred on specific days the boys deposited their money almost exclusively on those days. In Exp. IV, point consequences contingent on the number of correct answers on a news quiz produced the greatest increase in the percentage of boys who watched the news and, to a lesser extent, increased the percentage of correct answers for the boys who watched the news. The results indicate that "pre-delinquent" behaviors are amenable to modification procedures and that a token reinforcement system provides a practical means of modifying these behaviors.

Token economies have been developed by Ayllon and Azrin (1968) to initiate and maintain the work and self-care behaviors of institutionalized psychotics; by Cohen, Filipczak, and Bis (1965) to improve and maintain the academic skills of institutionalized delinquents; and by Birnbrauer, Wolf, Kidder, and Tague (1965), Clark, Lachowicz, and Wolf (1968), and Wolf, Giles, and Hall (1968) to decrease behavioral problems and increase the academic behavior of children in special classrooms. Experimental evaluations of these token economies have indicated that teachers, therapists, and ward personnel can produce dramatic changes in many behaviors by manipulating their consequences. Phillips (1968) described the use of a token economy at Achievement Place, a community based, family style behavior modification program for pre-delinquents. Phillips provided evidence that indicated that contingent tokens could be used to decrease the incidence of aggressive statements and poor grammar and increase tidiness, punctuality, and amount of homework completed.

The aims of the present research, which was also conducted at Achievement Place, were to evaluate the effects of the token economy on promptness at meal time, room cleaning, saving money, and accuracy of answers on a news quiz. An additional aim was to examine the effects of threats, a fading procedure, and a "fixed-interval schedule of reinforcement" on behavior in an applied setting.

## PROGRAM

### Subjects

All the youths in Achievement Place were adjudicated by the local juvenile court and

[1]The authors wish to thank Jon Bailey for his assistance in Exp. II and Gary Timbers and Kathy Kirigan for preparing the news questions in Exp. IV.

[2]This investigation was supported by grant MH 16609 from the National Institutes of Mental Health (Center for Studies of Crime and Delinquency) and by grant HD 03144 from the National Institute of Child Health and Human Development, University of Kansas. Preparation of the manuscript was supported by PHS training grant HD 00183 from the National Institute of Child Health and Human Development to the Kansas Center for Research in Mental Retardation, University of Kansas.

JOURNAL OF APPLIED BEHAVIOR ANALYSIS, 1971, Vol. 4, pp. 45-59.

custody was given to the county Department of Social Welfare. In the opinion of the juvenile court, all of the youths were in danger of becoming habitual law breakers if some corrective action was not taken. Some of the descriptive terms used in records made by parents, teachers, and court officials to describe the youths later committed to Achievement Place were "aggressive", "inferior attitude", "dangerous to other children", "openly hostile toward teachers", "poor motivation", "general lack of cleanliness", and "low interest". Four boys participated in Exp. I and Exp. II, five boys in Exp. III, and six boys in Exp. IV. The boys' ages ranged from 12 to 15 yr.

*Token Reinforcement System*

The token economy at Achievement Place has been described by Phillips (1968). The tokens continue to be points that are earned for specified appropriate behaviors and lost for specified inappropriate behaviors. As points are earned or lost, the number of points and the behavior are recorded on a 3 by 5 in. index card each boy carries with him. At the end of each day, each boy subtracts the total number of points lost from the total number of points earned and the resulting point difference is used to buy privileges for the following day or is accumulated until the end of the week, as described below. Thus, points are made directly contingent on the occurrence of some behavior and are later used by the youths to purchase less-easily manipulated but more important consequences (privileges).

In the 2 yr since the Phillips report, the following changes have been made in the token system at Achievement Place. Originally, there was only one point system, the weekly point system, whereby the youths earned and lost points each day, the points were accumulated over a seven-day period, and privileges were purchased with those points for the following week. After noting the behavior of the youths on the weekly point system, two problems became apparent. First, the youths earned fewer points on the first few days after purchasing their privileges than on the few days preceding the next purchase day. Thus, when privileges were purchased on Friday for the following week, the youths earned fewer points on Saturday, Sunday, and

Monday than they did on Wednesday, Thursday, and Friday. To remedy this situation, each youth was required to earn a point difference of at least 1500 points each day in order to engage in his weekly privileges on the following day. Thus, although a youth bought privileges for an entire week, he had to make a point difference of 1500 points each day in order to engage in those privileges the following day.

The second problem was that for some youths entering the Achievement Place program, the point consequences did not produce large, reliable effects on some important behaviors for several weeks. To increase the effectiveness of the point system during those first weeks, a daily point system was arranged for all youths entering Achievement Place. On the daily point system, the point difference at the end of each day was used to buy privileges for the next day. Thus, the delay between earning points and purchasing privileges was minimized.

The privileges the youths could buy with their points have also changed somewhat. Table 1 describes the privileges and their price in points under the daily and weekly point system. The "basic" privileges were sold as a package and included the use of tools, telephone, radio, recreation room, and the privilege of going outdoors. The basic privileges had to be purchased before any other privilege because these were difficult for the teaching-parents to monitor. The other privileges could be purchased in any order. As shown in Table 1, a youth could live comfortably by earning a point difference of

Table 1

Privileges that can be earned with points on the daily and weekly point systems.

| | Price in Points | |
|---|---|---|
| Privileges | Weekly System | Daily System |
| Basics (hobbies and games) | 3000 | 400 |
| Snacks | 1000 | 150 |
| TV | 1000 | 150 |
| Allowance (per $1.00) | 2000 | 300 |
| Permission to leave Achievement Place (home, downtown, sports events) | 3000 | * |
| Bonds (savings for gifts, special clothing, *etc.*) | 1000 | 150 |
| Special privileges | Variable | * |

*Not available

226

10,000 each week. In contrast, Phillips (1968) reported a point difference of only 7000 each week was required for approximately the same privileges. Thus, inflation has occurred in the Achievement Place token economy.

## EXPERIMENT I

### PROMPTNESS

Phillips (1968) conducted an analysis of promptness at school, bedtime, and on errands and found that point losses for each minute each youth was late produced punctual behavior. In the time since that study, promptness at the evening meal became a problem. This led to the following systematic replication of the Phillips (1968) procedures.

### PROCEDURES

Promptness was recorded for each evening meal, seven days a week. Approximately 5 min before dinner each evening, the boys were told "Dinner will be ready in about five minutes." A bell that could be heard throughout the house was rung when dinner was ready and a stopwatch was started at the same time. The stopwatch was stopped when the last boy sat down at the table. The time between starting and stopping the watch defined "minutes late". If a boy sat down at the table with dirty hands, uncombed hair, etc., his presence was counted and he was asked to go clean up after the last boy was seated.

### Conditions

All conditions were announced, except Baseline.

*Baseline.* The time elapsed between ringing the bell and the last boy seating himself at the table was recorded by the teaching-parents each evening. There were no reprimands, reminders, or other scheduled consequences for being early or late.

*Points.* Each boy lost 100 points for each minute he was late. Other than being initially informed of the change in procedure, the boys were given no verbal reprimands or reminders. There were no scheduled consequences for being early. Point losses, if any, were delivered to each boy after he sat down at the table.

*Threats no points.* Identical to the Baseline condition, except on the sixth, tenth, thirteenth, fourteenth, and eighteenth days of this

condition the following threat was given to the boys after the last boy was seated: "If you are late for dinner tomorrow night, you will lose points." None of these threats were backed up with point consequences on the following day.

### RESULTS

There were 22 reliability checks during the study. With two observers independently recording minutes late to the nearest second, they never differed more than 6 sec.

As shown in Fig. 1, during Baseline the last boy to sit down at the table was about 10 min late. When the 100-point fine was made contingent on each minute late, the boys were more prompt and, by the end of the Points condition, all the boys were seated at the table less than 60 sec after the dinner bell rang. Under the Threats No Points condition, the behavior reverted to about 10 min late; during the final Points condition the boys were again prompt in coming to dinner. These data indicate that point losses were effective in producing punctual behavior at dinner time. Although not shown in Fig. 1, the "last boy to sit down at the table" varied from day to day among all the youths. Thus, the data in Fig. 1 represent all four youths in the experiment and not just one habitually tardy youth.

For an analysis of threats in the Threats No Points condition, Fig. 2 shows the average minutes late on the days before each threat was made (including the day of the threat) and the minutes late on the day following each threat. It can be seen in Fig. 2 that only the first three threats to reinstate the point loss condition produced improvements in punctuality on the day following the threat. The last two threats produced no appreciable change in punctuality, possibly because none of the threats were backed up with point losses on the next day.

## EXPERIMENT II

### ROOM CLEANING

Another problem involved a general lack of cleanliness and tidiness, which was typical of the youths when they arrived at Achievement Place. Reports by social workers and probation officers suggested that in many cases the homes of the boys were unkempt and disar-

## Promptness At Meals

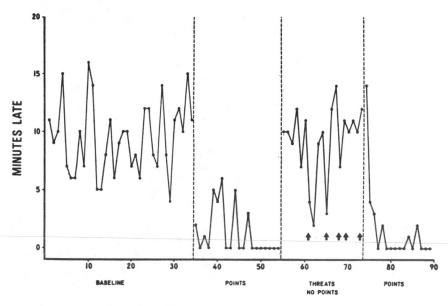

SESSIONS

Fig. 1. Minutes late for each evening meal under Baseline conditions where there were no consequences for promptness and under Points conditions where each boy lost 100 points for each minute he was late. The arrows in the Threats No Points condition mark the day following a threat to reinstate point consequences for promptness.

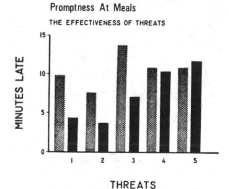

## Promptness At Meals
### THE EFFECTIVENESS OF THREATS

THREATS

Fig. 2. The cross-hatched bars represent the average minutes late on the days before each threat was made (including the day of the threat) and the solid bars represent the minutes late on the day following the threat.

ranged. Teachers' reports also commented on the poor hygiene habits and inappropriate clothing of the youths.

To alleviate a portion of this problem, token reinforcement procedures were designed to establish the cleanliness of the boys' rooms and to maintain the room-cleaning behavior in the absence of daily consequences.

### PROCEDURES

*Response Definition*

Room cleaning was divided into 10 major areas, which were explicitly defined according to a set of objective criteria. In addition, each major area was scored for the number of items that met the definition, up to a maximum. For example, *Dirty Clothes*, a major area, was defined as follows: "All clothes not neatly placed in the wardrobe, dresser, or closet should be in the dirty clothes hamper (in the utility room). There should be no clothes visible without opening doors or drawers (maximum = 13)." Thus, if all clothes were put away and met the definition, a score of 13 was assigned to the area *Dirty Clothes.* Each piece of clothing that was visible or improperly put away was subtracted from the score of 13. The other nine areas and their maximum scores were *Shades and Windows* (max. = 4), *Bed* (max. = 20), *Floor* (max. = 15), *Closet* (max. = 15), *Doors and Drawers* (max. = 4), *Furniture* (max. = 4), *Desk* (max. = 10), *Surface Tops* (max. = 10), and *Baskets* (max. = 5). Therefore, the maximum number of items totalled 100 for each of the four boys in this experiment.

*Conditions*

A list of room-cleaning definitions was posted on a bulletin board at the beginning of the study and remained there throughout the experiment. The boys were free to remove the list of definitions to check their rooms at any time. All conditions were announced. Without telling the boys, data were recorded each week-day morning shortly after the boys left for school.

*Points.* Under the Points condition, each boy made 500 points if his total score was 80 or above and lost 500 points if his score fell below 80. In addition to the point consequences, each boy was given feedback concerning the exact nature and location of the items that did not meet the definitions of room cleaning.

*No points.* During this condition there were no point consequences for room cleaning. However, several probes were made during the No-Points condition: the feedback was discontinued and reinstated; the boys were threatened that "If you boys don't start cleaning your rooms it will be necessary to start points on rooms again"; they were given instructions that "Boys, your rooms are a mess. Clean them up as soon as possible"; and it was demanded that "Boys, your rooms are a mess. I want you to go up and clean your rooms now!"

*Fading points.* The Points condition was reinstated with the exception that no feedback was given. After 13 days of recording data and delivering consequences for room cleaning each day, the percentage of days the contingency occurred and consequences were delivered was reduced from 100% to 50% for eight days, then to 33% for nine days, to 16% for 27 days, and then to 8% for 25 days. Although the points were given on a variable and intermittent schedule, the cleanliness of the rooms was measured every day.

When the intermittency was introduced, an "adjusting consequence" was added to avoid reducing both the frequency and magnitude of the points at the same time. The potential number of points that could be earned or lost accumulated each day the contingency did not occur. Thus, if the contingency was finally applied after five days, five times as many points would be earned or lost than if the contingency had occurred on each successive day. The adjusting consequence was discontinued after 38 days and a fixed number of points occurred as the consequence for each intermittent contingency thereafter. The value of this new consequence was equal to a five-day accumulation of points under the adjusting consequence.

*Post checks.* During this condition, room cleaning was measured and point consequences were delivered on 8% of the days for over six months. Thus, data were recorded only on the days the consequences were to be delivered.

Inter-observer agreement among three observers was measured on 22 occasions throughout the study; agreement, computed by dividing the total number of agreements by the total number of agreements plus disagreements, ranged from 96% to 100% and averaged 99%.

## RESULTS

Figure 3 shows the almost perfect level of cleanliness of the boys' rooms under the Points condition. At this time, the Points condition had been in effect for nearly two months. When the contingency was removed during the No Points condition, the number of items completed decreased. The effects of a number of variables were probed during this reversal period. Precise feedback was supplied to each boy during the Points condition and was continued during the beginning of the No Points condition. The feedback consisted of a diagram of the rooms and indicated the exact nature of the items that did not meet the criteria. Neither discontinuing nor reinstating

229

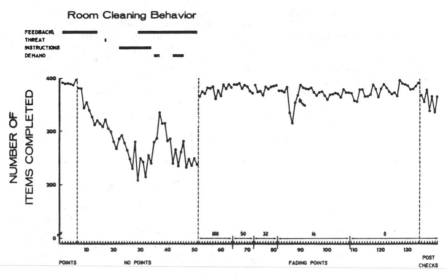

## SESSIONS

Fig. 3. The total number of items completed for all four boys each week day. The bars over portions of the Points and No Points conditions indicate the sessions Feedback, Threats, Instructions, and Demands were given. The numbers above the abscissa in the Fading Points condition indicate the percentage of days the point contingency occurred. The arrow in the Fading Points condition indicates the session where the "adjusting consequence" was discontinued.

this procedure during the reversal stage appeared to have any effect. Also, when the Points condition was reinstated without the feedback there did not seem to be any loss of control. Apparently, while precise feedback may have been functional in the beginning, it clearly no longer was.

Instructions that they clean their rooms and a threat to reinstate the point contingency if they did not produced no change in the youths' room-cleaning behavior. Demands resulted in the boys going to their rooms and engaging in apparent room-straightening behavior. The first group of demands also produced an increase in room-cleaning behavior. However, the remaining demands had almost no effect on the room cleanliness measure.

In the Fading Points condition, when the daily point contingency was reinstated, the room-cleaning behavior immediately increased to the level seen in the initial Points condition. As the percentage of days on which the point consequences were delivered was reduced from 100% to 8%, the room-cleaning

behavior remained at a stable, high level. At the arrow in Fig. 3, the adjusting consequence was discontinued and a fixed number of points occurred as the consequence for each intermittent contingency with no loss of control. During the Post Checks condition, when the behavior was measured and consequences were delivered on only 8% of the days, room cleaning decreased slightly over the six month period but was still above the criterion of 80% items completed for all the boys.

These data indicate that the point consequences were effective in maintaining the boys' room-cleaning behavior and that the consequences for room cleaning remained effective even when they were delivered on as few as 8% of the days.

### EXPERIMENT III

#### SAVINGS

One set of goal behaviors at Achievement Place may be described as "planning for the future". Obviously, "planning ahead" involves a large class of behaviors. Considering the financial history of many of the families of the boys in Achievement Place, one member of this class which was of immediate practical interest was saving money.

To encourage saving money the teaching-parents purchased a plastic "piggy bank" for each of the boys and labelled each one with a boy's name. Each piggy bank had a narrow slot at the top to insert coins and bills and did not have any means of removing the money short of breaking the bank open. Before beginning the study, each boy was asked to specify what he was saving his money for, the price of his anticipated purchase was established, and the money was removed from the bank only when that purchase price was equalled or exceeded. The boys saved their money for records, a record player, model cars, and a bicycle. Money that was removed from the bank had to be spent on the originally specified item or some other item that was equal in cost. Thus, withdrawls could not be re-deposited.

## PROCEDURES

Saving was recorded by having each boy bring his bank and the money he wished to deposit to the teaching-parents. The teaching-parents noted the amount of the deposit in the boy's "savings account book" and watched as the money was inserted into the bank. The "savings account book", therefore, provided a data record for the experimenters' use. At the end of the experiment, the total amount deposited was compared with the money actually removed from the banks. The "savings account book" was found to be in agreement with the actual withdrawls within a few pennies.

### Conditions

*Baseline.* The date and amount of each deposit were recorded in the "savings book". There were no scheduled consequences for deposits.

*Points.* Under the Points condition, each boy was given 10 points for every penny he deposited. Points could be earned for deposits that occurred on any day of the week.

*Points specific days.* Each boy was given 10 points for every penny he deposited but points could be earned only for deposits that oc-

curred on certain days of each week, as described in the Results section.

## RESULTS

Figure 4 shows the cumulative dollars saved each day for each condition of the study for all the boys. The arrows mark Friday of each week for all conditions. Under Baseline conditions very little money was saved. Under the Points conditions, where deposits earned points on any day of the week, a considerable amount of money was saved and there was a strong positive correlation between the amount saved and Friday of each week. For the first Points Specific Days condition, it was announced that saving money would earn points only if the deposits occurred on a specific day each week, namely, Saturday, Monday, Wednesday, and Monday, respectively, for the next four weeks. As shown in Fig. 4, deposits occurred exclusively on the designated day each week. When the baseline condition was again replicated there were no deposits made. Under the third Points condition, the cumulative dollars saved increased

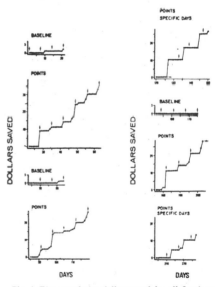

Fig. 4. The cumulative dollars saved for all five boys each day of the experiment. The arrows mark Friday (the day points were exchanged for privileges) of each week for all conditions.

231

and the correlation between amount saved and Friday was replicated. During the second Points Specific Days condition, deposits again occurred almost exclusively (there were two exceptions) on the designated day, Monday of each week.

The data in Fig. 4 clearly show that saving behavior never became independent of the point consequences. In order to promote saving money it seems to be necessary to pay the boys "interest" on their deposits.

## EXPERIMENT IV

### NEWS

Many of the boys who come to Achievement Place have little knowledge of events that occur in the United States and the world. Some of the boys had never read any part of the newspaper except the comic section and seldom, if ever, watched a TV news program. Since knowledge of current national and international events had a conversational value in general and was particularly stressed in classes concerning government in school, token reinforcement procedures were designed to increase news watching and comprehension.

### PROCEDURES

An observer watched the Huntley-Brinkley news broadcast each weekday evening. During the broadcast the observer composed several "fill in the blank" questions concerning news items that were given special attention in the broadcast (i.e., usually a film clip with accompanying dialogue concerning a major news event). After the broadcast the observer telephoned the questions and answers to the teaching-parents, these were recorded on audio tape, and within 1 hr after the broadcast, the boys were given a news quiz over the evening news. The news quiz consisted of the boys listening to the recorded questions and independently writing down the answers in the presence of the teaching-parents. The boys' answers were then compared with the answers supplied by the observer and the per cent correct was recorded. A percentage measure was used because the number of questions on the news quiz varied from seven to nine during the course of the experiment. All boys were required to take the news quiz each evening. The observer was not told when conditions were changed and did not receive any

information on the results of the study until the end of the experiment.

On four occasions during the study an assessment of variations in the difficulty of the questions asked was made by having two observers watch the same program and submit an equal number of questions to the teaching-parents. On each occasion, half of the boys were given one observer's questions and half were given the other observer's questions with the boys counterbalanced across the two observers across all four occasions. On the first occasion, all boys were required to watch the news and the two groups were 43% and 54% accurate in answering the news questions. On the next two occasions, none of the boys was allowed to watch the news and the accuracy scores were 20% and 20% and 12% and 17% for the two groups on the second and third occasions, respectively. On the fourth occasion, all boys were again required to watch the news and the accuracy for the two groups was 67% and 67%. Thus, with two observers independently composing questions, the two groups of boys responded to the questions with equal accuracy on two occasions and the greatest difference in accuracy was 11%.

On one other occasion during the study two boys were not allowed to watch the news, two boys were required to watch the CBS news with Walter Cronkite, and two boys were required to watch the NBC news with Huntley-Brinkley. The observer composed the questions while watching Huntley-Brinkley. All the boys then took the same news quiz. The two boys who did not watch the news were 11% and 15% accurate in answering the news questions, the two boys who watched Walter Cronkite were 15% and 19% accurate, and the two boys who watched Huntley-Brinkley were 45% and 66% accurate. These data suggest that the proportion of correct answers on the news quiz depended to a great extent on watching the appropriate newscast and not on information available on other newscasts or on information from other sources available to the boys.

### Conditions

All conditions, except Baseline, were announced and a description of the point consequences in effect was available on the bulletin board during each condition.

Baseline. There were no point consequences

for watching news or for correct questions on the quiz.

*Sampling 100+.* Each boy was given 100 points for each question he answered correctly. In addition, a sampling procedure was used such that two of the five boys available during this condition were required to watch the news each night. The sampling procedure consisted of having the boys rotate watching news in the order AB, BC, CD, DE, EA, *etc.*

*100+.* This condition was the same as the Sampling 100+ condition except none of the boys was required to watch the news.

*600+.* Each boy was given 600 points for each question he answered correctly. No one was required to watch the news.

*600±.* In this condition, each boy earned 600 points for each correct answer only if 40% or more of the questions were answered correctly. If a boy failed to reach the 40% criterion he lost 600 points for each answer below the criterion. Thus, if there were seven or eight questions, a boy would make 1800 points for three correct answers, 2400 points for four correct answers, 3000 points for five correct answers, and so forth. However, he would lose 600 points for only two correct answers, lose 1200 points for one correct answer, and lose 1800 points if he answered none of the questions correctly. If there were nine questions the same point scale applied, except the requirement for making points was four correct answers instead of three (four correct answers earned 2400 points, three correct lost 600 points). No one was required to watch the news.

*600−.* This condition was identical to the 600± condition except no points could be earned. Thus, the lost side of the point scale used for the 600± condition was again used but, instead of earning points for 40% or more correct answers, the boys simply avoided losing points. No one was required to watch the news.

*Sampling 1000+ for watching news.* In this condition, about half of the boys were required to watch the news each evening. The sampling procedure was similar to that used in the Sampling 100+ condition. The 1000-point consequence, however, was contingent on watching the newscast and not on answering the news questions correctly. There were no consequences for correct or incorrect answers on the news quiz.

*Sampling 600±.* This condition was identical to the 600± condition except that about half of the boys were required to watch the news each evening.

RESULTS

Figure 5 shows the mean per cent correct for all boys on the news quiz within each condition. During Baseline the boys answered less than 20% of the questions correctly. When the Sampling 100+ condition was initiated, the mean per cent correct increased to about 25%. When the sampling procedure was discontinued in the 100+ condition, the mean percent correct decreased across days to less than 20%. After the 100-point consequence for each correct answer was replaced by a 600-point consequence in the 600+ condition, there was an initial increase in the mean per cent correct but this faded across days to less than 20%. The next two conditions replicated these results; the 600+ condition, relative to the 100+ condition, did not produce a reliable, durable effect on the mean percentage of correct answers on the news quiz and both the 100+ and 600+ conditions resulted in a lower mean per cent correct than the sampling 100+ condition. When the 600± condition was instituted there was an immediate increase in the percentage of questions answered correctly to about 60%. When the 600+ condition was again replicated the boys answered about 20% of the questions correctly, slightly more than in the previous 600+ conditions. To test the effects of the lost side of the 600+ point scale, the 600− condition was next employed. Under the 600− condition, the boys answered about 35% of the questions correctly, which was less than the 60% that resulted from the 600± condition but more than the 10% to 20% in the previous 600+ conditions. Following the 600− condition, the boys were returned to the 600+ condition and the mean per cent correct decreased to less than 15%. The 600± condition was then replicated and the result once again was about 60% of the news questions answered correctly. When the Sampling 1000+ for Watching News procedure was used, the mean per cent correct decreased to about 10%. This was about 15% lower than the mean per cent correct found under the Sampling 100+ procedure where there was a 100 point consequence contingent on each correct answer. Under the next Sam-

## NEWS QUESTIONS

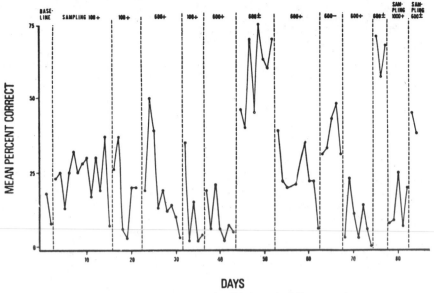

Fig. 5. The mean per cent correct for all boys on the daily news quiz.

pling 600± condition the boys answered about 40% of the news questions correctly.

The results presented in Fig. 5 indicate that the 600± and, to a lesser extent, the 600– conditions produced a greater percentage of correct answers on the news quiz relative to the other conditions. These results may have been due to (a) actual changes in the percentage of correct answers for those who watched the news or, since the number of boys who watched the news broadcast was controlled only during the sampling conditions, (b) changes in the number of boys who watched the news, or (c) some combination of (a) and (b). To determine which of these alternatives best fit the data, the results were further analyzed into the mean per cent correct of those who watched the news, the mean per cent correct of those who did not watch the news, and the percentage of boys who watched the news each day. These data appear in Fig. 6. "Watching news" was defined as a boy sitting in the room looking at the TV for at least 25 min of the 30-min newscast. In practice, the boys who did not meet this definition were not in the

room at all and thus did not watch any of the newscast. Rarely, a boy would watch TV for 5 to 10 min then leave the room and not watch the remainder of the newscast.

Figure 6 shows that the point consequence produced a clear effect on the percentage of boys who watched the news and did not substantially effect the mean per cent correct of those who watched or did not watch the news. The boys who watched the news averaged about 50% of the news questions answered correctly and the boys who did not watch the news averaged about 5% to 10% correct across most of the conditions. The large changes in mean per cent correct in Fig. 5 thus appear to have been more a function of the number of boys who watched the news than of actual changes in the mean per cent of those who watched the news.

There is some evidence in Fig. 6, however, that suggests that the changes in point contingencies produced changes in the mean per cent correct for those who watched news. The mean per cent correct under the 600± conditions appeared to be slightly greater than

234

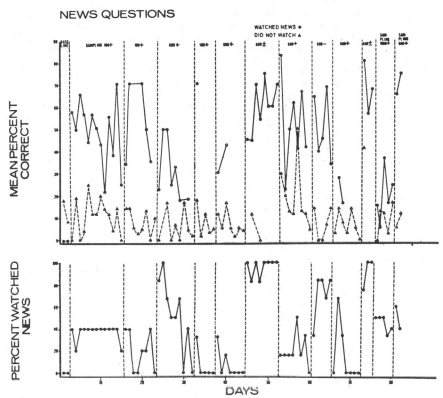

## NEWS QUESTIONS

WATCHED NEWS ●
DID NOT WATCH ▲

Fig. 6. The mean per cent correct for the boys who watched the news, the mean per cent correct for the boys who did not watch the news, and the percentage of boys who watched the news each day for all conditions.

that resulting from the other conditions but, due to the wide variability across all conditions, no unequivocal conclusion can be stated. To test whether the points contingent on number of correct answers had any effect at all, the point consequences were discontinued for correct answers and placed on merely watching the news during the Sampling 1000+ for Watching News condition. These results in Fig. 6 show that the curves for those who watched and those who did not watch the news did not differ substantially. Furthermore, the mean per cent correct for those who watched the news was appreciably lower than during the Sampling 100+ condition where there was a 100-point contingency for each correct answer. When the sampling procedure was maintained and the 600± point conse-

quences were made contingent on number of correct answers in the Sampling 600± condition, the mean per cent correct of the boys who were required to watch the news increased from about 20% to about 70% and the mean per cent correct for those who did not watch the news remained at about 10%.

It appears then that the point consequences had their greatest effect on the percentage of boys who watched the news but also effected the percentage of correct answers for those who watched the news.

## DISCUSSION

The results of these experiments indicated that point consequences contingent on promptness, room cleaning, saving money, and accuracy of answers on a news quiz produced significant and reliable improvements in each behavior. Furthermore, the results of Exp. I showed that threats to reinstate the point consequences were only temporarily effective in improving promptness at meal time. Similarly, the threats and instructions given in Exp. II had very little effect on the cleanliness of the boys' rooms. Demands in Exp. II initially produced an improvement in room-cleaning behavior but this effect was not replicated with the second group of demands. These data indicate that threats, instructions, and demands, when they are not discriminative stimuli for future point losses or loss of privileges, at best produce only temporary changes in behavior. In this light, it is interesting to note in Fig. 1 that the announcement of the first Points condition produced an immediate improvement in promptness but the announcement of the second Points condition, which occurred after several threats had been made and not backed up, had no immediate effect on promptness. On the second day of the second Points condition, a large improvement in promptness occurred, possibly because the last "threat" (the announcement) had been backed up with point consequences.

The results of the Fading Points condition in Exp. II indicated that a high level of room-cleaning behavior could be maintained over a considerable period of time when point consequences were delivered on only 8% of the days. To achieve these results, a fading procedure was employed that systematically reduced the percentage of days on which the contingency occurred and, at the same time, increased the point consequences of each contingency. While this was done to avoid reducing the total number of points that could be earned for room cleaning while decreasing the percentage of days on which the contingency occurred, no functional analysis of the importance of the adjusting consequence was attempted.

In Exp. III, the systematic changes in the probability of the boys making deposits each day of the week during the Points conditions resembled the "scallops" that characterize behavior under control of fixed-interval schedules of reinforcement. The scallops initially appeared even though the point consequences for deposits were available any day of the week. On an *a priori* basis one might expect

the boys to deposit most of their money on Saturday or Sunday because they bought their allowance on Friday ($1.00 to $4.00 a week depending on the number of points each boy was willing to pay) and many of the boys did odd jobs on Saturday for which they earned money. However, Friday was the day the boys used the points they had earned for the week (up to and including Friday) to purchase privileges for the following week. Thus, by depositing money in their banks on Friday, the boys earned points which were almost immediately exchanged for the back-up privileges.

To test the effects of point consequences when the purchase of back up privileges was delayed, it was announced that saving money would earn points only if the deposits occurred on a specific day each week. Throughout this time, points continued to be exchanged for privileges on Friday evening, so the delay between earning points for deposits and exchanging those points for privileges was as much as six days when Saturday was the designated day. Under the Points Specific Days condition, deposits occurred almost exclusively on the designated day. Thus, the point consequences increased savings even when there was a delay between earning points for deposits and buying privileges. These data are similar to those obtained with human subjects by Weiner (1969) who used a response cost procedure and a fixed-interval schedule to produce the characteristic scallops. With this procedure reinforcement in the form of 100 points on a counter (points were later exchanged for money) was available on a fixed-interval schedule. However, each response the subject made cost one point, *i.e.*, one point was subtracted from the counter. Subjects on the fixed-interval response cost schedule made very few responses, almost all of which were correlated with the end of the fixed interval. Although there was no scheduled response cost procedure in Exp. III, deposits made early in the week under the Points condition "cost" the boys the potential use of that money later in the week. Therefore, the "natural" consequences of spending money (*i.e.*, not having that money available for future purchases) may have partially controlled the emergence of the fixed-interval scallops noted in the Points conditions.

The results of Exp. IV indicated that point

consequences contingent on number of correct answers on the news quiz significantly increased the percentage of correct answers, but changes in the value of the point consequences produced little effect on the number of correct answers for the boys who watched the news. Similarly, Tyler and Brown (1968) found only a small (about one-half answer) difference between one group of delinquent boys that was given tokens for the number of news questions answered correctly and another group that was given tokens noncontingently. However, in the present experiment changes in the value of the point consequences did have a large, reliable effect on the percentage of boys who watched the news. It appeared that the 600± condition also produced an increase in the mean per cent correct of those who watched news (Fig. 6) to about 60% to 70% relative to 50% or less for the other conditions. In addition, the 600± condition resulted in nearly 100% of the boys watching the news. The 600− condition had no observable effect on the mean per cent correct for those who watched news but did result in about 80% of the boys watching the news. In addition to these data, the teaching-parents reported that during the 600± conditions the boys appeared to take notes during the news cast, seemed to discuss the news among themselves, and appeared to study their notes before the news quiz. These behaviors were not noted by the teaching-parents during any other condition in the experiment. Thus, the 600± consequences on output (i.e., number of correct answers) resulted in nearly 100% participation by the boys, slightly increased accuracy for the boys who watched the news, and appeared to have generated and maintained a long chain of "study" behaviors.

Taken together, the results of these four experiments indicate that "pre-delinquent" behaviors are amenable to modification procedures and that a point system administered by two professionally trained teaching-parents and backed up with privileges naturally available in most homes provides a practical means of modifing these behaviors.

When any token economy is developed, the goal is to establish or modify certain target behaviors with the reinforcing consequences that are available. Although this goal is common to all token economies, the arrangement of the economy itself can vary across at least two important dimensions. The first dimension concerns the relationship between the tokens and behavior. An economy can be "all positive", that is, tokens can be given for certain specified behaviors but they cannot be removed. Or, an economy can be "all negative" where each youth starts off each day with a full complement of tokens and can only lose them for certain behaviors. Another possibility is an economy where tokens can be both earned and lost, a "positive and negative" economy. A second important dimension in a token economy concerns the relationship between the number of tokens that can be earned and the cost of privileges. It would be possible to construct an economy where there was a fixed number of tokens available for specified behaviors each day and where an equal number of tokens was required to purchase the desired privileges. In such a "fixed" system it would be somewhat arbitrary whether the consequences were all in terms of earning tokens for behavior, losing tokens for behavior, or a combination of the two. For example, in a fixed economy, failure to earn 100 tokens would be equal to losing 100 tokens since each would result in the direct loss of some privilege. In a fixed token economy there would be no way to make-up unearned or lost tokens. Thus, it is not really possible to distinguish between positive reinforcement and punishment in a fixed economy. Nevertheless, it would also be possible to construct a token economy where there were nearly unlimited opportunities to earn tokens for specified behaviors but where a certain number of tokens was required to purchase the desired privileges. In this "flexible" economy tokens that are unearned or lost can be made up in a variety of ways. Thus, the loss of tokens does not necessarily mean the loss of privileges, only additional effort to earn tokens in order to buy the privileges.

In the Achievement Place token economy, points could be earned and lost, it was a "positive and negative" system. Second, a set number of points were required to earn the privileges described in Table I. Third, the opportunities for earning points were almost unlimited and, therefore, there existed the opportunity to earn more points than were required each day. Thus, it was also a "flexible" economy. There are several advantages to the Achievement Place system. First, certain appropriate behaviors that have an initially low baseline rate can be strengthened using only positive points (no points can be lost). An example of this was seen in Exp. III. Second, certain inappropriate behaviors that have an initially high baseline rate can be eliminated by using only negative points (no points can be earned). An example of this was seen in Exp. I. Third, there are certain appropriate behaviors that are critical to the overall treatment program or to the operation of the home. For these behaviors, a positive and negative consequence can be used (points can be either made or lost depending upon the level of the behavior). Examples of this procedure were seen in Exp. II and IV. The fourth advantage is that points can be earned in a variety of ways and point losses can be made up. In a flexible system such as this, point losses do not necessarily correlate with the loss of privileges. Rather, point losses mean that additional appropriate behaviors must be engaged in in order to recoup the lost points so all the privileges can be acquired. This is, in fact, what the Achievement Place boys generally do. In a recent 13-week period, only one of the seven boys in the home failed to earn a sufficient point difference in one week to buy all of the first five privileges in Table I; he was unable to buy "permission to leave Achievement Place" that one week.

Thus, while the Achievement Place token economy depends partially on mild punishment (contingent loss of points) for its effectiveness, the flexibility in the economy means that, in reality, the boys seldom suffer the loss of their privileges. On the other hand, one can conceive of a more "fixed" token economy based entirely on "positive reinforcement" but where the participants would frequently fail to earn all the back-up reinforcers. The aversiveness of a token economy would seem to be better measured by the degree of success that the participants have in earning the back-up reinforcers, rather than by the presence or absence of contingent point losses.

The results of Exp. IV indicated that losing points was more effective than making an equal number of points (compare the 600+ and 600− conditions in the bottom half of Fig. 6). This result can be explained in terms of the general token economy at Achievement Place. There were many opportunities for the

boys to make points each day and the boys were free to choose among the tasks that would earn them points. After the daily point difference requirement (1500 points) was surpassed, the boys would tend to choose those tasks that maximized the points they could earn and minimized the time and effort required, or select tasks that they most enjoyed. Thus, earning 600 points for each correct answer on the news quiz was only one of many choices the boys had for earning points. However, losing 600 points for each incorrect answer below the 40% criterion meant that the boy who lost points would have to earn additional points to recoup his losses. That is, he would have to expend greater effort in order to achieve his required daily point difference.

One final point should be made. The point system is the "work horse" of the treatment program at Achievement Place. By making points contingent upon objectively defined behaviors, major changes have been effected in each boy's social, academic, and self-help behaviors. Point consequences provide immediate, concrete feedback to the youths each day and provide a powerful treatment tool. However, the world outside Achievement Place does not always provide systematic consequences for appropriate and inappropriate behavior. For this reason, a merit system was devised. To be advanced to the merit system, a youth must display exceptionally good behavior on the weekly point system over a period of several weeks. On the merit system, all privileges are free and only social consequences are supplied for the youth's behavior. If the youth continues to behave appropriately for several weeks on the merit system he becomes a candidate for the homeward bound system, his parents are prepared for his return, and he begins a gradual transition from Achievement Place to his natural home. If, however, the youth engages in inappropriate behavior that is considered to be critical to his eventual success in the community, he can be taken off the merit system and returned to the weekly point system for further training until, once again, he earns his way onto the merit system. Therefore, the point system provides the motivation needed to change the youths' behaviors and the merit system is used to reduce the dependence of those behaviors on immediate consequences.

## REFERENCES

Ayllon, T. and Azrin, N. H. *Token economy: a motivational system for therapy and rehabilitation*. New York: Appleton-Century-Crofts, 1968.

Birnbrauer, J., Wolf, M., Kidder, J., and Tague, C. Classroom behavior of retarded pupils with token reinforcement. *Journal of Experimental Child Psychology*, 1965, 2, 119-135.

Clark, M., Lachowicz, J., and Wolf, M. A pilot basic education program for school dropouts incorporating a token reinforcement system. *Behavior Research and Therapy*, 1968, 6, 183-188.

Cohen, H., Filipczak, J., and Bis, J. Case project: contingencies applicable to special education. In J. Shlien (Ed.), *Research in psychotherapy*. Washington: American Psychological Association, 1968. Pp 34-53.

Phillips, E. L. Achievement Place: token reinforcement procedures in a home-style rehabilitation setting for pre-delinquent boys. *Journal of Applied Behavior Analysis*, 1968, 1, 213-223.

Tyler, V. O. and Brown, G. D. Token reinforcement of academic performance with institutionalized delinquent boys. *Journal of Educational Psychology*, 1968, 14, 413-423.

Weiner, H. Controlling human fixed-interval performance. *Journal of the Experimental Analysis of Behavior*, 1969, 12, 349-373.

Wolf, M., Giles, D., and Hall, R. Experiments with token reinforcement in a remedial classroom. *Behavior Research and Therapy*, 1968, 6, 51-64.